MW00861216

Praxis II
Special Education: Preschool/Early Childhood (5691) Exam

SECRETS

Study Guide
Your Key to Exam Success

Praxis II Test Review for the
Praxis II: Subject Assessments Exam

Dear Future Exam Success Story:

First of all, **THANK YOU** for purchasing Mometrix study materials!

Second, congratulations! You are one of the few determined test-takers who are committed to doing whatever it takes to excel on your exam. **You have come to the right place.** We developed these study materials with one goal in mind: to deliver you the information you need in a format that's concise and easy to use.

In addition to optimizing your guide for the content of the test, we've outlined our recommended steps for breaking down the preparation process into small, attainable goals so you can make sure you stay on track.

We've also analyzed the entire test-taking process, identifying the most common pitfalls and showing how you can overcome them and be ready for any curveball the test throws you.

Standardized testing is one of the biggest obstacles on your road to success, which only increases the importance of doing well in the high-pressure, high-stakes environment of test day. Your results on this test could have a significant impact on your future, and this guide provides the information and practical advice to help you achieve your full potential on test day.

Your success is our success

We would love to hear from you! If you would like to share the story of your exam success or if you have any questions or comments in regard to our products, please contact us at **800-673-8175** or **support@mometrix.com**.

Thanks again for your business and we wish you continued success!

Sincerely,
The Mometrix Test Preparation Team

Need more help? Check out our flashcards at: http://MometrixFlashcards.com/PraxisII

Secret Key #2 – Make Your Studying Count

You're devoting a lot of time and effort to preparing for this test, so you want to be absolutely certain it will pay off. This means doing more than just reading the content and hoping you can remember it on test day. It's important to make every minute of study count. There are two main areas you can focus on to make your studying count:

Retention

It doesn't matter how much time you study if you can't remember the material. You need to make sure you are retaining the concepts. To check your retention of the information you're learning, try recalling it at later times with minimal prompting. Try carrying around flashcards and glance at one or two from time to time or ask a friend who's also studying for the test to quiz you.

To enhance your retention, look for ways to put the information into practice so that you can apply it rather than simply recalling it. If you're using the information in practical ways, it will be much easier to remember. Similarly, it helps to solidify a concept in your mind if you're not only reading it to yourself but also explaining it to someone else. Ask a friend to let you teach them about a concept you're a little shaky on (or speak aloud to an imaginary audience if necessary). As you try to summarize, define, give examples, and answer your friend's questions, you'll understand the concepts better and they will stay with you longer. Finally, step back for a big picture view and ask yourself how each piece of information fits with the whole subject. When you link the different concepts together and see them working together as a whole, it's easier to remember the individual components.

Finally, practice showing your work on any multi-step problems, even if you're just studying. Writing out each step you take to solve a problem will help solidify the process in your mind, and you'll be more likely to remember it during the test.

Modality

Modality simply refers to the means or method by which you study. Choosing a study modality that fits your own individual learning style is crucial. No two people learn best in exactly the same way, so it's important to know your strengths and use them to your advantage.

For example, if you learn best by visualization, focus on visualizing a concept in your mind and draw an image or a diagram. Try color-coding your notes, illustrating them, or creating symbols that will trigger your mind to recall a learned concept. If you learn best by hearing or discussing information, find a study partner who learns the same way or read aloud to yourself. Think about how to put the information in your own words. Imagine that you are giving a lecture on the topic and record yourself so you can listen to it later.

For any learning style, flashcards can be helpful. Organize the information so you can take advantage of spare moments to review. Underline key words or phrases. Use different colors for different categories. Mnemonic devices (such as creating a short list in which every item starts with the same letter) can also help with retention. Find what works best for you and use it to store the information in your mind most effectively and easily.

Secret Key #3 – Practice the Right Way

Your success on test day depends not only on how many hours you put into preparing, but also on whether you prepared the right way. It's good to check along the way to see if your studying is paying off. One of the most effective ways to do this is by taking practice tests to evaluate your progress. Practice tests are useful because they show exactly where you need to improve. Every time you take a practice test, pay special attention to these three groups of questions:

- The questions you got wrong
- The questions you had to guess on, even if you guessed right
- The questions you found difficult or slow to work through

This will show you exactly what your weak areas are, and where you need to devote more study time. Ask yourself why each of these questions gave you trouble. Was it because you didn't understand the material? Was it because you didn't remember the vocabulary? Do you need more repetitions on this type of question to build speed and confidence? Dig into those questions and figure out how you can strengthen your weak areas as you go back to review the material.

Additionally, many practice tests have a section explaining the answer choices. It can be tempting to read the explanation and think that you now have a good understanding of the concept. However, an explanation likely only covers part of the question's broader context. Even if the explanation makes sense, **go back and investigate** every concept related to the question until you're positive you have a thorough understanding.

As you go along, keep in mind that the practice test is just that: practice. Memorizing these questions and answers will not be very helpful on the actual test because it is unlikely to have any of the same exact questions. If you only know the right answers to the sample questions, you won't be prepared for the real thing. **Study the concepts** until you understand them fully, and then you'll be able to answer any question that shows up on the test.

It's important to wait on the practice tests until you're ready. If you take a test on your first day of study, you may be overwhelmed by the amount of material covered and how much you need to learn. Work up to it gradually.

On test day, you'll need to be prepared for answering questions, managing your time, and using the test-taking strategies you've learned. It's a lot to balance, like a mental marathon that will have a big impact on your future. Like training for a marathon, you'll need to start slowly and work your way up. When test day arrives, you'll be ready.

Start with the strategies you've read in the first two Secret Keys—plan your course and study in the way that works best for you. If you have time, consider using multiple study resources to get different approaches to the same concepts. It can be helpful to see difficult concepts from more than one angle. Then find a good source for practice tests. Many times, the test website will suggest potential study resources or provide sample tests.

Practice Test Strategy

When you're ready to start taking practice tests, follow this strategy:

Untimed and Open-Book Practice

Take the first test with no time constraints and with your notes and study guide handy. Take your time and focus on applying the strategies you've learned.

Timed and Open-Book Practice

Take the second practice test open-book as well, but set a timer and practice pacing yourself to finish in time.

Timed and Closed-Book Practice

Take any other practice tests as if it were test day. Set a timer and put away your study materials. Sit at a table or desk in a quiet room, imagine yourself at the testing center, and answer questions as quickly and accurately as possible.

Keep repeating timed and closed-book tests on a regular basis until you run out of practice tests or it's time for the actual test. Your mind will be ready for the schedule and stress of test day, and you'll be able to focus on recalling the material you've learned.

Secret Key #4 – Pace Yourself

Once you're fully prepared for the material on the test, your biggest challenge on test day will be managing your time. Just knowing that the clock is ticking can make you panic even if you have plenty of time left. Work on pacing yourself so you can build confidence against the time constraints of the exam. Pacing is a difficult skill to master, especially in a high-pressure environment, so **practice is vital**.

Set time expectations for your pace based on how much time is available. For example, if a section has 60 questions and the time limit is 30 minutes, you know you have to average 30 seconds or less per question in order to answer them all. Although 30 seconds is the hard limit, set 25 seconds per question as your goal, so you reserve extra time to spend on harder questions. When you budget extra time for the harder questions, you no longer have any reason to stress when those questions take longer to answer.

Don't let this time expectation distract you from working through the test at a calm, steady pace, but keep it in mind so you don't spend too much time on any one question. Recognize that taking extra time on one question you don't understand may keep you from answering two that you do understand later in the test. If your time limit for a question is up and you're still not sure of the answer, mark it and move on, and come back to it later if the time and the test format allow. If the testing format doesn't allow you to return to earlier questions, just make an educated guess; then put it out of your mind and move on.

On the easier questions, be careful not to rush. It may seem wise to hurry through them so you have more time for the challenging ones, but it's not worth missing one if you know the concept and just didn't take the time to read the question fully. Work efficiently but make sure you understand the question and have looked at all of the answer choices, since more than one may seem right at first.

Even if you're paying attention to the time, you may find yourself a little behind at some point. You should speed up to get back on track, but do so wisely. Don't panic; just take a few seconds less on each question until you're caught up. Don't guess without thinking, but do look through the answer choices and eliminate any you know are wrong. If you can get down to two choices, it is often worthwhile to guess from those. Once you've chosen an answer, move on and don't dwell on any that you skipped or had to hurry through. If a question was taking too long, chances are it was one of the harder ones, so you weren't as likely to get it right anyway.

On the other hand, if you find yourself getting ahead of schedule, it may be beneficial to slow down a little. The more quickly you work, the more likely you are to make a careless mistake that will affect your score. You've budgeted time for each question, so don't be afraid to spend that time. Practice an efficient but careful pace to get the most out of the time you have.

Secret Key #5 – Have a Plan for Guessing

When you're taking the test, you may find yourself stuck on a question. Some of the answer choices seem better than others, but you don't see the one answer choice that is obviously correct. What do you do?

The scenario described above is very common, yet most test takers have not effectively prepared for it. Developing and practicing a plan for guessing may be one of the single most effective uses of your time as you get ready for the exam.

In developing your plan for guessing, there are three questions to address:

- When should you start the guessing process?
- How should you narrow down the choices?
- Which answer should you choose?

When to Start the Guessing Process

Unless your plan for guessing is to select C every time (which, despite its merits, is not what we recommend), you need to leave yourself enough time to apply your answer elimination strategies. Since you have a limited amount of time for each question, that means that if you're going to give yourself the best shot at guessing correctly, you have to decide quickly whether or not you will guess.

Of course, the best-case scenario is that you don't have to guess at all, so first, see if you can answer the question based on your knowledge of the subject and basic reasoning skills. Focus on the key words in the question and try to jog your memory of related topics. Give yourself a chance to bring the knowledge to mind, but once you realize that you don't have (or you can't access) the knowledge you need to answer the question, it's time to start the guessing process.

It's almost always better to start the guessing process too early than too late. It only takes a few seconds to remember something and answer the question from knowledge. Carefully eliminating wrong answer choices takes longer. Plus, going through the process of eliminating answer choices can actually help jog your memory.

Summary: Start the guessing process as soon as you decide that you can't answer the question based on your knowledge.

How to Narrow Down the Choices

The next chapter in this book (**Test-Taking Strategies**) includes a wide range of strategies for how to approach questions and how to look for answer choices to eliminate. You will definitely want to read those carefully, practice them, and figure out which ones work best for you. Here though, we're going to address a mindset rather than a particular strategy.

Your chances of guessing an answer correctly depend on how many options you are choosing from.

How many choices you have	How likely you are to guess correctly
5	20%
4	25%
3	33%
2	50%
1	100%

You can see from this chart just how valuable it is to be able to eliminate incorrect answers and make an educated guess, but there are two things that many test takers do that cause them to miss out on the benefits of guessing:

- Accidentally eliminating the correct answer
- Selecting an answer based on an impression

We'll look at the first one here, and the second one in the next section.

To avoid accidentally eliminating the correct answer, we recommend a thought exercise called **the $5 challenge**. In this challenge, you only eliminate an answer choice from contention if you are willing to bet $5 on it being wrong. Why $5? Five dollars is a small but not insignificant amount of money. It's an amount you could afford to lose but wouldn't want to throw away. And while losing $5 once might not hurt too much, doing it twenty times will set you back $100. In the same way, each small decision you make—eliminating a choice here, guessing on a question there—won't by itself impact your score very much, but when you put them all together, they can make a big difference. By holding each answer choice elimination decision to a higher standard, you can reduce the risk of accidentally eliminating the correct answer.

The $5 challenge can also be applied in a positive sense: If you are willing to bet $5 that an answer choice *is* correct, go ahead and mark it as correct.

Summary: Only eliminate an answer choice if you are willing to bet $5 that it is wrong.

Which Answer to Choose

You're taking the test. You've run into a hard question and decided you'll have to guess. You've eliminated all the answer choices you're willing to bet $5 on. Now you have to pick an answer. Why do we even need to talk about this? Why can't you just pick whichever one you feel like when the time comes?

The answer to these questions is that if you don't come into the test with a plan, you'll rely on your impression to select an answer choice, and if you do that, you risk falling into a trap. The test writers know that everyone who takes their test will be guessing on some of the questions, so they intentionally write wrong answer choices to seem plausible. You still have to pick an answer though, and if the wrong answer choices are designed to look right, how can you ever be sure that you're not falling for their trap? The best solution we've found to this dilemma is to take the decision out of your hands entirely. Here is the process we recommend:

Once you've eliminated any choices that you are confident (willing to bet $5) are wrong, select the first remaining choice as your answer.

Whether you choose to select the first remaining choice, the second, or the last, the important thing is that you use some preselected standard. Using this approach guarantees that you will not be enticed into selecting an answer choice that looks right, because you are not basing your decision on how the answer choices look.

This is not meant to make you question your knowledge. Instead, it is to help you recognize the difference between your knowledge and your impressions. There's a huge difference between thinking an answer is right because of what you know, and thinking an answer is right because it looks or sounds like it should be right.

Summary: To ensure that your selection is appropriately random, make a predetermined selection from among all answer choices you have not eliminated.

Test-Taking Strategies

This section contains a list of test-taking strategies that you may find helpful as you work through the test. By taking what you know and applying logical thought, you can maximize your chances of answering any question correctly!

It is very important to realize that every question is different and every person is different: no single strategy will work on every question, and no single strategy will work for every person. That's why we've included all of them here, so you can try them out and determine which ones work best for different types of questions and which ones work best for you.

Question Strategies

Read Carefully

Read the question and answer choices carefully. Don't miss the question because you misread the terms. You have plenty of time to read each question thoroughly and make sure you understand what is being asked. Yet a happy medium must be attained, so don't waste too much time. You must read carefully, but efficiently.

Contextual Clues

Look for contextual clues. If the question includes a word you are not familiar with, look at the immediate context for some indication of what the word might mean. Contextual clues can often give you all the information you need to decipher the meaning of an unfamiliar word. Even if you can't determine the meaning, you may be able to narrow down the possibilities enough to make a solid guess at the answer to the question.

Prefixes

If you're having trouble with a word in the question or answer choices, try dissecting it. Take advantage of every clue that the word might include. Prefixes and suffixes can be a huge help. Usually they allow you to determine a basic meaning. Pre- means before, post- means after, pro - is positive, de- is negative. From prefixes and suffixes, you can get an idea of the general meaning of the word and try to put it into context.

Hedge Words

Watch out for critical hedge words, such as *likely, may, can, sometimes, often, almost, mostly, usually, generally, rarely*, and *sometimes*. Question writers insert these hedge phrases to cover every possibility. Often an answer choice will be wrong simply because it leaves no room for exception. Be on guard for answer choices that have definitive words such as *exactly* and *always*.

Switchback Words

Stay alert for *switchbacks*. These are the words and phrases frequently used to alert you to shifts in thought. The most common switchback words are *but, although*, and *however*. Others include *nevertheless, on the other hand, even though, while, in spite of, despite, regardless of*. Switchback words are important to catch because they can change the direction of the question or an answer choice.

Characteristics of infants and young children with intellectual disabilities

Newborns with intellectual disabilities, especially of greater severity, may not demonstrate normal reflexes, such as rooting and sucking reflexes, necessary for nursing. They may not show other temporary infant reflexes such as the Moro, Babinski, swimming, stepping, or labyrinthine reflexes, or they may demonstrate weaker versions of some of these. In some babies, these reflexes will exist but persist past the age when they normally disappear. Babies with intellectual disabilities are likely to display developmental milestones at later-than-typical ages. The ages when they do display milestones vary according to the severity of the disability and by individual. Young children with intellectual disabilities are likely to walk, self-feed, and speak later than normally developing children. Those who learn to read and write do so at later ages. Children with mild intellectual disabilities may lack curiosity and have quiet demeanors; those with profound intellectual disabilities are likely to remain infantile in abilities and behaviors throughout life. Intellectually disabled children will score below normal on standardized IQ tests and adaptive behavior rating scales.

Learning disabilities

Variables with the potential to cause learning disabilities

LDs are basically neurological disorders. Though they are more specific to particular areas of learning than global disorders like intellectual disabilities, scientific research has found correlations between LDs and many of the same factors that cause intellectual disabilities, including prenatal influences like excessive alcohol or other drug consumption, diseases, and so on. Once babies are born, glandular disorders, brain injuries, exposure to secondhand smoke or other toxins, infections of the central nervous system, physical trauma, or malnutrition can cause neurological damage resulting in LDs. Hypoxia and anoxia (oxygen loss) before, during, or after birth is a cause, as are radiation and chemotherapy. These same influences often cause behavioral disorders as well as LDs. Another factor is genetic: Both LDs and behavior disorders have been observed to run in families. While research has not yet identified specific genetic factors, heritability does appear to be a component in influencing learning and behavioral disorders.

Types of neurological damage

Various neurological research studies have revealed that children diagnosed with LDs and ADHD have at least one of several kinds of structural damage to their brains. Scientists have found smaller numbers of cells in certain important regions of the brains of some children with learning and behavioral disorders. Some of these children are found to have brain cells of smaller than normal size. In some cases, dysplasia is discovered; that is, some brain cells migrate into the wrong area of the brain. In some children with learning and behavioral disorders, blood flow is found to be lower than normal to certain regions in the brain. Also, the brain cells of some children with learning and behavioral disabilities show lower levels of glucose metabolism; glucose (blood sugar) is the brain's main source of fuel, so inadequate utilization of glucose can affect the brain's ability to perform some functions related to cognitive processing, as in LDs, and to attention and impulse control, as in ADHD.

Types of learning disabilities

Dyslexia, the most common LD, means deficiency or inability in reading. It primarily affects reading but can also interfere with writing and speaking. Characteristics include reversing letters and words, for example, confusing b and d in reading and writing; reading won as now, confusing similar speech sounds like /p/ and /b/, and perceiving spaces between words in the wrong places when reading. Dyscalculia is difficulty doing mathematical calculations; it can also affect using money and telling time. Dysgraphia means difficulties specifically with writing, including omitting words in writing sentences or leaving sentences unfinished, difficulty putting one's thoughts into writing, and poor handwriting. Central auditory processing disorder causes difficulty perceiving small differences in words despite normal hearing acuity; for example, couch and chair may be perceived as cow and hair. Background noise and information overloads exacerbate the effects. Visual processing disorders affect visual perception despite normal visual acuity, causing difficulty finding information in printed text or from maps, charts, pictures, graphs, and so on; synthesizing information from various sources into one place; and remembering directions to locations.

Attachment styles identified by Mary Ainsworth

Mary Ainsworth worked with John Bowlby, discovering the first empirical evidence supporting his attachment theory. From her Strange Situation experiments, she identified secure, insecure and avoidant, insecure and resistant, and insecure and disorganized attachment styles. Securely attached children show normal separation anxiety when mother leaves and happiness when she returns, avoid strangers when alone but are friendly with mother present, and use mother as a safe base for environmental exploring. Insecure and resistant children show exaggerated separation anxiety, ambivalence and resistance to mother upon reuniting, fear strangers, cry more, and explore less than secure or avoidant babies. Insecure and avoidant children show no separation anxiety or stranger anxiety and little interest on reunions with mother and are comforted equally by mother or strangers. Insecure and disorganized types seem dazed and confused, respond inconsistently, and may mix resistant and ambivalent and avoidant behaviors. Secure styles are associated with sensitive, responsive caregiving and children's positive self-images and other images, resistant and ambivalent styles with inconsistent caregiving, and avoidant with unresponsive caregivers. Avoidant, resistant, and disorganized styles, associated with negative self-images and low self-esteem, are most predictive of emotional disturbances.

Emotional disturbances and symptoms classified as anxiety disorders

Anxiety disorders include generalized anxiety disorder (GAD), obsessive-compulsive disorder (OCD), posttraumatic stress disorder (PTSD), panic disorder, social phobia, and specific phobias. All share a common characteristic of overwhelming, irrational, and unrealistic fears. GAD involves excessive worrying about anything or everything and free-floating anxiety. Anxiety may be about real issues but is nonetheless exaggerated and spreads, overtaking the child's life. OCD involves obsessive and preoccupied thoughts and compulsive or irresistible actions, including often bizarre rituals. Germ phobia, constant hand washing, repeatedly checking whether tasks are done or undone, and collecting things excessively are common. PTSD follows traumatic experiences/events. Children have frequent, extreme nightmares, crying, flashbacks wherein they vividly perceive or believe they are experiencing the traumatic event again, insomnia, depression, anxiety, and social withdrawal. Symptoms of panic disorder are panic attacks involving extreme fear and physical symptoms like a racing heart, cold hands and feet, pallor, hyperventilation, and feeling unable to move. Children with social phobia develop fear and avoidance of day care, preschool, or other social settings. Specific phobias are associated with specific objects, animals, or persons and are often triggered by traumatic experiences involving these.

Emotional disturbances in young children

Researchers have investigated emotional disturbances but have not yet established known causes for any. Some disturbances, for example the major mental illness schizophrenia, seem to run in families and hence include a genetic component; childhood schizophrenia exists as a specific diagnosis. Factors contributing to emotional disturbances can be biological or environmental but more often are likely a combination of both. Dysfunctional family dynamics can often contribute to child emotional disorders. Physical and psychological stressors on children can also contribute to the development of emotional problems. Some people have attributed emotional disturbances to diet, and scientists have also researched this but have not discovered proof of cause and effect. Bipolar disorder is often successfully treated with the chemical lithium, which affects sodium flow through nerve cells, so chemical imbalance may be implicated as an etiology. Pediatric bipolar disorder, which has different symptoms than adult bipolar disorder, correlates highly with histories of bipolar and other mood disorders or alcoholism in both parents.

Symptoms of pediatric bipolar disorder

Bipolar, formerly called manic-depressive disorder, has similar depressive symptoms in children as adults. However, children's mood swings often occur much faster, and children show more symptoms of anger and irritability than other adult manic symptoms. Bipolar children's most common symptoms include frequent mood swings; extreme irritability; protracted (up to several hours) tantrums or rages; separation anxiety; oppositional behavior; hyperactivity, impulsivity, and distractibility; restlessness and fidgetiness; silly, giddy, or goofy behavior; aggression; racing thoughts; grandiose beliefs or behaviors; risk-taking; depressed moods; lethargy; low self-esteem; social anxiety; hypersensitivity to environmental or emotional triggers; carbohydrate (sugar or starch) cravings; and trouble getting up in the morning. Other common symptoms include bed-wetting (especially in boys), night terrors, pressured or fast speech, obsessive or compulsive behaviors, motor and vocal tics, excessive daydreaming, poor short-term memory, poor organization, learning disabilities, morbid fascinations, hypersexuality, bossiness and manipulative behavior, lying, property destruction, paranoia, hallucinations, delusions, and suicidal ideations. Less common symptoms include migraines, bingeing, self-injurious behaviors, and animal cruelty.

Conduct disorder

Factors contributing to conduct disorders in children include genetic predispositions, neurological damage, child abuse, and other traumatic experiences. Children with conduct disorders display characteristic emotional and behavioral patterns. These include aggression: They bully or intimidate others, often start physical fights, will use dangerous objects as weapons, exhibit physical cruelty to animals or humans, and assault and steal from others. Deliberate property destruction is another characteristic—breaking things or setting fires. Young children are limited in some of these activities by their smaller size, lesser strength, and lack of access; however, they show the same types of behaviors against smaller, younger, weaker, or more vulnerable children and animals, along with oppositional and defiant behaviors against adults. Also, while truancy is impossible or unlikely in preschoolers, and running away from home is less likely, young children with conduct disorders are likely to demonstrate some forms of seriously violating rules, another symptom of this disorder.

Childhood-onset schizophrenia

The incidence of childhood-onset schizophrenia is rare, but it does exist. One example of differential diagnosis involves distinguishing qualitatively between true auditory hallucinations and young children's "hearing voices" otherwise: In the latter case, a child hears his or her own or a familiar adult's voice in his or her head and does not seem upset by it, while in the former, a child may hear other voices, seemingly in his or her ears, and is frightened and confused by them. Tantrums, defiance, aggression, and other acting-out, externalized behaviors are less frequent in childhood-onset schizophrenia than internalized developmental differences, for example, isolation, shyness, awkwardness, fickleness, strange facial expressions, mistrust, paranoia, anxiety, and depression. Children demonstrate nonpsychotic symptoms earlier than psychotic ones. However, it is difficult to use prepsychotic symptoms as predictors due to variance among developmental peculiarities. While psychiatrists find the course of childhood-onset schizophrenia somewhat more variable than in adults, child symptoms resemble adult symptoms. Childhood-onset schizophrenia is typically chronic and severe, responds less to medication, and has a more guarded prognosis than adolescent- or adult-onset schizophrenia.

Diagnosing the emotional disturbances

Psychosis is a general psychiatric category referring to thought disturbances or disorders. The most common symptoms are delusions that is, believing things that are not true, and hallucinations, that is, seeing, hearing, feeling, tasting, or smelling things that are not there. While early childhood psychosis is rarer than at later ages, psychiatrists confirm it does occur. Moreover, prognosis is poorer for psychosis with onset in early childhood than in adolescence or adulthood. Causes can be from known metabolic or brain disorders or unknown. Younger children are more vulnerable to environmental stressors. Also, in young children, thoughts distorted by fantasy can be from normal cognitive immaturity, due to lack of experience and a larger range of normal functioning, or pathology; where they lie on this continuum must be determined by clinicians. Believing one is a superhero who can fly can be vivid imagination or delusional; having imaginary friends can be pretend play or hallucinatory. Other developmental disorders can also cloud differential diagnosis.

Visual impairments

Developmental characteristics

Historically, it was thought that VI children developed more slowly than normal; however, it is now known that ages for reaching developmental milestones are equally variable in VI babies as in others and that they acquire milestones within equal age ranges. One developmental difference is in sequence: VI children tend to utter their first words or subject-verb 2-word sentences earlier than other children. Some VI children also demonstrate higher levels of language development at younger-than-typical ages. For example, they may sing songs from memory or recall events from the past at earlier ages than other children. This is a logical development in children who must rely more on input to their hearing and other senses than to their vision when the latter is impaired. Totally blind babies reach for objects later, hence explore the environment later; hand use, eye-hand coordination, and gross and fine motor skills are delayed. Blind infants' posture control develops normally (rolling, sitting, all-fours, and standing), but mobility (raising on arms, pulling up, and walking) are delayed.

Causes of visual impairments

Syndrome-related and other malformations like cleft iris or lens dislocation causing VI can have prenatal origins. Cataracts clouding the eye's lens can be congenital, traumatic, or due to maternal rubella. Eyes can be normal, but impairment in the brain's visual cortex can cause VI. Infantile glaucoma, like adult glaucoma, causes intraocular fluid buildup pressure and VI. Conjunctivitis and other infections cause VI. Strabismus and nystagmus are ocular-muscle conditions, respectively causing eye misalignments and involuntary eye movements. Trauma damaging the eyeball(s) is another VI cause. The optic nerve can suffer from atrophy (dysfunction) or hypoplasia, that is, developmental regression, usually prenatally due to neurological trauma; acuity cannot be corrected. Refractive errors like nearsightedness, farsightedness, and astigmatism are correctable. Retinoblastoma, or behind-the-eye tumors, can cause blindness and fatality; surgical or chemotherapeutic treatment is usually required before age 2. Premature infants can have retinopathy of prematurity or retrolental fibroplasia. Cryotherapeutic treatment seems to stop disease progression. Its effects range from none to severe VI (approximately 25% of children) to complete blindness.

neurological damage, seizure-controlling medications also frequently cause drowsiness, interfering with attention and cognition. Attention deficit and attention deficit hyperactivity disorders (ADD and ADHD) limit attention span, focus, and concentration and thus are sometimes classified as health impairments requiring special education services.

Characteristics of babies and children with physical and health impairments

The characteristics of children having various physical or health impairments can range from having no limitations to severe limitations in their activities. Children with cerebral palsy, for example, usually have deficiencies in gross and fine motor development and deficits in speech-language development. Physical and health conditions causing severe debilitation in some children not only seriously limit their daily activities but also cause multiple primary disabilities and impair their intellectual functioning. Other children with physical or health impairments function at average, above-average, or gifted intellectual and academic levels. An important consideration when working with babies and young children having physical or health impairments is handling and positioning them physically. Correctly picking up, holding, carrying, giving assistance, and physically supporting younger children and arranging play materials for them based on their impairment is not only important for preventing injury, pain, and discomfort; it also enables them to receive instruction better and to manipulate materials and perform most efficiently. Preschoolers with physical impairments also tend to have difficulty with communication skills, so educators should give particular attention to facilitating and developing these.

Factors leading to developmental delays

Developmental delays can come from genetic or environmental causes or both. Infants and young children with intellectual disabilities are most likely to exhibit developmental delays. Their development generally proceeds similarly to that of normal children but at slower rates; milestones are manifested at later-than-typical ages. Sensory impairments such as with hearing and vision can also delay many aspects of children's development. Children with physical and health impairments are likely to exhibit delays in their motor development and performance of physical activities. Another factor is environmental: Children deprived of adequate environmental stimulation commonly show delays in cognitive, speech-language, and emotional and social development. Children with autism spectrum disorders often have markedly delayed language and speech development; many are nonverbal. Autistic children also typically have impaired social development, caused by and inability or difficulty with understanding others' emotional and social nonverbal communications. When they cannot interpret these, they do not know how to respond and also cannot imitate them; however, they can often learn these skills with special instruction.

Characteristics indicating developmental delays

Developmental delays mean that a child does not reach developmental milestones at the expected ages. For example, if most babies normally learn to walk between 12 and 15 months of age, a 20-month-old who is not beginning to walk is considered as having a developmental delay. Delays can occur in cognitive, speech-language, social-emotional, gross motor skill, or fine motor skill development. Signs of delayed motor development include stiff or rigid limbs, floppy or limp body posture for the child's age, using one side of the body more than the other, and clumsiness unusual for the child's age. Behavioral signs of children's developmental delays include inattention, or shorter than normal attention span for the age; avoiding or infrequent eye contact; focusing on unusual objects for long times or preferring objects over social interaction; excessive frustration when attempting tasks normally simple for children their age; unusual stubbornness; aggressive and acting-out behaviors; daily violent behaviors; rocking; excessive talking to oneself; and not soliciting love or approval from parents.

Traumatic brain injury (TBI)

TBI is defined by the IDEA law (the Individuals with Disabilities Education Act) as "an acquired injury to the brain from external physical force, resulting in total or partial functional disability or psychosocial impairment, or both, that adversely affect a child's educational performance." This definition excludes injuries from birth trauma, congenital injuries, and degenerative conditions. TBI is the foremost cause of death and disability in children (and teens) in the USA. The most common causes of TBI in children include falls, motor vehicle accidents, and physical abuse. In spite of the IDEA's definition, aneurysms and strokes are examples of internal traumas that can also cause TBI in babies and young children. External head injuries that can result in TBI include both open and closed head injuries. Shaken baby syndrome is caused by forcibly shaking an infant. This causes the brain literally to bounce against the insides of the skull, causing rebound injuries, resulting in TBI and even death.

Characteristics of infants and young children who have sustained traumatic brain injuries

TBI can impair a child's cognitive development and processing. It can impede the language development of children, which is dependent upon cognitive development. Children who have sustained TBI often have difficulties with attention, retention and memory; reasoning, judgment, understanding abstract concepts and thinking abstractly, and problem-solving abilities. TBIs can also impair a child's motor functions and physical abilities. The sensory and perceptual functions of children with TBI can be abnormal. Their ability to process information is often compromised. Their speech can also be affected. In addition, TBIs can impair a child's psychosocial behaviors. Memory deficits are commonest, tend to be longer lasting, and are often area specific; for example, a child may recall personal experiences but not factual information. Other common characteristics of TBI include cognitive inflexibility or rigidity, damaged conceptualization and reasoning, language loss or poor verbal fluency, problems with paying attention and concentrating, inadequate problem solving, and problems with reading and writing.

Etiologies and characteristics of multiple disabilities

The term multiple disabilities refers to any combination of more than one disabling condition. For example, a child may be both blind and deaf due to causes such as having rheumatic fever in infancy or early childhood. Anything causing neurological damage before, during, or shortly after birth can result in multiple disabilities, particularly if it is widespread rather than localized. For example, infants deprived of oxygen or suffering traumatic brain injuries in utero, during labor or delivery, or postnatally can sustain severe brain damage. So can babies having encephalitis or meningitis and those whose mothers abused drugs prenatally. Infants with this type of extensive damage can often present with multiple disabilities, including intellectual disabilities, cerebral palsy, physical paralysis, mobility impairment, visual impairment, hearing impairment, and speech-language disorders. They may have any combination of or all of these disabilities as well as others. In addition to a difficulty or inability with normal physical performance, multiply disabled children often have difficulty acquiring and retaining cognitive skills and transferring or generalizing skills among settings and situations.

Prematurity or preterm birth

Babies born before 37 weeks' gestation are classified as premature or preterm. Premature infants can have difficulty with breathing, as their lungs are not fully developed, and with regulating their body temperatures. Premature infants may be born with pneumonia, respiratory distress, extra air or bleeding in the lungs, jaundice, sepsis or infection, hypoglycemia (low blood sugar), severe intestinal inflammation, bleeding into the brain or white-matter brain damage, or anemia. They pennies arranged in 3 rows of 4 each. Conservation is one type of mental operation. The hallmark of concrete operations is the ability to perform mental operations and reverse them, but only using concrete objects. Abstract operations develop later in the formal operations stage, around age 11. Significantly, concrete operations coincide with beginning formal schooling and enables children to learn and use arithmetic, grammar, and so on because they can think logically.

Preoperational vs. Concrete Operational

Piaget called the stage of most children aged 2–6 years Preoperational because children these ages cannot yet perform mental operations, i.e. manipulate information mentally. At around 6–7 years old, children begin to develop Concrete Operations. A key aspect of this stage is the ability to think logically. This ability first develops relative to concrete objects and events. Concrete Operational children still have trouble understanding abstract concepts or hypothetical situations, but they can apply logical sequences and cause and effect to things they can see, feel, and manipulate physically. For example, Concrete Operational children develop the understanding that things have the same amount or number regardless of their shape or arrangement, which Piaget termed conservation. They develop proficiency in inductive logic, i.e. drawing generalizations from specific instances. However, deductive logic, i.e. predicting specific results according to general principles, is not as well-developed until the later stage of Formal Operations involving abstract thought. Another key development of Concrete Operations is reversibility, i.e. the ability to reverse an action or operation.

Example of Preoperational and Concrete Operations stages

The different thinking found between Piaget's Preoperational and Concrete Operations stages is exemplified in experiments he and others conducted to prove his theory. For example, the absence/presence of ability to conserve liquid volume across shape/appearance has been shown in experiments with differently aged children. A preschooler is shown a tall, thin beaker and a short, wide one. The experimenter also shows the child two identically sized and shaped containers with identical amounts of liquid in each. The experimenter then pours the equal amounts of liquid into the two differently shaped beakers. The preschooler will say either the thin beaker holds more liquid because it is taller or the short beaker holds more because it is wider. Piaget termed this "centration"—focusing on only one property at a time. An older child "decentrates," can "conserve" the amount, and knows both beakers hold identical amounts. Older children also use reversibility and logic, e.g. "I know they are still equal, because I just saw you pour the same amount into each beaker."

Human prenatal development

The first stage of development is the germinal period in the first 2 weeks after conception. Cells divide rapidly and begin to differentiate. Within 1 week 100 to 150 cells have formed. The zygote (fertilized egg) differentiates into layers: The innermost layer, which will become the embryo, is the blastocyst; the outermost layer of cells, which will support and nourish the embryo, is the trophoblast. Approximately 10 days following conception, the zygote becomes implanted in the uterine wall (endometrium). From 2 to 8 weeks after conception is the embryonic period. The embryonic cells further differentiate into three layers. Innermost is the endoderm, which will develop into respiratory and digestive systems and some other internal body parts. The middle layer is the mesoderm, which will develop into bones, muscles, and the reproductive and excretory systems. The outermost layer, the ectoderm, will develop into the nervous system and sensory receptors—eyes, ears, nose, and skin. The amniotic sac, umbilical cord, and placenta develop along with the embryo.

Fetal period of human prenatal development

The fetal period follows the germinal and embryonic periods. It begins 2 months after conception and continues for an average of 7 months. At 3 months following conception, a fetus is almost 4 inches (about 10 cm) long and weighs a bit more than 2 ounces (60 grams). The fetus becomes physically active during this period, moving its limbs and head and opening and closing its mouth. The fetal forehead, face, eyelids, nose, chin, and hands are discernible. The lower fetal body parts undergo a growth spurt at around 4 months. Toenails and fingernails develop by 5 months; fetal activity increases. By the end of 6 months, fetal eyelids and eyes are completely formed; the fetus has developed the grasping reflex and begins to breathe intermittently. During the eighth and ninth months, the fetus develops fatty tissues; the functioning of the heart, kidneys, and other organs increases; and sensory systems begin working, especially hearing. Some children report memories of sounds like the maternal heartbeat; some remember music they heard in utero.

Principles of development

Human development in utero follows three basic principles. One is cephalocaudal, or literally, from head to tail; that is, physical structures closer to the head develop earlier than those closer to the toes. Another principle is from more basic to more specialized. In other words, body organs and systems do not first appear as completely formed miniatures but in simpler earlier forms that only later develop finer details. For example, the heart first forms with 2chambers and later develops into an organ with four chambers. A third principle of human prenatal development is in the order of importance. The organs most important to survival, such as the brain and the heart, develop earliest, while other organs not as important for surviving develop later.

Formation of the brain during the embryonic period

The human brain begins forming 18 days after conception. It is among the slowest-developing organs and continues development after birth for many years. In a 9-weeks fetus, the brain makes up 25% of body weight, which decreases as the rest of the body develops. The brain is 10% of a newborn's body weight and 2% of an adult's. In the embryonic period, by the third week, the embryonic disc, which will become the baby, has formed the three germ layers of ectoderm, mesoderm, and endoderm. Cells in the ectoderm thicken, forming the neural plate, and a groove forms in this plate at around 18 days. This groove begins to close, creating the neural tube, which normally closes fully by 4 weeks. Failed or incomplete closure results in neural tube birth defects like anencephaly or spina bifida. Neural tube walls thicken to form the neuroepithelium, where glia, neurons, and all brain cells will develop.

Structures that develop prenatally

After the neural tube closes at around 4 weeks in gestation, the forebrain, midbrain, and hindbrain differentiate. During this fourth week, the forebrain additionally divides into the diencephalon and telencephalon. Near the fourth week's end, the hindbrain divides into the metencephalon and myelencephalon. The forebrain's telencephalon grows to cover its diencephalon, forming the cerebral hemispheres and cortices by 11 weeks. The brain stem and the hindbrain develop earliest; then the midbrain and, finally, the forebrain's cerebral cortices develop. This sequence is believed by scientists to be connected to basic biological processes, like breathing and digestion, which must function immediately at birth, before the gray matter of the cerebral cortices, needed for thinking and other mental processes, will develop in the forebrain.

Stages of cellular development in the human brain

The first stage of neuronal development, which occurs prenatally and is complete by the end of the second trimester of gestation, is proliferation, that is, the production of nerve cells. The second stage is cellular migration, occurring between the fourth and ninth months of gestation. Cells are first formed in the wall of the neural tube and then migrate to their ultimate destinations. Alongside of the developing neurons, radial glial cells grow to guide the formation of neural pathways for neurons to migrate to their final locations. The third stage of neuronal development continues beyond birth and involves two processes: myelinization and synaptogenesis. Myelinization is the process whereby myelin, a sheath of fatty tissue, develops around the neurons to insulate them from other cells, protect them, and facilitate the transmission of neural impulses along the nerves. Synaptogenesis is the process whereby neurons establish synapses—connections to communicate with each other and with end organs, enabling transmission of neural impulses throughout the brain and between the brain and other organs.

Prenatal vs. postnatal brain development

Research has found that all of the neurons (brain cells) a human will ever have are produced by the end of the second trimester of gestation. As many as 250,000 cells per minute are formed between the 10th and 26th weeks after conception. Cellular overproduction is normal during prenatal development. Also normal is natural cellular death, known as apoptosis or pruning, which takes place before and after birth; an estimated 50% to70% of this pruning occurs postnatally. Once formed, neurons establish connections. Those not making connections or making improper ones die, that is, they are pruned, as part of the developmental process. Ultimately, the adult human brain contains approximately 100 billion neurons.

Prenatal developmental milestones

The first fetal movements are observed by 7 weeks of gestation. Startling and general motions occur at 8 weeks. Hiccups, isolated arm and leg movements, and isolated backward head bending occur at 9 weeks; isolated head rotation happens at 9 to 10 weeks. Isolated downward head bending, breathing movements, arm and leg twitches, stretching, rotation, and hand-face touching emerge at 10 weeks. Jaw movements appear at around 10 to 11 weeks, and fetuses have been observed to yawn at 11 weeks. Movements of the fingers, and sucking and swallowing movements, typically develop by 12 weeks of fetal development. Clonic movements, meaning short, spasmodic motions, of the fetal arms and legs are observed to occur by 13 weeks. The developing fetus will demonstrate motions associated with the rooting reflex (physically searching for the nipple to nurse) at 14 weeks of gestation. The fetus is found to make its first eye movements by the gestational age of 16 weeks.

Fetal behavioral states

Human fetuses are generally active throughout gestation. However, as they develop, their movements more clearly differentiate into active and inactive periods. Behavioral states, that is, well-defined, distinguishable sets of factors with stability across time and discrete transitions between them, have been observed by 36 weeks of gestation and identified based on newborn behavioral states as referents. Some describe these states as evidence of increased central nervous system integration. Quiet sleep (1F) involves a stable heart rate, no eye movements, and occasional startling. This occurs at c. 15% at 36 weeks; 32% at 38 weeks; and 38% at term. Active sleep (2F) includes eye movements, gross body movements, and heart rate often accelerating with movements. This occurs c. 42% to 48% of the time. Quiet awake (3F) involves eye movements; no body movements, no heart rate accelerations, and wider oscillation bandwidth than quiet sleep (1F) occur briefly and rarely. Active awake (4F) involves eye movements, constant activity, and an unstable and faster heart rate, occurring c. 6% to 7% of the time at 36 to 38 weeks and 9% c. 40 weeks, just before birth.

Human prenatal development of senses

Development of smell and taste

From roughly 12 weeks of gestation, the human fetus begins swallowing amniotic fluid. This means that anything the mother ingests, which diffuses into the amniotic fluid, can be received by the fetus. Also, any changes in the maternal diet or other substances ingested change the kind of stimulation the fetus experiences. Because the sensory receptors for smell and taste in the fetal brain are both bathed in amniotic fluid, these two senses are difficult for scientists to separate. Hence, fetal responses to olfaction, or smell, and gustation, or taste, are typically combined under the term chemosensation. Researchers have found that, when they inject sugar into the amniotic fluid, fetuses swallow more; when a harmful substance, like iodinated poppy seed, is injected into the amniotic fluid, they swallow less. The facts that newborn infants orient toward their own amniotic fluid and prefer the odors of their mothers over those of other women are interpreted by scientists as additional evidence that babies experience smells and tastes before birth.

Development of hearing

By 22 to 24 weeks of gestation, the fetus shows responses to sound by changes in movement. Frequency and pitch, intensity and loudness, and duration of sounds affect fetal responses. Louder sounds cause greater movement. Fetal hearing begins developing at 250 to 500 Hz, the lower range of frequencies humans can hear. This increases with development toward the adult hearing range of 20 to 20,000 Hz. Researchers have found fetuses also respond discriminatively to speech sounds, like different vowels. Fetuses can hear their mothers' heartbeats, blood flow, and digestive sounds. They can also hear sounds outside the womb, though these are attenuated (damped) by maternal tissues. Higher-frequency or pitched sounds above 2,000 Hz are attenuated by up to 40 dB (decibels), so the fetus likely cannot hear these. It is interesting to note that the basic frequency range of human speech, 125 to 250 Hz, is attenuated the least of all frequencies, enabling unborn babies to hear speech sounds coming from both the mother and from others around her.

Development of touch

Touch is the earliest fetal sense to develop at around 8 weeks' gestation. Fetuses around 8 to 9 weeks move their heads away from touch stimuli to the cheeks or lips; however, they move toward touch stimuli in the second trimester. Excepting the back and top of the head, most of the fetal body responds to touch by 14 weeks. Fetuses touch their faces with arms or hands from around 13 weeks, supplying tactile stimulation; twins, triplets, or other multiple pregnancies afford greater touch stimulation. Pregnant mothers report more fetal movement when they take hot baths; otherwise, the temperature regulation of normal pregnancy prevents fetuses from feeling much temperature variation. Neural pathways for pain develop around 26 weeks. Pain is subjective and can only be measured indirectly in fetuses, so whether they feel pain is controversial. However, behavioral reactions have been observed in fetuses when touched by a needle during amniocentesis, and after fetal scalp blood sampling during labor, and biochemical stress responses have been measured after needle punctures during blood transfusions from 23 weeks' gestation.

Development of vision

Of all senses, vision is the least stimulated and used in utero as there is no light source inside the womb and the fetus sees little more than a "diffuse orange glow," which may become lighter if very bright light is shined on the mother's abdomen or transvaginally at the cervix. Thus, infant vision is less developed than other senses upon birth, when infants receive all the same visual stimuli that adults do. The pupillary reflex, which expands and contracts the pupils to admit more or less light, is underdeveloped at birth. Visual accommodation for focusing on nearer or farther objects is also restricted at birth. It is clearest at around 7 to 20 inches, corresponding to the distance of the baby's eyes from the mother's face when nursing. The combination of poor pupillary reflexes and visual accommodation in neonates makes much of their vision unfocused. However, these abilities develop quickly after birth. As the baby grows, processes of tracking, scanning, and other eye movements additionally develop, enhancing eyesight.

Reflexes in human newborn infants

Reflexes are involuntary motor movements that are elicited by sensory or kinetic stimulation, for example, visual stimuli like light, tactile stimulation (touch), or changes in body position. Brain structures below the cerebral cortices control these reflexive motor behaviors. Many reflexes appear in newborns and disappear when they are several months old, for example, the Babinski reflex (when the sole of the foot is stroked, the toes fan out and then curl up), the Moro reflex (startling, extending the head and limbs at loud noises or sudden slipping), and rooting (searching for the nipple) and sucking reflexes. Rooting and sucking disappear as they are replaced by nonreflexive or voluntary eating behaviors. Reflexes like breathing and swallowing are necessary to survive and persist throughout life, as do blinking and yawning reflexes. Infant reflexes are important for indicating normal brain functioning and integrity, ensuring newborns' survival, and providing foundations for future motor development. Infant reflexes that are weaker than normal, or persist past ages when they normally end can indicate cerebral palsy or other neurological problems.

Different reflexes demonstrated by newborn human infants

From birth to 4 or 5 months, infants demonstrate the rooting reflex when their cheeks or mouth edges are touched. From birth to 4 to 6 months, the sucking reflex is activated by touching their mouths. From birth to 4 months, babies show the grasping reflex when their hands are touched. The Moro, or startling, reflex results from sudden loud sounds, such as objects being dropped, and occurs from birth to 4 to 6 months. The Babinski reflex, wherein the baby's toes fan out and then curl up when the sole of the foot is stroked, appears from birth to 9 to 12 months. Babies demonstrate the swimming reflex, holding their breath and making swimming motions with their limbs when placed in water, from birth to 4 to 6 months. When infants are held above a surface and their feet touch it, they show the stepping reflex from birth to 3 to 4 months. From birth to 4 months, babies exhibit the labyrinthine reflex, extending limbs when placed on their backs and flexing limbs when placed on their stomachs. These reflexes normally disappear by the ends of the time ranges given.

Principles of physical growth of children

1. *General to specific*: Movements become more defined with development. Infants wave their limbs; older children can walk and draw.
2. *Differentiation and integration*: Differentiation is locating or isolating specific body parts and gaining control over them. Once differentiated, children integrate the movements of each part with those of others, enabling more complex motor activities like walking, riding bicycles, and so on.
3. *Growth variations*: Various body parts grow at different rates; children's motor abilities vary by age.
4. *Optimal tendencies*: Growth tends to seek optimal realization of its potential. If development is delayed, for example, by malnutrition, it tends to catch up when possible; hence children with such environmental delays can develop skills at later ages.

- 33 -

5. *Sequential growth*: Development proceeds in an ordered sequence, seen in the growth of individual body parts and motor behaviors—rolling over, then sitting up, then crawling, then walking.
6. *Critical periods*: Just as the first few years are critical for brain development, ages 1½ to 5 years are critical for motor development.

Types of physical movement

One type of physical movement is (1) *locomotor movement*, that is, the child's movement of his or her body from one location to another. Locomotor movement includes crawling, walking, running, jumping, hopping, skipping, galloping, and leaping. Locomotor movement helps to develop the child's gross motor skills. (2) *Non-locomotor movement* refers to the child's body movements made while remaining in the same location. Sitting down, standing up, wriggling, turning around, twisting, pulling, and pushing are activities that demonstrate non-locomotor movement, which helps to develop the child's skills of coordination and balance. (3) *Manipulative movement* is the child's controlled usage of the hands and feet, with and without objects. Activities like opening and closing the hands, grasping, waving, throwing, and catching are examples of manipulative movement, which helps to develop a child's hand-eye coordination and fine motor skills.

Normative vs. dynamic development

Normative development refers to normal or typical abilities and limits of the majority of children in the same age and cultural groups. Developmental norms help parents know what their children should be able or unable to do at certain ages and what to expect. Developmental milestones identify certain physical abilities, behaviors demonstrating them, and ages when they typically emerge. For example, knowing the fine motor development of 3-year-olds is typically not ready to operate zippers informs parents that expecting this ability would be unrealistic. Dynamic development refers to physical changes occurring during children's development as they grow older and gain experience, the order of changes, and their interactions. Children's bodies grow in three directional patterns: (1) from large muscle to small muscle, or gross motor to fine motor—large trunk, neck, and limb muscles develop before small wrist, hand, finger, and eye muscles; children walk before self-feeding, scribbling, and so on; (2) top-to-bottom, or head to toe—infants can hold up their heads before they can crawl or walk; (3) proximodistal, or inner to outer. Central muscles nearer the trunk develop before extremity (hands, feet) muscles.

Motor development in children

Motor development means children's physical growth and growth in their abilities to use their bodies and bodily skills. The process whereby children gain skills and patterns in physical movement is also a common definition of motor development. Variables influencing motor development include genetic factors; the child's birth size, body composition, and body build; nutritional elements; birth order of the child; aspects of child rearing; the family's social class and socioeconomic status; the child's temperament type; the child's and family's ethnic group; and family cultural influences. Gross motor development involves use of the large muscles for sitting, standing, walking, running, jumping, reaching, throwing, and so on. Fine motor development involves the use of small muscles for self-feeding by hand and with utensils; picking up small objects, drawing, writing, tying shoes, brushing teeth, and so on.

Erikson psychosocial development stages

First stage

Erikson proposed eight stages of psychosocial development or ages of man through adulthood. He later added a ninth stage to include very old age. Each of Erikson's stages focuses on a nuclear conflict that the individual must resolve. According to Erikson's theory, from birth through 1½ to 2 years, children are in the stage of Basic Trust Versus Mistrust. In this first stage, if an infant's needs, such as feeding, changing, bathing, pain relief, physical holding and cuddling, and overall nurturing, are met timely, to satisfaction, and consistently, the infant develops a sense of basic trust in the world, emerging with a sense of security and optimism toward life. If the infant's needs are not met, are only met after delays, are insufficiently satisfied, or are met inconsistently or unpredictably, the child emerges with emotional and social characteristics of mistrust in the world and basic insecurity. Erikson's positive outcome for this stage is Hope.

Second stage

Of nine developmental stages covering the entire human life span, Erikson identified his second stage as centering on resolving the nuclear conflict of Autonomy Versus Shame and Self-Doubt, transpiring between about 1½ to 2 years and 3½ to 4 years of age. Children are learning to control their bodies during this stage, as exemplified by toilet training. They extend this developing ability from controlling their bodily functions to exerting control over their environments. As they experience control, they begin to assert their independence. Parents are familiar with the temper tantrums, loud expressions of "No," and so on, associated with what is often called the Terrible Twos. Children successfully resolving this conflict feel proud and self-assured; those who overexert control or are punished feel ashamed and doubt their own abilities. Erikson found that the positive outcome for successfully completing this stage is Will.

Fourth stage

Of nine stages covering human life, Erikson identified his fourth stage with what he termed the school age. This stage begins around age 5 to 6 years, coinciding with when children begin formal education in Western and developed societies, and continuing until adolescence. Hence, only the beginning of this stage applies to children through age 6. Erikson called this stage and its nuclear conflict to resolve Industry Versus Inferiority. Children beginning school must learn to follow formal rules. Unstructured, free preschool play is replaced by structured play with complex rules, often requiring teamwork, as in sports. Children's activities of making and getting along with friends are extended as their social circles expand. Homework and structured extracurricular activities require increasing self-discipline. Children who have previously learned trust, autonomy, and initiative in Erikson's three earlier stages are prepared to develop industry for accomplishing tasks; those who learned mistrust, shame or self-doubt, and guilt will likely experience defeat, developing a sense of inferiority. Erikson's positive outcome for this stage is Competence.

Scaffolding

Toddlers allowed to explore their environments, play, and pursue their own interests learn better than those who are overly directed or controlled. The concept of scaffolding involves supplying only as much support as a child needs to accomplish a task or activity he or she cannot perform independently and gradually withdrawing this support as the child's skills develop and performance becomes more autonomous. The aim is to prevent excessive frustration while still allowing the child to attack and master new challenges. For example, if a younger toddler is trying to insert a square peg into a round hole, the adult can show him or her how to move the peg over each hole and then drop it into the hole that fits. An adult can give an older toddler time to figure out how to put on shoes or boots. If the child shows frustration, the adult can align the shoes or boots with the corresponding feet and suggest holding onto a chair while balancing on one leg to insert the other foot. Praising process and effort, not just product or outcome, promotes confidence.

Erikson's third stage of emotional and social child development

Erikson's theory encompasses the whole life span of humans, from birth to death. He associated the third stage with the ages between 3½ and 5 to 6 years, a period which he termed the play age. Erikson named this stage for the nuclear conflict that the child must resolve, of Initiative Versus Guilt. Children increase their exploration of the environment in this stage. Their imaginations develop. They engage in active play, including fantasy, which expands their repertoire of skills. An important social development in this stage is learning to cooperate with others. Whereas many 2-year-olds cannot share, most 4-year-olds have learned how. Children learn to lead and to follow. Those not allowed to take the initiative or those punished for it feel guilty and fearful, remain overly dependent on adults, and are not included or marginalized by peer groups. Their play skills and imagination are limited. While Erikson's negative outcome for this stage is Guilt, he deemed its successful completion as Purpose.

Salient aspects of the emotional and social development

As babies become toddlers, they begin to develop self-awareness. They realize they are individuals, independent and separate from other people. Hence, they begin developing the ability to realize others may have their own feelings. Developing the capacity to imagine what others feel enables toddlers to begin developing empathy for others. While toddlers also become more interested in their peers, they are not as likely to play interactively as young children at later ages (e.g., 3 to 4 years) do. Instead, they are most likely to engage in parallel play, wherein they play next to another child rather than directly with him or her. For example, a toddler might approach an older toddler and watch him or her play. With encouragement to play with the older child, the younger toddler will start playing alongside of the older one, observing and sometimes imitating him or her.

Emotional and social characteristics affecting ability to resolve conflict

Toddlers and young children have not yet developed much self-control and impulse control. This means they want immediate gratification and have difficulty deferring it; they also have difficulty not acting on their impulses. These characteristics make it difficult for young children to share things with others and to follow rules. The fact that toddlers are also learning control of their bodies and environments, and thus asserting their wills, further impinges on sharing, cooperating, and conforming to rules. Adults can model sharing for them. They can set kitchen timers to illustrate the duration waiting for a turn in group activities. Young toddlers are unable to resolve conflicts through discussing them; when they become frustrated with waiting, adults can distract or redirect their attention with other stimuli or activities. Adults can help toddlers learn and practice the art of sharing by initiating games involving playing together, passing or tossing balls around a circle of children, taking turns hitting a Nerf ball, and so on.

Emotional and social development in 3- to 4-year-old children

As toddlers grow older, they begin playing more interactively with peers. They also engage in pretend play. For example, children might use toys like blocks to simulate food, "serve" playmates, pretend to exchange money, operate a toy cash register, and so on. They may act out killing monsters using toy weapons or dress up in parents' clothing and imitate adult behaviors like going to work. Most 3- to 4-year-olds are developing better abilities to share and take turns with peers than 1- to 2-year-olds, but they are still learning. Adults can encourage early friendships by providing some activities without sharing, such as individual artwork, playing musical instruments, and so on. When a child refuses to play with a peer, saying "Look at his (or her) face; how do you think he (or she) feels?" helps the child imagine how his or her actions affect others. Explaining others' feelings, for example, "Billy is sad because his daddy said good-bye," and suggesting pro-social comfort, for example, "Let's see if Billy wants to read a story with us," helps children see others' viewpoints, promoting empathy.

Examples of emotional and social developmental needs

Toddlers often feel emotions quite clearly but have not yet developed the language skills to express them. This, combined with their limited abilities to control their behavior and refrain from acting on their impulses, is why they so frequently act out their feelings physically through tantrums, hitting others, and so on. Adults can help by putting emotions into words. For example, they can explain, "You are angry because your brother took your toy." They can also provide modeling by verbally articulating their own emotions: "I am frustrated because I can't find my keys." Helping them verbally label emotions and practice ways of managing them helps children eventually learn to practice these behaviors independently. Explaining consequences of children's actions, for example, "Stevie is crying because it hurt when you hit him—he feels sad and mad," helps them develop empathy and responsibility. Adults can ask or suggest what better choices the child can make next time to promote learning.

Language development - Conception to 6 months

Characteristics of children's language development

Scientists have found evidence that fetuses can hear speech sounds made by their mothers and others around her while still in the womb. They learn to recognize their mother's voice before birth. Newborns listen to people speaking around them. They awaken at loud noises and startle or cry at unexpected noises. They quiet and attend to new sounds. From birth to 3 months, babies turn toward people speaking and smile at the sounds of their voices. They recognize familiar voices and stop crying upon hearing them. They also cease whatever activity they are involved in on hearing the sound of an unfamiliar voice, paying close attention. When someone speaks in comforting tones to babies up to 4 months old, they frequently respond to these whether they are familiar with the speaker's voice or not. By 3 months, they make sounds differentially expressing pleasure, hunger, pain, and so on. At around 4 to 6 months, babies respond to the word "no" and vocal tone changes, begin babbling, and communicate needs through sounds and gestures.

Features of child language development

At 6 months, most babies vocalize expressively, especially babbling. They incorporate the same intonational patterns into babbling that they hear in adult speech, imitating adult rhythms, pitch changes, and so on. Receptively, they respond to hearing their names. Without visual input, they respond to others' voices by turning their heads or eyes toward the speakers. They show emotional understanding of voices by responding appropriately to friendly and angry tones. From 7 to 12 months, babies listen when spoken to, start enjoying games like peekaboo and patty-cake, and recognize names of familiar people or things like mommy, daddy, car, phone, key, and so on. They begin to respond to requests such as "Give the book to Mommy" and questions like "More milk?" By 12 months, babies understand simple directions, especially when accompanied by physical or vocal cues. They can use one or more words meaningfully. They realize the social import of speech. They practice using intonations and begin to utter their first words, for example, Mama, doggie, night-night, and bye-bye.

<u>Milestones of children's language development</u>

Typically, 1-year-olds can point to pictures of things named by adults and point to some body parts on request. They can follow simple directions, for example, "Hot! Don't touch!" or "Pull the wagon" and understand simple questions, like "Where's the kitty?" or "What do you have in your bag?" They enjoy hearing adults recite rhymes and sing songs and listening to simple stories. They like having the same rhyme, game, or story repeated multiple times. By 18 months, most children have expressive vocabularies of around five to twenty words, mostly nouns. Their speech includes much "jargon," that is, nonword or unintelligible speech, which however, expresses emotional content through tone, volume, pitch, rhythm, and so on. They may display some echolalia, that is, repeating what others say or repeating the same word or phrase over and over. Children from 18 months to 2 years old generally speak in utterances of one or two words at a time, though these utterances can express the same meaning as sentences, for example, "Heavy!" upon lifting something or "Watch this!" before doing something.

Examples of play activity of young children

It is important to allow young children to choose the topics of play because this allows them to explore their own interests. For example, if a toddler is fascinated with trucks, adults can help him or her to construct pretend trucks, read books about trucks, and visit a local U-Haul to look at real trucks. When parents follow the child's lead by participating in children's pretend play, they teach him or her about playing interactively with others and its enjoyment and impart feelings of being important, competent, and loved in the child. They can also build upon child pretend play to promote learning. For example, if a child is pretending to have a picnic, the adult can ask the child, "What is good (or bad) weather for a picnic?" and "What kinds of foods are good (or bad) to pack for a picnic?"

Social and emotional skills

By 3 years old, most children comprehend and utilize language well enough to understand simple verbal explanations. Adults can use children's linguistic development to promote their ongoing learning of social skills using simple language they can follow. For example, they can define limits and offer alternatives: "Hitting hurts; you may not hit. When you are mad, you can stomp your feet, jump up and down, rip up paper, throw soft toys, or ask me for a hug." Explaining natural consequences for their actions teaches cause-and-effect relationships: Throwing a hard toy has the consequence of putting the toy away; the positive consequence of cooperatively putting on coats is more time at the playground. Adults should explain the benefits of rules to children: Sharing toys gives everyone a chance to play; helping after-meal cleanup by taking their plates to the kitchen allows more time for stories. This enables children to understand reasons for limits and requests, teaches them to follow rules, and helps them eventually learn to make positive choices.

Language development - 3 and 4 years old

<u>Characteristics of children's language development</u>

Typically, 3-year-olds comprehend who, what, or where questions and respond when called from another room. They should not be expected to answer all questions asked of them even when they understand. A child should be able to say his or her name, age, and sex when asked. They can now think through and answer questions like what they should do when hungry, thirsty, sleepy, or cold. They understand most simple questions about their surroundings and activities. They can recount their experiences understandably to adults. About 90% of 3-year-olds' speech should be intelligible to adults. They know the main body parts and can either name or point to them. Between 3 and 4 years, children develop expressive vocabularies of around 900 to 1,000 words. They can easily

- 38 -

utter 3-word sentences. Verbs become more prevalent than earlier nouns. They correctly use the pronouns I, me, and you and begin using some past tenses and plurals. They commonly use the prepositions in, on, and under and may know more than three prepositions.

Typical developments

Commonly, 5-year-olds are able to count verbally to 10 and know numerical concepts of 4 or more. They understand and use most basic opposite concepts, for example, heavy versus light, hard versus soft, and big versus little. They can now speak with spontaneous use of adjectives and adverbs to describe things. While some may have imperfect articulation, all of their speech should be intelligible to others. They should be able to pronounce all vowels and, in addition to consonants /p/, /b/, /m/, /w/, and /n/ mastered earlier, have added /h/, /k/, /g/, /t/, /d/, /ŋ / (ng), and /y/. They should also be able to repeat heard sentences up to nine words long. They typically can follow uninterrupted 3-step directions. They know their age. They understand basic temporal concepts of day, night, morning, afternoon; today, yesterday, tomorrow; and while, after, and later. They should be able to define common terms like chair, shoe, or hat by their uses. They speak in longer sentences, including some complex and compound sentences. Overall, 5-year-old children's speech is grammatically correct.

Features of emerging language

Generally, 2-year-olds can follow 2-step directions, for example, "Take your shirt off, and put it in the hamper." They now understand the concept of words indicating opposites, like hot and cold or stop and go. They can name more familiar objects in their environments. They can use at least two prepositions, commonly in, on, or under. They can utter short sentences; even two-word utterances are now chiefly noun–verb combinations. Normally, at this age ⅔ of what a child says should be intelligible to adults. From ages 2 to 3 years, children's vocabularies expand greatly to around 150 to 300 words. The fluency and rhythm of their speech is normally still not well developed, and they do not yet control the loudness and pitch of their voices well. While they frequently confuse I and me, they can use you and I or me appropriately. They begin to use the possessives mine and my. They can follow requests such as "Show me your ears (or nose, eyes, mouth, or hair)."

Salient characteristics of normal child language development

Most 4-year-olds understand almost everything they hear, speak more clearly, and can answer simple questions about stories they hear. They know familiar animals' names. They understand and can use at least four prepositions. They can name common objects in pictures and one or more colors. They usually can repeat four-syllable words they hear and repeat four numerical digits if dictated slowly. They show comprehension of the concepts denoted by the prepositions over and under and of comparatives like longer or shorter and bigger or smaller. Between the ages of 4 and 5 years, children can easily follow directions even when the objects referenced in the directions are out of their sight. They do much practice, repeating speech sounds, syllables, phrases, and words. They tend to verbalize copiously during activities, narrating their actions. Psychologist Lev Vygotsky termed this private speech. They engage in much pretend play with narration. They can now correctly pronounce most vowels and the bilabial consonants /p/, /b/, /m/, /w/, and also /n/. They are likely still to distort other consonants somewhat.

Elements demonstrated by age 6 years

Most children have mastered vowel sounds and the consonants /p/, /b/, /m/, /w/, /n/, /h/, /k/, /g/, /t/, /d/, /ŋ / (ng), and /y/ by around the age of 5 years. By the age of 6 years, they generally have also mastered the more difficult consonants /f/, /v/, /ʃ/ (sh), /ʒ/ (zh), and /ð/ (voiced th as in the). Most 6-year-olds should have numerical concepts up to 7. By age 6, children's speech normally is completely understandable to others and is also useful for social purposes. When a 6-year-old is shown a picture, he or she should be able to tell a contiguous story about it, including relationships among the elements. At 6 years old, children should also be able to verbalize relationships between things, people, and events in a connected fashion. Many 6-year-olds have not perfected pronunciation of the most difficult consonants /s/, /z/, /r/, /θ/ (devocalized th as in earth), /tʃ/ (ch), /dʒ/ (j), and /wh/, usually mastering these by age 7. Typically, 6-year-olds are learning to read and write.

Monitoring and adjusting speech based on auditory feedback

When adults and older children are speaking, they tend to rely on their hearing to monitor their own speech for correct pronunciation. As a violinist plays, if a note produced is out of tune, the player will adjust his or her finger position, raising or lowering the pitch to correct it. Adult and older child speakers use an analogous process. Recent research (2011, 2012) has confirmed this: When participants wear headphones and hear altered vowel sounds while speaking, they adjust their spoken vowels accordingly. However, researchers have found that 2-year-olds do not use this process of responding to the auditory feedback of hearing their own voices to adjust their speech sounds. Scientists still do not know exactly what strategies toddlers might use in learning to control their speech. Some speculate that they may depend on the interaction with their listener(s), using visual, nonverbal, and verbal feedback from the other person(s) to assess the accuracy of the speech sounds they produce.

Perceptual development - up to around 18 months

Children 9 to 17 months old stop crawling when they reach the edge of a surface. They will nuzzle fresh laundry to smell it; crumple and tear paper; touch, pat, push, squeeze, and otherwise explore textures; and manipulate substances like play dough. They remember the locations of objects they have seen before. They react to extreme temperatures and tastes. Between the ages of 12 and 18 months, toddlers learn to adjust their gaits according to the surfaces they are walking on, such as walking faster on smooth surfaces and slower on bumpy or rocky ones. Toddlers may decide to slide down a hill on their bottoms rather than walk after using perception to judge its steepness. When standing, toddlers often sway, bounce, or swing their arms to music. They pull their hands away from slimy or unfamiliar textures they touch. When playing at the beach or in a sandbox, they often spend a long time burying their hands or feet in the sand. They will stop pouring sand into a pail when they see it is full.

Importance of perceptual development

Perceptual development is important because it informs the motor activities of babies. They use their perception, for example, of slippery, slanted, rigid, or bumpy surfaces to gauge how to crawl or walk on them. Babies 6 to 9 months old will pick up, look at, and mouth objects to explore them. Hearing footsteps in a dark room, they may turn their heads to look for the source. They may display excitement when recognizing the color of a preferred food. Intersensory redundancy, that is, the overlapping of senses, provides multimodal perception, a foundation of perceptual development, as when an infant turns his or her head upon simultaneously seeing a face and hearing a voice. Perceptual development informs cognitive development. For example, perceiving differences and similarities enables the cognitive ability of classification. Perceptual development is also important to the emotional and social development of young children. For example, they observe others' facial expressions and learn to interpret them as associated with particular emotional states and with social messages, such as encouragement, warning, or disapproval.

<u>Behaviors of perceptual development</u>

From 18 to 24 months, toddlers are likely to engage in and enjoy rough-and-tumble play. Around 2 years of age, they learn to handle fragile objects gently. Most 2-year-olds enjoy books with tactile stimuli, like fuzzy, fake fur; soft, plush fabric; and sandpaper. At 2 to 3 years, many children enjoy playing with sand and water by digging, filling pails, and pouring. By age 3, children can identify blankets and other familiar objects by touch alone. They can identify distinctive toy shapes buried in sand by feeling them. They learn to climb more slowly near the tops of ladders. They know to press harder on clay than play dough and to walk more slowly and carefully when carrying an uncovered container of liquid than when carrying one with a lid. Most 3-year-olds have developed the ability to use their eyesight to follow the lines that they mark on paper when scribbling. They can also observe an adult or older child draw a circle and then try to imitate it.

Responding directly vs. representing ymbolically to environments

Just as children's cognitive development generally proceeds from more concrete to more abstract, this progression can be seen in their responses to the environment moving from the sensorimotor or behavioral to the symbolic or representational. For example, very young children can navigate their homes by recalling visual images of objects, their locations, and other sensory information; as they grow older, they learn abstract concepts like left and right or how to read a floor plan of their home. Researchers find that young children aged around 2 years start reconstructing and symbolically representing what they know. Toddlers often use available objects to symbolize other objects during pretend play. For example, a child might pretend a broom is a horse to ride or a guitar to strum, or a calculator is a smartphone, and so on. Their capacity to employ different media and modalities expands: By preschool ages, they may incorporate gestures, body, and spoken language; drawing, painting, or sculpture; construction; dramatic enactions; and written language. These multimodal play representations of concepts reciprocally improve children's actual knowledge.

Sensorimotor Stage of Piaget's Theory of Cognitive Development

From birth until about 2 years of age, infants are in what Piaget termed the Sensorimotor stage of cognitive development. They learn through environmental input they receive through their senses; motor actions they engage in; and through feedback they receive from their bodies and the environment about their actions. For example, a baby kicks his legs, sees his feet moving, and reaches for them. He sees objects, reaches for them, and grasps them. Eventually, babies learn they can make some objects move by touching or hitting them. They learn through repeated experiences that when they throw objects out of their cribs, their parents retrieve them. They will seem to make a game of this, not to annoy parents, but as a way of learning rules of cause and effect by repeating actions to see the same results. They also enjoy their ability to be causal agents and their power to achieve effects through their actions.

<u>First Three Substages of the Sensorimotor Stage</u>

From birth to 1 month old, infants learn to comprehend their environment through their inborn reflexes, such as the sucking reflex and the reflex of looking at their surroundings. From 1–4 months old, babies begin to coordinate their physical sensations with new schemas, i.e. mental constructs/concepts they form to represent elements of reality. For example, an infant might suck her thumb by chance and feel pleasure from the activity; in the future, she will repeat thumb-sucking because the pleasure is rewarding. Piaget called this second substage "Primary Circular Reactions." In the third substage, around 4–8 months, which he called "Secondary Circular Reactions," children also repeat rewarding actions, but now they are focused on things in the environment that they can affect, rather than just the child's own person. For example, once a baby learns to pick up an object and mouth it, s/he will repeat this. Thus, babies learn an early method of environmental exploration through their mouths, an extension of their initial sucking reflex.

Last Three Substages of the Sensorimotor Stage

According to Piaget, babies about 8–12 months are in the "Coordination of Reactions" substage of the Sensorimotor stage. Having begun repeating actions purposely to achieve environmental effects during the previous substage of Secondary Circular Reactions, in Coordination of Reactions, infants begin further exploring their surroundings. They frequently imitate others' observed behaviors. They more obviously demonstrate intentional behaviors. They become able to combine schemas (mental constructs) to attain certain results. They develop object permanence, the understanding that unseen objects still exist. They learn to associate certain objects with their properties. For example, once a baby realizes a rattle makes a noise when shaken, s/he will deliberately shake it to produce the sound. In "Tertiary Circular Reactions," at about 12–18 months, children begin experimenting through trial-and-error. For instance, a child might test various actions or sounds for getting parents' attention. From 18–24 months, in the substage of "Early Representational Thought," children begin representing objects and events with symbols. They begin to understand the world via not only actions, but mental operations.

Object Permanence

One of the landmarks of infant cognitive development is learning that concrete objects are not "out of sight, out of mind"; in other words, things still continue to exist even when they are out of our sight. Babies generally develop this realization around 8–9 months old, though some may be earlier or later. Some researchers after Piaget have found object permanence in babies as young as 3½ months. Younger infants typically attend to an object of interest only when they can see it; if it is removed or hidden, they are upset/confused at its disappearance and/or shift their attention to something else. A sign that they have developed object permanence is if they search for the object after it is moved or hidden. Babies only become interested in "hide and seek" types of games once they have developed this understanding that the existence of objects and people persist beyond their immediate vision or proximity. Another example of emerging object permanence is the delight babies begin to take in "peek-a-boo" games.

Schema and Schemata Development in Infants

Piaget proposed we form mental constructs or concepts that he called schemata, representing elements of the environment, beginning in infancy. A schema does not represent an individual object, but a category or class of things. For example, a baby might form a schema representing "things to suck on," initially including her bottle, her thumb, and her pacifier. Piaget said assimilation is when we can fit something new into an existing schema: the child in this example assimilates "Daddy's knee" into her schema of things she can suck on when she discovers this action. When something new cannot be assimilated into an existing schema, we either modify that schema or form a new schema, which both constitute accommodation. The baby in our example, becoming a toddler, might modify her schema of things to suck to include straws, which require a different sucking technique. Piaget said assimilation and accommodation combined constitute the process of adaptation, i.e. adjusting, to our environment through interacting with it.

Piaget's Schema Examples

A toddler on an airplane sees a nearby stranger who is male, about 5'8", with white hair and eyeglasses. Both of his grandfathers have these same general appearances. He murmurs to himself, "Hi, Granddaddy." Explain this according to Piaget's concept of the schema in his cognitive-developmental theory.

The toddler in this example did not actually mistake a complete stranger for either one of his grandfathers. Notice that he did not directly address the stranger as "Granddaddy" with conversational loudness, but murmured it to himself. He recognized this man was not someone he knew. However, he recognized common elements with his grandfathers in the man's appearance. According to Piaget's theory of cognitive development, the explanation for this is that the child had formed a schema, i.e. a mental construct, to represent men about 5'8" with white hair and eyeglasses, based initially on his early knowledge of two such men he knew, his grandfathers, and then extending to include other similar-appearing men, through the process of assimilation of new information into an existing schema. His description did not mean he thought the stranger was named "Granddaddy." Rather, the word "Granddaddy" was not only the name he called one grandfather, but also the word he used to label his schema for all men who appeared to fit into this category.

A toddler sees a large, brown dog through the window and says, "Moo." Explain this according to Piaget's theory of cognitive development.

Piaget found that forming schemas, or mental constructs to represent objects and actions, is how babies and children learn about themselves and the world through their interactions with their bodies and the environment. If they can fit a new experience into an existing schema, they assimilate it; or when necessary, they change an existing schema or form a new one to accommodate a new stimulus. Therefore, in this example, the toddler had seen cows in picture books, photos, or on a farm, and learned to associate the sound "Moo" with cows, reinforced by the teaching of toys, books, and adults. She had formed a schema for large, brown, four-legged, furry animals. Because the dog she saw fit these properties, she assimilated the dog into her cow schema. If she were then told this was a dog that says "Bow-wow," she would either form a new schema for dogs; or, if she had previously only seen smaller dogs, accommodate (modify) her existing dog schema to include larger dogs.

Conservation

Conservation is the cognitive ability to understand that objects or substances retain their properties of numbers or amounts even when their appearance, shape, or configuration changes. Piaget found from his experiments with children that this ability develops around the age of five years. He also found children develop conservation of number, length, mass, weight, volume, and quantity respectively at slightly different ages. One example of a conservation experiment is with liquid volume: the experimenter pours the same amount of liquid into a short, wide container and a tall, thin one. Children who have not developed conservation of liquid volume typically say one container has more liquid, even though they saw both amounts were equal, based on one container's looking fuller. Similarly, children who have not developed conservation of number, shown equal numbers of beads, usually say a group arranged in a long row has more beads than a group clustered together. Children having developed conservation recognize the amounts are the same regardless of appearance.

Preoperational Versus Concrete Operational Stages

Piaget called the stage of most children aged 2–6 years Preoperational because children these ages cannot yet perform mental operations, i.e. manipulate information mentally. At around 6–7 years old, children begin to develop Concrete Operations. A key aspect of this stage is the ability to think logically. This ability first develops relative to concrete objects and events. Concrete Operational children still have trouble understanding abstract concepts or hypothetical situations, but they can apply logical sequences and cause and effect to things they can see, feel, and manipulate physically. For example, Concrete Operational children develop the understanding that things have the same amount or number regardless of their shape or arrangement, which Piaget termed conservation. They develop proficiency in inductive logic, i.e. drawing generalizations from specific instances. However, deductive logic, i.e. predicting specific results according to general principles, is not as well-developed until the later stage of Formal Operations involving abstract thought. Another key development of Concrete Operations is reversibility, i.e. the ability to reverse an action or operation.

The different thinking found between Piaget's Preoperational and Concrete Operations stages is exemplified in experiments he and others conducted to prove his theory. For example, the absence/presence of ability to conserve liquid volume across shape/appearance has been shown in experiments with differently aged children. A preschooler is shown a tall, thin beaker and a short, wide one. The experimenter also shows the child two identically sized and shaped containers with identical amounts of liquid in each. The experimenter then pours the equal amounts of liquid into the two differently shaped beakers. The preschooler will say either the thin beaker holds more liquid because it is taller or the short beaker holds more because it is wider. Piaget termed this "centration"—focusing on only one property at a time. An older child "decentrates," can "conserve" the amount, and knows both beakers hold identical amounts. Older children also use reversibility and logic, e.g. "I know they are still equal, because I just saw you pour the same amount into each beaker."

Preoperational Stage of Piaget's Theory of Cognitive Development

Children between (roughly) two and six years old are in Piaget's Preoperational stage of cognitive development. Having begun to use objects to represent other things, i.e. symbolic representation, near the end of the previous Sensorimotor stage, children now further develop this ability during pretend/make-believe play. They may pretend a broom is a guitar or a horse; or talk using a block as a phone. Toddlers begin to play "house," pretending they and their playmates are the mommy, the daddy, the mailman, the doctor, etc. The reason Piaget called this stage Preoperational is that children are not yet capable of performing mental "operations," including following concrete logic or manipulating information mentally. Their thinking is intuitive rather than following logical steps. Piaget termed Preoperational children "egocentric" in that they literally cannot adopt another's point of view, even concretely: in experiments, after seeing pictures of a scene as viewed from different positions, children could not match a picture to another person's position, selecting the picture showing the scene from their own viewpoint.

Animism and Magical Thinking

Piaget found that children in the Preoperational stage are not yet able to perform logical mental operations. Their thinking is intuitive during the toddler and preschool years. One characteristic of the thinking of young children is animism, or assigning human qualities, feelings, and actions to inanimate objects. For example, a child seeing an autumn leaf fall off of a tree might remark, "The tree didn't like that leaf and pushed it off of its branch." Or a child with a sunburn might say, "The sun was angry at me and burned me." A related characteristic is magical thinking, which is attributing cause and effect relationships between their own feelings and thoughts and environmental events where none exists. For example, if a child says "I hate you" to another person or secretly dislikes and wishes the other gone, and something bad then happens to that person, the child is likely to believe what s/he said/felt/thought caused the other's unfortunate event. This is related to egocentrism—seeing everything as revolving around oneself.

Stages of Growth and Development in Art

Austrian and German art scholars established six stages in art. (1) The Scribble stage: from 2–4 years, children first make uncontrolled scribbles; then controlled scribbling; then progress to naming their scribbles to indicate what they represent. (2) The Preschematic stage: from ages 4–6, children begin to develop a visual schema. Schema, meaning mental representation, comes from Piaget's cognitive-developmental theory. Without complete comprehension of dimensions and sizes, children may draw people and houses the same height; they use color more emotionally than logically. They may omit or exaggerate facial features, or they might draw sizes by importance, e.g. drawing themselves as largest among people or drawing the most important feature, e.g. the head, as the largest or only body part. (3) The Schematic stage: from 7–9 years, drawings more reflect actual physical proportions and colors. (4) Dawning Realism: from ages 9-11, drawings become increasingly representational. (5) Children aged 11–13 are in the Pseudorealistic stage, reflecting their ability to reason. (6) Children 14+ are in the Period of Decision stage, reflecting the adolescent identity crisis.

Viktor Lowenfeld

Viktor Lowenfeld (1903–1960) taught art to elementary school students and sculpture to blind students. Lowenfeld's acquaintance with Sigmund Freud, who was interested in his work with the blind, motivated Lowenfeld to pursue scientific research. He published several books on using creative arts activities therapeutically. Lowenfeld was familiar with six stages previously identified in the growth of art. He combined these with principles of human development drawn from the school of psychoanalytic psychology founded by Freud. In his adaptation, he named the six stages reflecting the development of children's art as Scribble, Preschematic, Schematic, Dawning Realism, Pseudorealistic, and Period of Decision. Lowenfeld identified adolescent learning styles as haptic, focused on physical sensations and subjective emotional experiences, and as visual, focused on appearances, each demanding corresponding instructional approaches. Lowenfeld's book Creative and Mental Growth (1947) was the most influential text in art education during the later 20th century. Lowenfeld's psychological emphasis in this text gave scientific foundations to creative and artistic expression, and identified developmentally age-appropriate art media and activities.

Involvement of Music in the Development of Infants and Young Children

Long before they can speak, and before they even comprehend much speech, infants respond to the sounds of voices and to music. These responses are not only to auditory stimulation, but moreover to the emotional content in what they hear. Parents sing lullabies to babies; not only are these sounds pleasant and soothing, but they also help children develop trust in their environment as secure. Parents communicate their love to children through singing and introduce them to experiences of pleasure and excitement through music. As children grow, music progresses to be not only a medium of communication but also one of self-expression as they learn to sing/play musical sounds. Music facilitates memory, as we see through commercial jingles and mnemonic devices. Experiments find music improves spatial reasoning. Children's learning of perceptual and logical concepts like beginning/ending, sequences, cause-and-effect, balance, harmony/dissonance and mathematical number and timing concepts is reinforced by music. Music also promotes language development. Children learn about colors, counting, conceptual relationships, nature, and social skills through music.

Enhancing the Emotional, Social, Aesthetic, and School Readiness Skills with Music

Young children who are just learning to use spoken language often cannot express their emotions very well verbally. Music is a great aid to emotional development in that younger children can express happiness, sadness, anger, etc., through singing and/or playing music more easily than they can with words. Children of preschool ages not only listen to music and respond to what they hear, they also learn to create music through singing and playing instruments together with other children. These activities help them learn crucial social skills for their lives, like cooperating with others, collaborating, and making group or team efforts to accomplish something. When children are given guided musical experiences, they learn to make their own judgments of what is good or bad music; this provides them with the foundations for developing an aesthetic sense. Music promotes preliteracy skills by enhancing phonemic awareness. As growing children develop musical appreciation and skills, these develop fundamental motor, cognitive, and social skills they need for language, school readiness, literacy, and life.

Premathematical Learning Experiences

Preschool children do not think in the same ways as older children and adults do, as Piaget observed. Their thinking is strongly based upon and connected to their sensory perceptions. This means that in solving problems, they depend mainly on how things look, sound, feel, smell, and taste. Therefore, preschool children should always be given concrete objects that they can touch, explore, and experiment with in any learning experience. They are not yet capable of understanding abstract concepts or manipulating information mentally, so they must have real things to work with to understand premath concepts. For example, they will learn to count solid objects like blocks, beads, or pennies before they can count numbers in their heads. They cannot benefit from rote math memorization, or "sit still and listen" lessons. Since young children "centrate" on one characteristic/object/person/event at a time, adults can offer activities encouraging decentration/incorporating multiple aspects, e.g. not only grouping all triangles, but grouping all red triangles separately from blue triangles.

Activities Assisting Children Develop Cognitive Abilities

As shown by Piaget, young children have difficulty reversing operations. Adults can ask them to build block structures, for example, and then dismantle them one block at a time to reverse the construction. They can ask children to retell rhymes or stories backward. They can take small groups of children for walks and ask them if they can return by the same route as they came. Young children often assume causal relationships where none exist. Adults can provide activities to produce and observe results, e.g. pouring water into different containers; knocking over bowling pins by swinging a pendulum; rolling wheeled toys down ramps; or blowing balls through mazes, and then asking them, "What happened when you did this? What would happen if you did this? What could you do to make this happen?" Young children are also often egocentric, seeing everything from their own viewpoint. Adults can help them take others' perspectives through guessing games wherein they must give each other clues to guess persons/objects and dramatic role-playing activities, where they pretend to be others.

Salient Aspects of Typical Early Childhood Physical Development

Early childhood physical growth, while significant, is slower than infant growth. From birth to 2 years, children generally grow to four times their newborn weight and 2/3 their newborn length/height. From 2–3 years, however, children usually gain only about 4 lbs. and 3.5 inches. From 4–6 years, growth slows more; gains of 5–7 lbs. and 2.5 inches are typical. Due to slowing growth rates, 3- and 4-year-olds appear to eat less food, but do not; they actually just eat fewer calories per pound of body weight. Brain growth is still rapid in preschoolers: brains attain 55 percent of adult size by 2 years, and 90 percent by 6 years. The majority of brain growth is usually by 4–4.5 years, with a growth spurt around 2 years and growth rates slowing significantly between 5 and 6 years. Larger brain size indicates not more neurons, but larger sizes; differences in their organization; more glial cells nourishing and supporting neurons; and greater myelination (development of the sheath protecting nerve fibers and facilitating their efficient intercommunication).

Gender Differences in Motor Development

On average, preschool boys have larger muscles than preschool girls, so they can run faster, climb higher, and jump farther. Boys at these ages tend to be more muscular physically. Preschool girls, while less muscular, are on the average more mature physically for their ages than boys. While boys usually exceed girls in their large-muscle, gross-motor abilities like running, jumping, and climbing, girls tend to surpass boys in small-muscle, fine-motor abilities like buttoning buttons, using scissors, and similar activities involving the manipulation of small tools, utensils, and objects. While preschool boys exhibit more strength in large-muscle, gross-motor actions, preschool girls are more advanced than preschool boys in large-muscle, gross-motor skills that do not demand strength so much as coordination, like hopping, balancing on one foot, and skipping. While these specific gender differences in preschoolers' physical and motor development have been observed consistently in research, it is also found that preschool girls' and boys' physical and motor development patterns are generally more similar than different overall.

Abilities in Perceptual Development Occurring in Infancy

In normal development, babies have usually established the ability to see, hear, smell, taste, and feel and also the ability to integrate such sensory information by the age of six months. Additional perceptual abilities, which are less obvious and more complex, continue to emerge throughout the early childhood years. For instance, young children develop increasing precision in recognizing visual concepts like size and shape. This development allows children to identify accurately the shape and size of an object no matter from what angle they perceive it. Infants have these capacities in place, but have not yet developed accuracy in using them. For example, a baby might realize that objects farther away occupy less of their visual fields than nearer objects; however, the baby has yet to learn just how much less of the visual field is taken up by the farther object. Young children attain this and similar kinds of learning by actively, energetically exploring their environments. Such activity is crucial for developing accurate perception of size, shape, and distance.

Signs of Progress in Typical Motor Development

Genetics, physiological maturation, nutrition, and experience through practice combine to further preschoolers' motor skills development. Newborns' reflexive behaviors progress to preschoolers' voluntary activities. Also, children's perception of the size, shape, and position of the body and body parts becomes more accurate by preschool ages. In addition, increases in bilateral coordination of the body's two sides enhance preschoolers' motor skills. Motor skills development entails both learning new movements and gradually integrating previously learned movements into smooth, continuous patterns, as in learning to throw a ball with skill. Both large muscles, for gross-motor skills like climbing, running, and jumping, and small muscles, for fine-motor skills like drawing and tying knots, develop. Eye-hand coordination involves fine-motor control. Preschoolers use visual feedback, i.e. seeing whether they are making things go where and do what they want them to, in learning to manipulate small objects with their hands and fingers.

Nature-Nurture Interaction in Early Childhood Physical Development

The physical development of babies and young children is a product of the interactions between genetic and environmental factors. Also, a child's physical progress is equally influenced by environmental and psychological variables. For the body, brain, and nervous system to grow and develop normally, children must live in healthy environments. When the interaction of hereditary and environmental influences is not healthful, this is frequently reflected in abnormal patterns of growth. Failure to thrive syndrome is a dramatic example. When children are abused or neglected for long periods of time, they actually stop growing. The social environments of such children create psychological stress. This stress makes the child's pituitary gland stop releasing growth hormones, and growth ceases. When such environmental stress is relieved and these children are given proper care, stimulation, and affection, they begin growing again. They often grow rapidly enough to catch up on the growth they missed earlier. Normal body and brain growth—as well as psychological development—depend upon the collaboration of nature and nurture.

Visual Perceptual Aspects of Interpreting Pictures and Eye Movements

As adults, our ability to look at pictures of people and things in the environment is something we usually take for granted. Researchers have established that 3-year-old children's responses indicate their ability to recognize shading, line convergence, and other cues of depth in two-dimensional pictures. However, scientists have also found that children's sensitivity to these kinds of visual cues increases as they grow older. The eye movements and eye fixation patterns of young children affect their ability to get the most complete and accurate information from pictorial representations of reality. When viewing pictures, adults sweep the entire picture to see it as a whole, their eye movements leaping around; to focus on specific details, adults use shorter eye movements. Preschool children differ from adults in using shorter eye movements overall, and focusing on small parts of the picture near the center or an edge. They therefore disregard, or do not see, a lot of the picture's available information.

Characteristics in Art Reflecting Perceptual, Cognitive, and Motor Development

Observations of young children find that while a 2½-year-old can grasp a crayon and scribble with it, by the age of 4 years, s/he can draw a picture we recognize as human. The typical 4-year-old drawing of a human being is called the "tadpole person" because it has no body, a large head, and stick limbs. Between the ages of 3 and 4 years, children typically make a transition from scribbling to producing tadpole person drawings. This development is enabled by greater development in motor control and eye-hand coordination, among other variables. Between the ages of 4 and 5 years, children make another transition by progressing from drawing tadpole persons to drawing complete figures with heads and bodies. Howard Gardner, psychologist and author of the Multiple Intelligences theory, stated that children achieve a "summit of artistry" by the end of their preschool years. He describes their drawings as "characteristically colorful, balanced, rhythmic, and expressive, conveying something of the range and...vitality associated with artistic mastery." (1980)

Self-Concept and Self-Esteem

Young children's self-concepts are founded on observable, readily defined, mainly concrete factors. Many young children also experience much adult encouragement. Because their self-concepts are more simple and concrete than those of older children and adults and because they typically receive abundant encouragement and positive reinforcement, preschoolers often have fairly high self-esteem, i.e. judgment regarding their own value. In general, young children tend to have positive, optimistic attitudes that they can learn something new, finish tasks, and succeed if they persist in their attempts. Self-esteem related specifically to one's ability to perform a given task is sometimes called "achievement-related attribution." Albert Bandura called it "self-efficacy." Young children derive self-esteem from multiple sources, including their relationships with their parents; their friendships; their abilities and achievements in tasks involving playing and helping others; their physical/athletic abilities; and their achievements in preschool/school.

Basic Temperament Types Influencing Personalities of Children

Psychologists studied the behavior of infants and classified their characteristics into three types of temperaments: easy, difficult, and slow to warm up. The majority of infants are easy babies. When they cry from hunger/needing changing/being tired/feeling discomfort/needing cuddling/attention, they are easily soothed by having these needs met. They typically sleep well. While they experience normal negative emotions, their predominant mood is good. Other than normal stranger anxiety at applicable ages, they respond positively to meeting people. In contrast, difficult babies are more likely to cry longer and be much harder to soothe. It is often hard to get them to sleep, and they may sleep fitfully, with many interruptions and/or for shorter times. They are more easily frightened by strange/new people and things, and more easily upset overall. Slow to warm up babies can initially seem difficult by not being as immediately responsive to people other than their parents like easy babies. However, given some time to adjust, they eventually "warm up" to new people and situations.

External Variables Influencing Self-Concepts, Self-Esteem, and Self-Efficacy

The way young children see themselves is affected by the feedback they receive from other people. When adults like parents, caregivers, and teachers give young children positive responses to their efforts—whether they succeed initially or not—the children are more likely to develop positive self-concepts, engendering higher self-esteem, and greater self-efficacy, the belief that they have the competency to succeed at a specific task or activity. On the other hand, when adults frequently give punitive/judgmental/indifferent/otherwise negative responses to young children's efforts, children develop poorer self-images. They feel they are not valued/good/important/worthy. They develop lower self-esteem, and their self-efficacy is weaker; they come to expect failure when they attempt tasks and may not even try. Peers also affect young children's self-concepts and self-esteem. When friends and classmates include a child in activities, this promotes a positive self-image and higher self-esteem and self-efficacy. If peers exclude, tease, or bully a young child, this can cause low self-esteem, make their self-concepts more negative, and lower their self-efficacy.

Learning Styles and Implications for Early Childhood Education

Young children with normal development learn in the same chronological sequences and learn the same types of skills. Even those with delayed development, as with intellectual disabilities, learn the same things in the same order, but simply at a slower rate and hence at later ages; and those with severe/profound impairment may never achieve certain developmental milestones. However, one aspect of learning that varies is learning style. For example, some children approach learning in a primarily visual manner. They focus on what they see and how things look. They learn best given visual stimuli, like colorful objects, pictures, and graphics. They understand abstract concepts and relationships better when these are illustrated visually. Other children approach learning in a primarily haptic or tactile way. They focus on textures and movements, learning through touch and kinesthetic senses. They learn best given concrete things to explore and manipulate, and physical activities to perform. They learn abstract concepts and relationships better through handling materials and engaging in physical movements and actions.

Internal Variable Influencing Self-Concepts, Self-Esteem, and Self-Efficacy

One major internal influence on self-concept is a child's basic temperament. Easy, difficult, and slow-to-warm-up temperaments in babies continue into early childhood (and throughout life). For example, children having easy temperaments are better prepared for coping with challenges and frustration. When they encounter difficulty attempting new tasks, they do not give up as easily and are more persistent. They are thus more likely to develop self-concepts of being good, valuable, and successful and hence have higher self-esteem. Since they experience more success through persistence, they develop greater self-efficacy, i.e. belief in their competence to perform specific tasks. Children with more difficult temperaments become frustrated more easily, after fewer attempts, and give up trying in discouragement or require extra help to perform new or challenging tasks. They are more at risk for believing they cannot succeed and hence are not valuable, leading to their developing lower self-esteem. This also affects self-efficacy: they are more likely to doubt their ability to perform a specific proposed task.

Locus of Control

Psychologist Julian Rotter originated the term and concept of locus of control. It refers to the place (locus) where we attribute causes for outcomes we experience, either externally or internally. An external locus control is something outside of us—another person and/or his/her actions; an environmental event; or an unknown but exterior influence, like good/bad luck or random chance. An internal locus of control is something inside of us—our native ability, our motivation, or our effort. For example, blaming another for failing—"The teacher gave me something too hard/wouldn't help me/didn't tell me how to do it" or "Johnny was bothering me" are examples of external locus of control. Blaming conditions, e.g. "It was too dark/hot/cold/noisy/the sun was in my eyes" is also external. Individuals may also attribute successes externally: "The teacher helped me" or "Johnny showed me how" or "I was lucky." Blaming/crediting oneself for failure/success is internal locus of control: "I didn't study the new words" or "I'm stupid" with failures or "I worked hard"/"I'm smart" with successes.

First Stage of Freud's Psychoanalytic Theory of Personality Development

Freud's orientation toward personality development was psychosexual. He believed the most important factors were the focus of erotic energy, which shifted in each developmental stage, and the child's early relationship with parents. Freud formulated five stages of development: Oral, Anal, Phallic, Latency, and Genital. He found if infants and children successfully complete each stage, they are well-adjusted; if not, they become fixated on one stage. Freud said infants from birth to 18 months are in the first Oral stage: their focus of pleasure is on the mouth as they suck to nurse. If a baby's oral need to nurse is met appropriately, s/he will progress to the following stage. However, if an infant's feeding needs are met either inadequately or excessively, s/he can develop an oral fixation. Signs of this in later life include tendencies to overeat, drink too much, smoke, bite one's nails, talk excessively, and other orally focused activities. Oral personalities either become overly dependent and gullible; or, when resisting oral compulsions, become pessimistic and aggressive to others.

Second Stage of Freud's Psychoanalytic Theory of Personality Development

Freud's theory divided personality development into five stages, each based on the corresponding erogenous zone: Oral, Anal, Phallic, Latency, and Genital. Infants 0–18 months are in the Oral stage as the focus is on nursing. Children 18–36 months are in the second Anal stage. The focus of pleasure sensations is on the anus as they are engaged in toilet training. Society and parents demand they control retaining/expelling waste; they must learn to control anal stimulation. This can be a power struggle between child and parents. Children this age are also learning to assert their individual independence and will, mirroring the battle of wills over toileting. Success contributes to healthy development; when unsuccessful, individuals develop anal fixation. Signs of this in later life take two extremes: those who resisted parental control and asserted personal control by retaining their feces develop anal-retentive personalities, becoming rigid, controlling, and overly preoccupied with neatness and cleanliness. Conversely, those who asserted themselves by expelling their feces develop anal-expulsive personalities, with sloppy, messy, disorganized, defiant behavior.

Effect of the Oedipal Conflict on Later Development

In his theory of personality development, Freud placed children ages 3–6 in his third Phallic stage when pleasure is focused on the genitals. He proposed that boys undergo an Oedipal conflict at this age, which he named after Greek tragedian Sophocles' Oedipus Rex, wherein the title character killed his father and married his mother. He said a boy unconsciously desires his mother, competing for her affection with his father, which equals aggression toward the father, and fears retaliation by the father through castration. He resolves these unacceptable impulses by "identifying with the aggressor," wanting to be like his father. Unsuccessful conflict resolution/fixation leads to later confusion/weakness of sexual identity, and either excessive or insufficient sexual activity. Because Freud focused only on males, later psychologists proposed a female counterpart, the Electra conflict. They pointed out how girls at the same ages become "Daddy's girls," often rejecting their mothers, and then around ages 4–5 want to be "just like Mommy," adopting feminine behaviors, paralleling male development. Freud rejected this notion.

Functions of the Basic Personality Structures in Freud's Developmental Theory

Freud proposed that the personality is governed by three structures or forces: the Id, the Ego, and the Superego. The Id, the "pleasure principle," represents the source of our powerful, instinctual urges, such as sexual and aggressive impulses. It is necessary as it energizes us to act, but cannot go unrestrained. The Ego, the "reality principle," represents our sense of self within reality. It is necessary for telling us what will happen if we act on the Id's impulses and knowing how to control them to protect ourselves. The Superego, the "conscience," represents our sense of morality. It is necessary when Ego protects ourselves but not others, so we also control our social interactions to be ethical and nonharmful to others. For example, when a young child sees a cookie or a toy belonging to someone else, his Id says, "I want that." His Ego says, "If I take that and get caught, I will be in trouble." His Superego says, "Whether I get caught or not, stealing is wrong."

Third Stage of Freud's Psychoanalytic Theory of Personality Development

Freud described developmental stages as focusing on particular erogenous zones. Nursing infants are in his Oral stage; toilet-training toddlers are in his Anal stage. His third stage, when children are aged 3–6 years, is the Phallic stage. Pleasure is focused on the genitals as children discover these. Freud focused his theory on males, proposing that at this age, boys develop unconscious sexual desires for their mothers and corresponding unconscious rivalries with their fathers for mother's attention. The rivalry represents aggression toward the father. Therefore they also unconsciously fear retaliation by the father in the form of castration. Freud named this the Oedipal conflict after the Greek tragic hero Oedipus, who unwittingly slew his father and married his mother. Since these unconscious impulses are socially unacceptable, boys resolve the conflict through a process Freud called "identification with the aggressor." This explains the common behavior of boys around ages

4–5, imitating and wanting to be "just like Daddy." They repress desires for mother and adopt masculine characteristics.

Fourth and Fifth Stages of Freud's Psychoanalytic Theory of Personality Development

Each of the stages in Freud's theory centered on an erogenous zone. Infants are in the Oral stage as they nurse; toddlers in the Anal stage as they are toilet-trained; preschoolers are in the Phallic stage as they focus on genital discovery, unconscious sexual impulses toward their opposite-sex parent, and unconscious aggressive impulses toward their same-sex parent, and resolving conflicts over these urges. Freud labeled the stage when children are six years old to puberty the Latency stage. During this time, children begin school. They are occupied with making new friends, developing new social skills; participating in learning, developing new academic skills; and learning school rules, developing acceptable societal behaviors. Freud said that children in the Latency stage repress their sexual impulses, deferring them while developing their cognitive and social skills takes priority. Thus sexuality is latent. From puberty on, children are in Freud's Genital stage, when sexuality reemerges with physical maturation and adolescents are occupied with developing intimate relationships with others.

Ego Defense Mechanisms of Freud's Psychoanalytic Theory of Personality Development

Freud identified and described many ego defense mechanisms in his theory. He said these are ways the ego finds to cope with impulses threatening it, and hence the person. Just a few of these that can be apparent in young children's behavior include the following. Regression—for example, if a child has received parental attention exclusively for four years, but then the parents introduce a new baby, not only is parental attention divided between two children, but the baby naturally needs and gets more attention by being a helpless infant. If the child feels displaced/threatened by the younger sibling, s/he may regress from normal four-year-old behaviors to more infantile ones in a bid for similar attention. Projection—if a child feels threatened by experiencing inner aggressive impulses, e.g. hating another person, s/he may project these feelings onto that person, accusing, "You hate me!" Denial—if a child cannot accept feelings triggered by losing a loved one through divorce or death, s/he may deny reality: "S/he will come back."

Key Differences Between Freud's and Erikson's Developmental Theories

Erikson's theory was based on Freud's, but whereas Freud's focus was psychosexual, Erikson's was psychosocial. Both emphasized early parent-child relationships. Freud believed the personality was essentially formed in childhood and proposed five stages through puberty and none thereafter; Erikson depicted lifelong development through nine stages. Each stage centers on a "nuclear conflict" to resolve, with positive/negative outcomes of successful/unsuccessful resolutions. Erikson's first, infancy stage (birth—18 months) is Basic Trust vs. Mistrust. When an infant's basic needs—such as being fed, changed, bathed, held/cuddled, having discomfort relieved, and receiving attention, affection, and interaction are met sufficiently and consistently, the baby develops basic trust in the world, gaining a sense of security, confidence, and optimism. The positive outcomes are hope and drive; negative outcomes are withdrawal and sensory distortion. If infant needs are inadequately and/or inconsistently met, the baby develops basic mistrust, with a sense of insecurity, worthlessness, and pessimism.

Second Stage in Erikson's Psychosocial Theory of Human Development

In each of Erikson's developmental stages, a central conflict must be resolved; success/failure dictates outcomes. Babies first develop basic trust or mistrust in the world during the first stage. Toddlers are in Erikson's second stage of Autonomy vs. Shame and Self-Doubt. In this stage, children 18 months—3 years are learning muscular control (walking, toilet-training) and developing moral senses of right/wrong. As they gain skills, they want to do more things independently, and they begin to assert their individual wills. Parents are familiar with the associated tantrums, "No!" and other common "Terrible Twos" behaviors. Children receiving appropriate parenting during this stage develop a sense of autonomy through being allowed to attempt tasks realistic for them; to fail and try again; and eventually to master them. Positive outcomes are will/willpower and self-control; negative outcomes are impulsivity and compulsion. Children with parenting at either extreme—being ignored and given no guidance or support; or overly controlled/directed, having everything done for them and never allowed freedom—develop shame, doubting their abilities.

Third Stage in Erikson's Psychosocial Theory of Human Development

Each of Erikson's nine developmental stages involves a "nuclear crisis" the individual must resolve; success or failure results in positive or negative outcomes. Babies develop basic trust or mistrust; toddlers develop autonomy or shame and self-doubt. Erikson's third stage, Initiative vs. Guilt, involves preschoolers. At this age, young children are exploring the environment further commensurately with their increasing physical/motor, cognitive, emotional, and social skills. They exercise imagination in make-believe/pretend play and pursue adventure. Having gained some control over their bodies in the previous stage, they now attempt to exercise control over their environments. When they succeed in this stage, the positive outcomes are purpose and direction. Children who receive adult disapproval for exerting control over their surroundings—either because they try to use too much control or because parents are overly controlling—feel guilt. Negative outcomes include excessive inhibition against taking action or ruthless, inconsiderate behavior at the opposite extreme.

Fourth Stage in Erikson's Psychosocial Theory of Human Development

Erikson formulated nine stages encompassing the entire human lifespan. The fourth stage corresponds to the end of the early childhood years, when children begin formal schooling. Erikson named this stage, which lasts from around ages 5–6 to puberty, Industry vs. Inferiority. Children in this stage are primarily occupied with learning new academic and social competencies as they attend school, meet more peers and adults, make new friends, and learn to interact in a wider environment. Whereas the focus of Stage 2, Autonomy vs. Shame and Doubt, was self-control and parents were the main relationship; and the focus of Stage 3, Initiative vs. Guilt, was environmental exploration and family was the main relationship; in Stage 4, Industry vs. Inferiority, the focus is on achievements and accomplishments. Friends, neighbors, school, and teachers are the most important relationships. Children's successful resolutions bring positive outcomes of competence and method; negative outcomes are narrowness of abilities and inertia (lack of activity).

Children's Development of Sexual/Gender Identification

Freud's View of Children's Development of Sexual/Gender Identification

While different psychological theories/schools of thought agree that sex as a social identity develops through the process of identification, they have different views and explanations for how children develop their social identities as boys or girls. In Freud's view, gender identity develops through processes of differentiation and affiliation. He said once children observe that certain other people have characteristics in common with themselves, they "endeavor to mold the ego after one that had been taken as a model." In other words, they identify with similar other people and try to attain the same attributes. Freud proposed that boys resolve their Oedipal conflicts through identification with the aggressor, i.e. adopting their fathers' characteristics and suppressing sexual impulses toward their mothers. While he focused exclusively on males in this respect, Neo-Freudian psychologists later proposed a female counterpart, the Electra conflict, wherein girls resolve desires for fathers by identifying with mothers and adopting their characteristics. In either case, children differentiate from their opposite-sex parent and identify/affiliate with their same-sex parent.

Explanation of Social Learning and Behaviorist Theories

Albert Bandura and other proponents of social learning theory maintain that children learn through a process of observing other people's behavior, observing certain behaviors of others that are rewarded, and then imitating those behaviors to obtain similar rewards. The concept of rewards reinforcing behaviors, i.e. increasing the probability of repeating them, comes from behaviorism or learning theory. Social learning theory is based on behaviorism, but includes additional emphasis on the ideas that learning occurs within a social context and that social interactions are primary influences on learning. According to social learning theory, children observe that males and females engage in different behaviors. They additionally observe that boys and girls receive different rewards for their behaviors. Based on these observations, children then imitate the behaviors appropriate to their own sex that they have seen rewarded in others of their sex to obtain the same rewards. Both behaviorist and social learning theories view gender identity development as being environmentally shaped by consequences; social learning theory focuses on the social environment.

Kohlberg's Cognitive-Developmental Theory

Kohlberg had developed a cognitive theory of moral development, based upon and expanding the concepts of morality Piaget included in his theory of cognitive development. Kohlberg also proposed a cognitive-developmental approach to children's acquisition of sex/gender roles. Piaget and Kohlberg discussed classification or categorization as one of the cognitive abilities that children develop. Just as they learn to categorize various things, e.g. foods, animals, people, etc., they learn that people include female and male categories. They then learn to categorize themselves as either female/girls or male/boys. When children are around 2 years old, they each begin to develop their distinctive sense of self. Once they have differentiated self from the rest of the world, they also begin to be able to develop complex mental concepts. These abilities enable them to develop self-concepts of gender. According to the cognitive-developmental view, once children have developed concepts of their sex/gender, these are maintained despite social contexts and are difficult to change.

Contribution of Psychoanalytic Theory to Early Childhood Care and Educational Practices

In his development of psychoanalytic theory, Freud (a physician) identified stages of childhood development according to the particular bodily zones where pleasure is focused during each age period. This identification still regularly informs early childhood care and educational practices. For example, infants are in the Oral stage, when nursing provides pleasure as well as nutrition and satisfying hunger. Knowing this, caregivers recognize that babies begin exploring their environments through oral routes. They thus will not punish mouthing of objects; will anticipate and prevent mouthing of unsafe/unsanitary objects; provide suitable objects and activities for oral inspection and orally oriented rewards. Toddlers engaged in toilet-training are in Freud's Anal stage. As they learn to control their bladders and bowels, they also learn to control their impulses and behaviors. Adults knowing this recognize toddlers' willful, stubborn behaviors as normal parts of the process of establishing individual identities and asserting their wishes. Thus, they will not punish these behaviors harshly/inappropriately, but strike a balance between permitting exploration and providing limits, guidance, and support.

Application of Freud's Third Stage of Psychoanalytic Theory

According to Freud's theory, preschoolers are in his Phallic stage of psychosexual development. This is the time when they discover their own genitals, so caregivers and educators knowing this will not be distressed at young children's attention to and manipulation of their genitals, and their curiosity and interest in others' genitals as these are not abnormal (unless excessive). Adults who are also aware of Freud's Oedipal conflict in boys and other Neo-Freudian psychologists' corresponding Electra conflict in girls should be neither surprised nor upset when little boys first focus more attention on mothers/female caregivers, and later abandon these attentions to focus on imitating fathers/male caregivers. Freud would say they are demonstrating the Oedipal desire for the mother, which includes fear of castration by the father, and then resolving this conflict through identification with the aggressor/father. Neo-Freudians would say little girls are undergoing a similar process in favoring their fathers and subsequently identifying with their mothers.

Fourth Stage of Psychosexual Development of Freud's Psychoanalytic Theory of Personality Development

Freud theorized that children are in his fourth Latency stage of development at around the same ages when they begin to attend formal schooling. Since Freud's emphasis on development was psychosexual, he identified an erogenous zone where pleasure was focused in each stage of development. The mouth, anus, and genitals are erogenous zones central to Freud's other developmental stages. However, in the stage he termed Latency, there is no erogenous zone of focus. This is because Freud believed that children's sexuality is repressed or submerged during this period. The child's attention is occupied at this time with learning new social and academic skills in the new environment of the school setting. Adults familiar with Freud's basic psychoanalytic concepts realize that children's focus shifts from their relationships with parents to their relationships with friends, classmates, teachers, and other adults during the Latency stage. Children are not rejecting/abandoning parents, but responding to widening social environments. They are more able to learn academic concepts and structures and more complex social interactions and behaviors.

Salient Characteristics of Piaget's Second Stage of Child Cognitive Development

Piaget's second cognitive-developmental stage is Preoperational. Toddlers and preschoolers in this stage typically begin to recognize rudimentary symbolic representation, i.e. that some objects represent other things. This understanding of symbols allows them to begin using words to represent things, people, feelings, and thoughts. Adults can support early childhood language development by frequently conversing with young children, reading books to them, introducing and explaining new vocabulary words, and playing games involving naming and classifying things. Children in this stage also begin pretend/make-believe play through understanding symbols; adults can encourage and support this play, which develops imagination and planning abilities. Preoperational children's thinking is intuitive, not logical; adults understanding this will not expect them to follow/use logical sequences such as doing arithmetic, as they cannot yet perform mental operations. Adults familiar with Piaget's concept of egocentrism realize Preoperational children cannot see others' viewpoints. They thus engage children's attention/interest by beginning from topics related to children's personal selves and activities.

Magical Thinking Concept of Piaget's Theory of Cognitive Development

According to Piaget, magical thinking is the belief that one's thoughts make external events happen. He identified this as a common characteristic of the way children in his Preoperational stage think.

Piaget said that preschool children have not yet developed the cognitive ability to perform mental operations. Because they cannot follow or apply logical thought processes, their thinking is irrational and intuitive rather than organized and based on real-world, empirical observations. For example, a Preoperational child may believe that something good happened because s/he wished hard enough for it. Preschoolers also commonly believe their saying/thinking/feeling/wishing something bad toward another caused the other's misfortune. They often blame themselves for divorce or death in the family, thinking these happened because they were "bad." Adults should explain to young children that what they wished, thought, felt, or said did not cause good or bad events, and reassign causes external to the child, e.g. "Mommy and Daddy were not getting along with each other"/"Grandpa was sick"/"It was an accident, not anybody's fault."

Major Characteristics of Piaget's Theory of Cognitive Development

According to Piaget's theory, infants are in the Sensorimotor stage of cognitive development. This means they learn through sensory input they get from the environment, motor actions they perform, and environmental feedback they receive from those actions. They also eventually coordinate their actions and reactions. For example, babies hear and attend to sounds; visually locate sound sources; and learn that some objects make sounds, like rattles. They learn to reach for, grasp, and manipulate objects. They learn when they shake a rattle, it makes a sound, and then repeat this action purposefully to generate the sound. Adults knowing these characteristics will provide infants with many toys they can manipulate, including toys that make noises/music, spin/twirl, or roll/bounce/fly; experiences affording input through all sensory modalities; and positive reinforcement when babies discover new body parts, objects, sights, sounds, textures, smells, and tastes; and demonstrate new behaviors interacting with these. They will not punish repetitive behaviors, like repeatedly throwing items from cribs/high-chair trays, which are part of learning in this stage.

Piaget's Egocentrism and Animism Concepts of Preoperational Children

Preoperational children are egocentric, i.e. they view everything as revolving around themselves. Adults aware of this understand that most two-year-olds, for example, neither want to share with others nor understand why they should. Egocentrism also means being unable to see others' perspectives. Adults who take this ability for granted may not realize the simplicity of both some early childhood problems and their solutions. For example, when a preschooler does something physically or emotionally hurtful to another, adults can guide identification of consequences: "Look at her face now. How do you think she feels?" and then guide perspective-taking: "How would you feel if somebody hit you like you just hit Sally?" This has not occurred to the preschooler, but once s/he is guided to think of it, it can be a revelation. Animism is Preoperational children's attributing human qualities to inanimate objects. Many children's books and TV shows accordingly appeal to young children by animating letters, numbers, or objects (e.g. SpongeBob SquarePants).

Piaget's New Developments of the Concrete Operations Stage Versus Previous Preoperational Stage

Piaget said that while preschoolers are in the Preoperational stage and do not think logically because they cannot yet perform mental operations, this ability emerges in the Concrete Operations stage, which tends to coincide with elementary school ages. Concrete Operational children can follow and apply logical sequences to concrete objects they can see and manipulate. This is why they can begin learning mathematical concepts and procedures like addition and subtraction, and grammatical paradigms like verb conjugations. While Preoperational children "centrate" or focus on one attribute of an object, like its appearance, Concrete Operational children "decentrate," accommodating multiple attributes, and can perform and reverse mental operations. For example, a Preoperational child can count pennies, but not understand ten pennies spread into a long row equal ten pennies clustered together. Children in Concrete Operations, instead of focusing on appearance, will use logic and simply count the pennies, showing that each group has the same number regardless of how they look.

Conservation in Piaget's Theory of Cognitive Development

Piaget identified conservation as a key ability, which Preoperational preschoolers have not yet developed. Piaget found elementary school-age Concrete Operational children develop conservation—the understanding that an object or substance conserves, or retains, its essential properties despite changes in appearance or configuration. For example, adults know a cup of liquid is the same amount regardless of the size or shape of the container holding it. Preoperational children, seeing equal amounts of liquid poured from a tall thin glass to a short wide one or vice versa, will "centrate" (focus exclusively) on either height or width and say one glass holds more. Concrete operational children know logically that the amounts are equal regardless of container shape/appearance. When asked how they know, they use empirical evidence and logic: "Of course it's the same amount; I just saw you pour it from the tall glass to the short one." A universal phenomenon is that after developing conservation, we take it for granted and cannot remember or believe our earlier Preoperational thinking.

Key Concepts of Bandura's Social Learning Theory

Psychologist Alfred Bandura developed the primary theory of social learning. While his theory incorporates elements of behaviorism in that environmental rewards and punishments that shape the behaviors and learning of children, Bandura focused more on the social dimension of learning in that he found the context of social interactions the most important medium and influence for learning. Bandura's theory also incorporates elements of cognitive theory by emphasizing the roles played by the cognitive processes of attention, memory, and motivation in learning. Bandura found children learn by observing and imitating the behaviors of models, including adults, older children, and peers. He proposed four conditions required for this learning: Attention, Retention, Reproduction, and Motivation. Adults understanding Bandura's theory realize children can learn new behaviors by seeing others be rewarded for performing these, and then imitating them; this greatly expands children's learning potential. Bandura also proved that children viewing violent video content engage in more aggressive behaviors, informing adults of the importance of monitoring and controlling children's exposure to media influences.

How Erikson's First Stage Informs Early Childhood Caregiving

Erikson's theory is based on Freud's, but focuses on psychosocial rather than psychosexual development. Erikson proposed infants are in his first stage, named for its nuclear conflict of Basic Trust vs. Mistrust. Erikson found if an infant's needs are met adequately and consistently, the baby will form a sense of trust in the world; but if they are not fully and/or regularly met, the baby will form a sense of mistrust in the environment and people. Erikson proposed a positive outcome for resolving the nuclear crisis in each stage; in this stage it is Hope. Caregivers understanding this theory and stage will feed a baby on a regular schedule and not leave the child crying from hunger for long times. They will change the baby's diaper timely when needed rather than letting him/her experience discomfort and cry too long. Moreover, caregivers will meet infant needs for interaction, especially holding and cuddling. Making care/nurturing predictable for babies establishes optimism. The negative outcome of Mistrust is linked to worthless feelings, even suicide.

How Erikson's Second Stage Informs Early Childhood Caregiving

Erikson's second stage of psychosocial development centers on the nuclear conflict of Autonomy vs. Shame and Doubt. Toddlers in this stage are engaged in learning to walk and toilet-training, involving motor control and self-control. They are also learning to assert themselves. This is one reason for tantrums characteristic of this age group. Toddlers who begin loudly saying "No!" are not merely obstinate or difficult, but are learning to express their wills. Erikson designated Will as the positive outcome of resolving the conflict in this stage, as well as self-control and courage. Children allowed to use their emerging skills to try things on their own become more independent, developing autonomy. Those not allowed to practice and progress in making choices and/or are made to feel ashamed during toilet-training/while learning other new skills, learn to doubt themselves and their abilities instead of developing independence. Adults appreciating this theory and stage let children express preferences and practice new skills, supplying needed encouragement, support, and positive reinforcement without overly restricting, controlling, or punishing them.

Relation of Erikson's Third Stage to Early Childhood Education

In his theory of psychosocial development, Erikson proposed his third stage revolves around the nuclear conflict of Initiative vs. Guilt. Erikson described 3- to 5-year-olds in this stage as being at the "play age." Having developed the ability for make-believe/pretend play, children imitate parents and other adults in their activities. At these ages, children begin taking the initiative to plan and enact scenarios wherein they play roles and use objects to symbolize other things. Through creating situations and stories, they experiment and identify socially with adult roles and behaviors. They are also more actively exploring their environments. Relationships expand from parents to family. The positive outcome/strength of this stage is Purpose. Children thwarted in fulfilling their natural goals and desires develop the negative outcome of Guilt through adults' punishing them for trying to control their environments and/or adults' controlling them too much. Adults understanding this encourage and support pretend play. They encourage and approve children for initiating activities rather than inhibiting or always directing their actions.

Relation of Erikson's Fourth Stage to Early Childhood Education

Erikson termed the fourth stage of his psychosocial theory of development as centering on the nuclear conflict of Industry vs. Inferiority. Children commonly enter this stage around the years beginning school, also coinciding with the close of the early childhood years. Children at elementary school ages acquire a great many new skills and much new knowledge. This enables them to attempt and accomplish many more things, which they are expected to do in school. Their increased ability and accomplishment engender a positive sense of Industry. Children's most important relationships are no longer only with their parents and family, but with friends, neighbors, classmates, teachers, and other school staff. Hence social interactions are central during this stage. Children feeling unequal to new tasks develop a sense of Inferiority compared to peers. Parents and educators who encourage and reinforce children's desires and attempts to learn and practice new skills and perform tasks help them develop senses of method and competence. Unsupportive/punitive adult responses result in restricted competencies and/or lack of motivation.

Hierarchy of Needs in Maslow's Humanistic Theory of Self-Actualization

Maslow proposed humans are driven by needs, and meeting the most basic needs is prerequisite to meeting more advanced needs. Maslow's needs hierarchy is depicted as a pyramid, with the most fundamental needs at the base. Its five levels are (1) physiological needs: air, water, sleep, and food necessary for survival; (2) security needs: shelter and a safe environment; (3) social needs: feeling loved, receiving affection, and belonging to a family and/or group; (4) esteem needs: feeling personal value, accomplishment, and social recognition; and (5) self-actualizing needs: achieving optimal personal growth and realizing one's full potential. For example, babies and young children must have clean air to breathe and be fed and rested to survive before other needs can be addressed. Children must have safe places to live, then their needs for love and belonging can be met. Once a child feels loved and part of a family/group, s/he can develop self-esteem through accomplishments and feeling valued by society. After satisfying these, children can self-actualize.

Organismic Valuing, Conditions of Worth, the Real Self, the Ideal Self, and Incongruence in Carl Rogers' Theory

Rogers said all organisms naturally pursue a tendency to actualize or make the best of life. Organismic valuing is the natural tendency to value what is healthy, e.g. avoiding bad-tasting foods, which can be poisonous or rotten. Organismic valuing leads to positive regard/esteem, engendering positive self-regard/self-esteem, reflecting what Rogers called the real self—the person one becomes under optimal conditions. Rogers observed society substitutes conditions of worth for organismic valuing, giving us things based not on our needs but on meeting society's required conditions. Children are taught early they will receive something they want on the condition they do what adults want. This establishes conditional positive regard, meaning children only feel esteemed by others on others' conditions; this develops conditional positive self-regard, or self-esteem dependent on others' esteem. This creates an unattainable ideal self-based on others' standards rather than the real self. For Rogers, incongruence between real and ideal self-causes neurosis. Rogers' required qualities for effective therapists—congruence/genuineness, empathy, and respect—are equally effective in early childhood education.

Rogers believed in actualization or realizing one's full potential as did fellow humanist Abraham Maslow. While Maslow applied self-actualization to humans, Rogers applied the "actualization tendency" to all life forms. Rogers gave the name "conditions of worth" to the process he observed whereby others give individuals things based not on need but worthiness. For example, while babies usually receive care based on need, as they grow older, adults establish conditions of worth: children get dessert if they finish dinner/vegetables; they get drinks or snacks after finishing a task/activity/lesson/class; and most significantly, they often get affection on condition of acceptable/desirable behavior. In behaviorism, this is called contingencies of reinforcement: rewards are given contingent on desired behaviors. Rogers would likely disagree with this practice, which he called conditional positive regard. He felt it makes children do what others want, not what they want or need, and teaches them conditional positive self-regard, i.e. self-esteem dependent on external standards. Rogers' remedy was unconditional positive regard—unconditional love and acceptance.

Fundamental Principles of Behaviorist or Learning Theory

Major principles of behaviorism include these: Organisms learn through interacting with the environment. Environmental influences shape behavior. Environmental stimuli elicit responses from organisms. Hypothetical constructs like the mind and/or inner physiological changes are unnecessary for scientifically describing behaviors—everything organisms do, including feeling and thinking. Learning and behavior change are achieved through arranging the learner's environment to elicit certain responses, increasing the probability of repeating those responses by rewarding them (positive reinforcement) and decreasing repetition of unwanted behaviors by punishing (positive punishment) or ignoring them (extinction). Just as Thorndike previously found all animals including humans learn the same way, Skinner also found his principles applied equally to rats, pigeons, and people. His methods have become so popular that early childhood educators routinely give positive reinforcement—verbal praise, treats, and privileges—for performing new skills and demonstrating socially desirable behaviors; teach young children complex tasks in steps (shaping/chaining/task analysis); take away privileges to punish unwanted behaviors (negative punishment); and remove aversive stimuli for complying (negative reinforcement).

Communication Development Normally Occurring Within a Child's First Five Years of Life

Language and communication development depend strongly on the language a child develops within the first five years of life. During this time, three developmental periods are observed. At birth, the first period begins. This period is characterized by infant crying and gazing. Babies communicate their sensations and emotions through these behaviors, so they are expressive; however, they are not yet intentional. They indirectly indicate their needs through expressing how they feel, and when these needs are met, these communicative behaviors are reinforced. These expressions and reinforcement are the foundations for the later development of intentional communication. This becomes possible in the second developmental period, between 6 and 18 months. At this time, infants become able to coordinate their attention visually with other people relative to things and events, enabling purposeful communication with adults. During the third developmental period, from 18 months on, children come to use language as their main way of communicating and learning. Preschoolers can carry on conversations, exercise self-control through language use, and conduct verbal negotiations.

Milestones of Normal Language Development by the 2 Years Old

By the time most children reach the age of 2 years, they have acquired a vocabulary of about 150 to 300 words. They can name various familiar objects found in their environments. They are able to use at least two prepositions in their speech, for example in, on, and/or under. 2-year-olds typically combine the words they know into short sentences. These sentences tend to be mostly noun-verb or verb-noun combinations (e.g. "Daddy work," "Watch this"). They may also include verb-preposition combinations (e.g. "Go out," "Come in"). By the age of 2 years, children use pronouns, such as I, me, and you. They typically can use at least two such pronouns correctly. A normally developing 2-year-old will respond to some commands, directions, or questions, such as "Show me your eyes" or "Where are your ears?"

Salient General Aspects of Human Language Abilities from Before Birth to 5 Years of Age

Language and communication abilities are integral parts of human life that are central to learning, successful school performance, successful social interactions, and successful living. Human language ability begins before birth: the developing fetus can hear not only internal maternal sounds, but also the mother's voice, others' voices, and other sounds outside the womb. Humans have a natural sensitivity to human sounds and languages from before they are born until they are about 4½ years old. These years are critical for developing language and communication. Babies and young children are predisposed to greater sensitivity to human sounds than other sounds, orienting them toward the language spoken around them. Children absorb their environmental language completely, including vocal tones, syntax, usage, and emphasis. This linguistic absorption occurs very rapidly. Children's first 2½ years particularly involve amazing abilities to learn language including grammatical expression.

6 Months, 12 Months, and 18 Months

Individual differences dictate a broad range of language development that is still normal. However, parents observing noticeably delayed language development in their children should consult

- 60 -

professionals. Typically, babies respond to hearing their names by 6 months of age; turn their heads and eyes toward the sources of human voices they hear; and respond accordingly to friendly and angry tones of voice. By the age of 12 months, toddlers can usually understand and follow simple directions, especially when these are accompanied by physical and/or vocal cues. They can intentionally use one or more words with the correct meaning. By the age of 18 months, a normally developing child usually has acquired a vocabulary of roughly 5 to 20 words. 18-month-old children use nouns in their speech most of the time. They are very likely to repeat certain words and/or phrases over and over. At this age, children typically are able to follow simple verbal commands without needing as many visual or auditory cues as at 12 months.

Three Years

By the time they are 3 years old, most normally developing children have acquired vocabularies of between 900 and 1,000 words. Typically they correctly use the pronouns I, me, and you. They use more verbs more frequently. They apply past tenses to some verbs and plurals to some nouns. 3-year-olds usually can use at least three prepositions; the most common are in, on, and under. The normally developing 3-year-old knows the major body parts and can name them. 3-year-olds typically use 3-word sentences with ease. Normally, parents should find approximately 75 to 100 percent of what a 3-year-old says to be intelligible, while strangers should find between 50 and 75 percent of a 3-year-old's speech intelligible. Children this age comprehend most simple questions about their activities and environments and can answer questions about what they should do when they are thirsty, hungry, sleepy, hot, or cold. They can tell about their experiences in ways that adults can generally follow. By the age of 3 years, children should also be able to tell others their name, age, and sex.

Four Years

When normally developing children are 4 years old, most know the names of animals familiar to them. They can use at least four prepositions in their speech (e.g. in, on, under, to, from, etc.). They can name familiar objects in pictures, and they know and can identify one color or more. Usually they are able to repeat four-syllable words they hear. They verbalize as they engage in their activities, which Vygotsky dubbed "private speech." Private speech helps young children think through what they are doing, solve problems, make decisions, and reinforce the correct sequences in multistep activities. When presented with contrasting items, 4-year-olds can understand comparative concepts like bigger and smaller. At this age, they are able to comply with simple commands without the target stimuli being in their sight (e.g. "Put those clothes in the hamper" [upstairs]). 4-year-old children will also frequently repeat speech sounds, syllables, words, and phrases, similar to 18-month-olds' repetitions but at higher linguistic and developmental levels.

Five Years

Once most children have reached the age of 5 years, their speech has expanded from the emphasis of younger children on nouns, verbs, and a few prepositions, and is now characterized by many more descriptive words, including adjectives and adverbs. 5-year-olds understand common antonyms, e.g. big/little, heavy/light, long/short, hot/cold. They can now repeat longer sentences they hear, up to about nine words. When given three consecutive, uninterrupted commands, the typical 5-year-old can follow these without forgetting one or two. At age 5 most children have learned simple concepts of time like today, yesterday, tomorrow; day, morning, afternoon, night; and before, after, and later. 5-year-olds typically speak in relatively long sentences, and normally should be incorporating some compound sentences (with more than one independent clause) and complex sentences (with one or more independent and dependent clauses). 5-year-old children's speech is also grammatically correct most of the time.

Personal Narratives

Personal narratives are the way that young children relate their experiences to others by telling the stories of what happened. The narrative structure incorporates reporting components such as: who was involved; where the events took place; and what happened. Understanding and using this structure is crucial to young children for their communication; however, many young children cannot follow or apply this sequence without scaffolding (temporary support as needed) from adults. Adults can ask young children guiding questions to facilitate and advance narratives. They can also provide learning tools that engage children's visual, tactile (touch), and kinesthetic (body position and movement) senses. This reinforces narrative use, increases the depth of scaffolding, and motivates children's participation. Children learn to play the main character; describe the setting; sequence plot actions; and use words and body language to express emotions. Topic-related action sequences or "social stories" are important for preschoolers to comprehend and express to promote daily transitions and self-regulation. Such conversational skills attainment achieves milestones in both linguistic and emotional-social development.

Achievements or Processes Enabled by Oral Language Skills Development

Crucial oral language development skills enable children to (1) communicate by listening and responding to others' speech; (2) comprehend meanings of numerous words and concepts encountered in their listening and reading; (3) acquire information on subjects they are interested in learning about; and (4) use specific language to express their own thoughts and ideas. Research finds young children's ability to listen to, understand, and use spoken and written language is associated with their later reading, spelling, and writing literacy achievement. Infants typically begin developing oral language skills, which continue developing through life. Babies develop awareness of and attend to adult speech, and soon begin communicating their needs via gestures and speech sounds. Toddlers express emotions and ideas and solicit information via language. They start uttering simple sentences, asking questions, and giving opinions regarding their likes and dislikes. Young preschoolers expand their vocabularies from hearing others' speech and from books. They describe past and possible future events and unseen objects; tell fictional/"make-believe" stories; and use complete sentences and more complex language.

Benefits of Play-Based Activities

When young children play, they often enact scenarios. Play scenarios tell stories that include who is involved, where they are, what happens, why it happens, and how the "actors" feel about it. Children engage in planning when they decide first what their playing will be about; which children are playing which roles; and who is doing what. This planning and the thought processes involved reflect narrative thinking and structure. Children who experience difficulties with planning play are more likely to avoid participating or to participate only marginally. Since playing actually requires these thought and planning processes, children who do not play spontaneously can be supported in playing by enabling them to talk about potential narratives/stories as foundations for play scenarios. When conflicts emerge during play, conversation is necessary to effect needed change. Narrative development constitutes gradual plot development; play conflicts are akin to fictional/personal narrative problems and result in changed feelings. Adults can help young children discuss problems, identify the changed feeling they cause, and discuss plans/actions for resolution.

Conversation of Adults with Young Children

Adults should converse with young children so the children get practice with: hearing and using rich and abstract vocabulary and increasingly complex sentences; using language to express ideas and ask questions for understanding; and using language to answer questions about past, future, and absent things rather than only about "here-and-now" things. To ensure they incorporate these elements in their conversations, adults can consider the following: in the home, care setting, or classroom, whose voices are heard most often and who does the most talking; the child, not the adult, should be talking at least half of the time. Adults should be using rich language with complex structures when conversing with young children. Adults should be talking with, not at children; the conversation should be shared equally rather than adults doing all the talking while children listen to them. Adults should also ask young children questions, rather than just telling them things. Additionally, adult questions should require that children use language to formulate and communicate abstract ideas.

Natural vs. Intentional

Children enjoy conversing with significant adults, including parents, caregivers, and teachers; and they require practice with doing so. Caregivers tend to talk with young children naturally, sometimes even automatically, throughout the day, which helps children develop significant language skills. However, caregivers can enhance young children's oral language development further through intentional conversations. One element of doing this is establishing an environment that gives the children many things to talk about and many reasons to talk. Another element of intentionally promoting oral language skills development is by engaging in shared conversations. When parents and caregivers share storybook reading with young children, this affords a particularly good springboard for shared conversations. Reading and conversing together are linguistic interactions supplying foundations for children's developing comprehension of numerous word meanings. Researchers find such abundant early word comprehension is a critical basis for later reading comprehension. Asking questions, explaining, requesting what they need, communicating feelings, and learning to listen to others talk are some important ways whereby children build listening, understanding, and speaking skills.

1:1 Conversations with Children

When parents, caregivers, or teachers converse 1:1 with individual children, children reap benefits not as available in group conversations. Caregivers should therefore try to have such individual conversations with each child daily. In daycare and preschool settings, some good times for caregivers to do this include when children arrive and leave; during shared reading activities with one or two children; and during center time. 1:1 talk allows the adult to repeat what the child says for reinforcement. It allows the adult to extend what the child said by adding more information to it, like new vocabulary words, synonyms, meanings, or omitted details. It allows the adult to revise what the child said by restating or recasting it. It allows the child to hear his or her own ideas and thoughts reflected back to them when the adult restates them. Moreover, 1:1 conversation allows adults to contextualize the discussion accordingly with an individual child's understanding. It also allows adults to elicit children's comprehension of abstract concepts.

Extended Conversations and Turn-Taking

When adults engage young children in extended conversations including taking many "back-and-forth" turns, these create the richest dialogues for building oral language skills. Adults make connections with and build upon children's declarations and questions. Adults model richer descriptive language by modifying/adding to children's original words with new vocabulary, adjectives, adverbs, and varying sentences with questions and statements. For example, a child shows an adult his/her new drawing, saying: "This is me and Gran in the garden," the adult can build on this/invite the child to continue: "What is your gran holding?" The child identifies what they planted: "Carrot seeds. Gran said to put them in the dirt so they don't touch." The adult can then encourage the child's use of language to express abstract thoughts: "What could happen if the seeds were touching?" The adult can then extend the conversation through discussion with the child about how plants grow or tending gardens. This introduces new concepts, builds children's linguistic knowledge, and helps them learn to verbalize their ideas.

In-Depth Comprehension of Word Meanings

To support deeper word-meaning comprehension, teachers can give multiple definitions and examples for the same word and connect new vocabulary with children's existing knowledge. For example, a teacher conducting a preschool classroom science experiment incorporates new scientific concepts with new vocabulary words and conversational practice: pouring water on a paper towel, the teacher asks children what is happening to the water. A child answers, "It's going into the paper." The teacher asks how. Another child says, "The paper's soaking it up." The teacher confirms this, teaches the word "absorb," compares the paper to a sponge, and asks how much more water will be absorbed. A child responds probably no more since water is already dripping out. The teacher pours water on a plastic lid, asking if it absorbs. Children respond, "No, it slides off." Confirming, the teacher teaches the word "repel." This teacher has introduced new science concepts and new vocabulary words; engaged the children in conversation; related new concepts and words to existing knowledge; and added information to deepen comprehension.

Adults' Narration of Child Activities and Actions

One oral language development technique adults can use is to narrate, i.e. describe what a child is doing as s/he does it. For example, a caregiver can say, "I see you're spreading paste on the back of your paper flower—not too much so it's lumpy, but not too little so it doesn't stick. Now you're pressing the flower onto your poster board. It sticks—good work!" Hence narration can be incorporated as prelude and segue to verbal positive reinforcement. This promotes oral language development by introducing and illustrating syntaxes. Communicating locations and directionality employs verbs and prepositions. Describing intensity and manner employs adverbs. Labeling objects/actions that are currently present/taking place with new vocabulary words serves immediately to place those words into natural contexts, facilitating more authentic comprehension of word meanings and better memory retention. Caregivers/teachers can narrate children's activities during formal instructional activities and informal situations like outdoor playtime, snack time, and cleanup time, and subsequently converse with them about what they did.

Topics That Young Children Enjoy Talking About

Personal content is important with young children, who enjoy talking about themselves; e.g., what their favorite color is or where they got their new shirt; about their activities, like what they are constructing with Legos or shaping with Play-Doh; or about familiar events and things that access their knowledge, like their family activities and experiences with neighbors and friends. Here is an example of how a teacher can make use of children's conversation to reinforce it, expand it, and teach new vocabulary and grammar. The teacher asks a child what s/he is building and the child answers, "A place for sick animals." The teacher asks, "You mean an animal hospital [or vet clinic]?" and the child confirms. When a child says someone was taken to a hospital "in the siren," the teacher corrects the usage: "They took him to the hospital in the ambulance with the siren was sounding?" This recasts "siren" with the correct word choice, "ambulance." It incorporates "siren" correctly and extends the statement to a complete sentence.

Storytelling

Young children like to communicate about their personal life experiences. When they can do this through narrative structure, it helps them use new words they are learning, organize their thoughts to express them coherently, and engage their imaginative powers. Teachers/caregivers can supply new words they need; model correct syntax for sentences by elaborating on or extending child utterances and asking them questions; and build further upon children's ideas. For example, a teacher asks a child what they did at her sister's birthday party. When the child describes the cake and makes gestures for a word she doesn't know, the teacher supplies "candles," which the child confirms and repeats. When the child then offers, "Mom says be careful with candles," the teacher asks what could happen if you're not careful, the child replies that candles can start a fire. In this way, teachers give young children models of sentence structure, teach vocabulary, and guide children in expressing their thoughts in organized sequences that listeners can follow.

Shared Book Reading

When teachers share books with preschoolers, they can ask questions and discuss the content, giving great opportunities for building oral language through conversation. Books with simple text and numerous, engaging illustrations best invite preschoolers to talk about the characters and events in the pictures, and the plotlines they hear. Children's listening and speaking skills develop; they learn new information and concepts; their vocabularies increase; and their ability to define words and explain their meanings is enhanced through shared reading. Many children's books include rich varieties of words that may not occur in daily conversation, used in complete-sentence contexts. Teachers should provide preschoolers with fictional and nonfictional books; poetry and storybooks; children's reference books like picture dictionaries/encyclopedias; and "information books" covering single topics like weather, birds, reptiles, butterflies, or transportation whereby children can get answers to questions or learn topical information. Detailed illustrations, engaging content, and rich vocabulary are strong elements motivating children to develop oral language and understand how to form sentences, how to use punctuation, and how language works.

Abstract thought is stimulated by asking young children to think about things not observed and/or current. During/after sharing books, teachers can ask children what else might happen in the story; what they imagine the story's characters could be feeling or thinking—which also engages their imaginations; and ask them the meaning of the story's events using questions necessitating children's use of language to analyze this meaning. Teachers can ask younger children vocabulary words: "What did we call this animal?" and encourage them to use language by asking them to describe story details, like "How do the firemen reach people up high in the building?" Once younger children are familiar with a story, teachers can activate and monitor their retention and recall: "Do you remember what happened to Arthur the day before that?" Teachers can ask older children to predict what they think will happen next in a story; to imagine extensions beyond the story ("What would you do if...?"); and make conclusions regarding why characters feel/behave as they do.

Enhancing the Effects of Shared Reading

According to researchers' findings, the effectiveness of shared reading experiences is related to the ways that adults read with young children. Rather than merely labeling objects or events with vocabulary words, teachers should ask young children to recall the shared reading, which monitors their listening comprehension and retention abilities. They should ask children to predict what will happen next based on what already happened in a book; speculate about what could possibly happen; describe characters, actions, events, and information from the shared reading; and ask their own questions about it. Shared reading with small groups of 1–3 children permits teachers to involve each child in the book by questioning and conversing with them about the pictures and plots. To teach vocabulary, teachers can tell children word meanings; point to illustrations featuring new words; relate new words to words the children already know; give multiple, varied examples of new words; and encourage children to use new words they learn in their conversations.

Repeating Shared Reading

Young children develop preferences for favorite books. Once they know a story's plot, they enjoy discussing their knowledge. Teachers can use this for extended conversations. They can ask children who the characters are; where the story takes place; and why characters do things and events occur. They can ask specific questions requiring children to answer how much/how many/how far a distance/how long a time, etc. Teachers can also help children via prompting to relate stories to their own real-life experiences. In a thematic approach, teachers can select several books on the same theme, like rain forests or undersea life. This affords richer extended conversations about the theme. It also allows teachers to "recycle" vocabulary by modeling and encouraging use of thematically related words, which enhances memory and in-depth comprehension of meanings. Teachers can plan activities based on book themes, like painting pictures/murals, sculpting, making collages, or constructing models, which gives children additional motivation to use the new language they learn from shared readings of books.

Reading Aloud

Just before reading a story aloud to young students, the teacher should identify vocabulary words in the story that s/he will need to go over with the children. The teacher can write these words on the board or on strips of paper. Discussing these words before the reading will give the children definitions for new/unfamiliar words, and help them understand word meanings within the story's context. Teachers can also give young children some open-ended questions to consider when listening to the story. They will then repeat these questions during and after the reading. Questions should NOT be ones children can answer with yes/no. When discussing vocabulary words, the teacher can also ask the children to relate words to personal life experiences. For example, with the word fish, some children may want to talk about going fishing with parents. Teachers can encourage children to tell brief personal stories, which will help them relate the story they are about to hear to their own real-life experience, making the story more meaningful.

Before reading a story aloud, adults should tell young children its title and the author's name. Then they can ask the children what an author does (children should respond "write stories" or something similar). Giving the illustrator's name, the adult also can then ask the children what illustrators do (children should respond "draw pictures" or something similar). Holding up the book, an adult can identify the front, spine, and back and ask the children if we start reading at the front or back (children should respond "at the front"). Adults can show young children the illustration on the front cover of the book and ask them, "From this picture, what do you think is going to happen in this story?" and remind them to answer this question in complete sentences. These exchanges before reading a story aloud activate children's fundamental knowledge regarding print and books, as well as the last example's exercising their imagination and language use.

When a teacher is reading a story aloud to young children, after reading each page aloud, s/he should have the children briefly discuss the picture illustrations on each page and how they relate to what the teacher just read aloud. After they read aloud each plot point, action, event, or page, they should ask the children open-ended (non yes/no) questions about what they just heard. This monitors and supports listening comprehension and memory retention/recall and stimulates expressive language use. When children associate something in the story with their own life experiences, teachers should have them explain the connection. As they read, teachers should stop periodically and ask the children to predict or guess what will happen next before continuing. This promotes abstract thinking, understanding of logical sequences, and also exercises the imagination. After reading the story, teachers should ask children whether they liked it and why/why not, prompting them to answer using complete sentences. This helps children to organize their thoughts and opinions and to develop clear, grammatical, complete verbal expression.

Environmental Print

Street signs, traffic signs, store and restaurant names, candy wrappers, food labels, product logos, etc.—all the print we see in everyday life—are environmental print. Just as parents often play alphabetic games with children in the car ("Find something starting with A...with B..." etc.), adults can use environmental print to enhance print awareness and develop reading skills. They can ask children to find letters from their names on colorful cereal boxes. They can select one sign type, e.g. stop, one-way, or pedestrian crossing, and ask children to count how many they see during a car trip. They can have children practice reading each sign and talk about the phonemes (speech sounds) each letter represents. Adults can take photos of different signs and compile them into a little book for children to "read." By cutting familiar words from food labels, they can teach capitalized and lowercase letters; associate letters with phonemes; have children read the words; and sort words by their initial letters and by categories (signs, foods, etc.).

Alphabetic Principle

The alphabetic principle is the concept that letters and letter combinations represent speech sounds. Children's eventual reading fluency requires knowing these predictable relationships of letters to sounds, which they can then apply to both familiar and unfamiliar words. Young children's knowing the shapes and names of letters predicts their later reading success: knowing letter names is highly correlated with the ability to view words as letter sequences and to remember written/printed words' forms. Children must first be able to recognize and name letters to understand and apply the alphabetic principle. Young children learn letter names first, via singing the alphabet song and reciting rhymes and alphabetical jump-rope chants ("A my name is Alice, I come from Alabama, and I sell Apples; B my name is Betty..." etc.). They learn letter shapes after names, through playing with lettered blocks, plastic/wood/cardboard letters, and alphabet books. Once they can recognize and name letters, children learn letter sounds after names and shapes and spellings after sounds.

To help young children understand that written or printed letters represent corresponding speech sounds, teachers should teach relationships between letters and sounds separately, in isolation, and should teach these directly and explicitly. They should give young children daily opportunities during lessons to practice with letter-sound relationships. These opportunities for practice should include cumulative reviews of sound-letter relationships they have already learned and new letter-sound relationships as well. Adults should begin early in providing frequent opportunities to young children for applying their increasing knowledge and understanding of sound-letter relationships to early experiences with reading. They can do this by providing English words that are spelled phonetically (i.e. spelled the same way that they sound) and have meanings that are already familiar to the young learners.

Print Awareness

Even before they have learned how to read, young children develop print awareness, which constitutes children's first preparation for literacy. Children with print awareness realize that spoken language is represented by the markings on paper (or computer screens). They understand

- 67 -

that the information in printed books adults read comes from the words, not the pictures. Children who have print awareness furthermore realize that print serves different functions within different contexts. They know that restaurant menus give information about the foods available; books tell stories or provide information; some signs show the names of stores, hotels, or restaurants, and other signs give traffic directions or danger warnings. Moreover, print awareness includes knowledge of how print is organized, e.g. that words are combinations of letters and have spaces in between them. Children with print awareness also know that [English] print is read from left to right and top to bottom; book pages are numbered; words convey ideas and meaning; and reading's purpose is to understand those ideas and acquire that meaning.

One way in which a teacher can get an idea of whether or to what extent a young child has developed print awareness is to provide the child with a storybook. Then the teacher can ask the child the following: "Show me the front of the book. Show me the back of the book. Show me the spine of the book. Where is the book's title? Where in the book are you supposed to start reading it? Show me a letter in the book. Now show me a word. Show me the first word of a sentence. Can you show me the last word of a sentence? Now will you show me the first word on a page? Please show me the last word on a page. Can you show me a punctuation mark? Can you show me a capital letter? Can you find a small letter/lowercase letter?" The teacher should also praise each correct response, supply the correct answers for incorrect responses, and review corrected answers.

Teachers should show young children the organization of books and the purpose of reading. When they read to them, they should use books with large print, which are more accessible for young children to view and begin to learn reading. Storybook text should use words familiar/predictable to young children. While reading together, teachers should point out high-frequency words like the, a, is, was, you; and specific letters, words, and punctuation marks in a story. Teachers can use index cards to label objects, areas, and centers in the classroom, pairing pictorial labels with word labels, and direct children's attention to them. They can invite preschoolers to play with printed words by making greeting cards, signs, or "writing" shopping lists and personal letters. They should point out print in calendars, posters, and signs. Also, teachers can have children narrate a story using a wordless picture book; write down their narrative on a poster; and reinforce the activity with a reward related to the story (e.g. eating pancakes after narrating the book Pancakes).

Self-Concept

Self-concept development begins during early childhood. Children come to identify characteristics, abilities, values, and attitudes that they feel define them. From 18–36 months, children develop the Categorical Self. This is a concrete view of oneself, usually related to observably opposite characteristics, e.g. child versus adult, girl versus boy, short versus tall, and good versus bad. A four-year-old might say, "I'm shorter than Daddy. I have blue eyes. I can help Mommy clean house!" Young children can also describe emotional and attitudinal aspects of self-concept, e.g. "I like playing with Joshua. I'm happy today." Preschoolers do not usually integrate these aspects into a unified self-portrait, however. Also, many preschoolers do not yet realize one person can incorporate opposite qualities; a person is either good or bad to them, rather than having both good and bad qualities. The Remembered Self develops with long-term memory, including autobiographical memories and things adults have told them, to comprise one's life story. The Inner Self is the child's private feelings, desires, and thoughts.

Phonics Instruction

Because children display individual differences in their speeds of learning sound-to-letter relationships, instruction should consider this; there is no set rate. Generally, a reasonable pace ranges from two to four sound-letter relationship per week. Relationships vary in utility: many words contain the sounds/letters m, a, t, s, p, and h, which are high-utility; but x as in box, gh as in through, ey as in they, and the sound of a as in want are lower-utility. High-utility sound-letter relationships should be taught first. Teachers should first introduce consonant relationships using f, m, n, r, and s, which are continuous sounds children can produce in isolation with less distortion than word-initial or word-medial stops like p, b, t, d, k, and g. Teachers should also introduce similar-sounding letters like b and v or i and e, and similar-looking letters like b and d or p and g, separately to prevent confusion. Single consonants versus clusters/blends should be introduced in separate lessons. Blends should incorporate sound-letter relationships children already know.

Language Experience Approach (LEA)

The LEA teaches beginning reading by connecting students' personal life experiences with written/printed words. A unique benefit is students using their own language and words, enabling them to interact with texts on multiple levels simultaneously. They thus realize they acquire knowledge and understanding through not just instruction, but also their own experiences. Four steps for implementing the LEA with EC groups: (1) Children and teacher choose a topic, like an exciting trip, game, or recent TV show, to discuss with teacher guidance. (2) Each child takes a turn saying a sentence using his/her own words that advances the discussion/story. The teacher writes the children's words verbatim without corrections, visibly and clearly. (3) Every few sentences or several words, the teacher stops and reads the record aloud for children to confirm accuracy. (4) Record review: the teacher points to each word, they read aloud together, or children repeat after the teacher. The teacher gives children copies of the record for independent review and possible compilation into books of LEA stories.

Whole Language Approach

The whole language approach concentrates on children's seeking, finding, and constructing meaning in language. As such, young children's early technical correctness is not the priority. Whole language teachers do not ignore children's errors. However, they do not make correction more important than overall engagement, understanding, and appreciation of reading, writing, and literature. Instead, teachers make formative assessments taking into account the errors each child makes. Then they design learning experiences for children that give them opportunities and assistance in acquiring mechanically correct linguistic forms and structures. While this holistic approach finds analytical techniques that break language down into components like phonemes and alphabet letters less useful, children with language processing/reading problems need to learn phonemic awareness, phonics, and other decoding skills to develop reading fluency. The National Reading Panel conducted a study (1997–2000) to resolve controversy over phonics vs. whole language as the best teaching method, finding that any effective reading instruction program must teach phonemic awareness, phonics, reading fluency, vocabulary development, and reading comprehension.

The whole language approach is based on constructivist philosophy and psychology: children construct their own knowledge through their interactions with their environments. In contrast to analytical approaches like phonics and alphabetic learning, constructivism views learning as an individual's unique cognitive experience of acquiring new knowledge, shaped by the individual's existing knowledge and personal perspective. Whole language instruction emphasizes helping children create meaning from their reading and express meaning in their writing. The whole-language philosophy emphasizes cultural diversity, integrating literacy instruction across subject domains, reading high-quality literature, and giving children many opportunities for independent reading, small-group guided reading, and being read to aloud by teachers. Whole language believes children learn to read by writing and vice versa. Realistically purposeful reading and writing are encouraged, as is using texts that motivate children to develop a love for literature. Early grammatical/spelling/technical correctness is not stressed, which can be problematic for children with reading/language processing disorders, who need explicit instruction in decoding skills and strategies.

Addressing Early Mechanical Errors in Learning Reading and Writing

The basal reader is America's commonest approach, used in an estimated 75–85 percent of K–8th-grade classrooms. The number of publishers offering basal reading series has decreased to about one-fourth of that in the 20th century, decreasing teacher responsibility for investigating/piloting readers for district approval. Using basal readers is a skills-based/bottom-up approach. Teaching smaller-to-larger reading subskills in systematic, rigid sequence assists students' transition from part to whole. Texts graded by reading level contain narration and exposition organized thematically by unit, including children's literature and diverse other genres. Phonics and other specific instructional strands with practice assignments develop skills, which are assessed with end-of-unit tests. For young children, text decoding is enabled through exact control of vocabulary items and word analysis skills, "big [enlarged] books," and word and picture cards. 20th-century and older series sacrificed comprehension and enjoyment for vocabulary control and skill acquisition, but 21st-century series vary methods more (like multiple story versions or book excerpts enabling selection sharing), affording children more motivation to read.

Directed Reading Activity (DRA) and the Directed Reading-Thinking Activity (DR-TA)

Using basal readers, the DRA comprises: (1) The teacher prepares children for reading by stimulating their motivation and introducing new concepts and/or vocabulary. (2) Students read silently, guided by teacher questions and statements. (3) The teacher develops student comprehension and students discuss characters, plots, or concepts to further comprehension. (4) After silent reading, students read aloud and read answers to teacher questions, known as "purposeful rereading." (5) Students' follow-up workbook activities/practice review comprehension and vocabulary. Some selections may include enrichment activities relating them to writing, art, drama, or music. The DR-TA approach is designed to develop critical readers through instruction in group comprehension. It requires children's active engagement in reading by processing information, asking questions, and receiving feedback as they read. The first phase of DR-TA is the teacher's direction of student thought processes throughout reading. The second phase involves developing student skills according to their needs as identified in phase 1, and additional extension or follow-up activities.

Differences Between DRA and DR-TA Approaches

(1) One main difference is that the DR-TA approach gives teachers all the responsibility and greater flexibility for developing lessons. As such it contains fewer directions than the DRA approach, which contains specific materials and questions to use, specific guidelines, and is more teacher-manual-oriented and materials-oriented. Therefore DR-TA can be used for not only basal readers, but also planning lessons in other curriculum areas involving reading; the DRA approach applies more directly to basal reader programs. (2) DRA manuals use mostly literal, factual questions, requiring only convergent thinking for student responses. However, in DR-TA, questions also demand divergent (creative) thinking of students, stimulating higher-level reading comprehension and interpretation. (3) New vocabulary is pretaught in the DRA approach before children read. The DR-TA approach excludes preteaching, realistically requiring student decoding of new vocabulary words during reading. (4) DRA manuals specify when to teach which skills for reading

comprehension. DR-TA approaches do not, requiring more questioning expertise and acceptance of some alternative student responses by teachers.

Aggression

Preschoolers typically demonstrate some aggressive behavior, which tends to peak around age 4. Instrumental Aggression is one basic type: younger preschoolers frequently shout, hit, or kick others to get concrete objects they want. Middle preschoolers are more likely to exhibit Hostile Aggression, i.e. getting even for wrongs or injuries they feel others have done to them. Hostile Aggression occurs in two subtypes: Overt and Relational. Overt Aggression involves physically harming others or threatening to do so, while Relational Aggression involves emotional/social harm, e.g. rejecting/excluding another from a group of friends or spreading malicious rumors about another. Young boys are more likely to engage in Overt Aggression, while young girls are more likely to engage in Relational Aggression. These gender preferences in aggressive behaviors tend to remain the same at all ages if aggression exists. While most young children eventually phase out aggression as they learn other ways of resolving social conflicts, some persist in verbally and/or physically aggressive behavior, causing problems.

Minimizing Aggressive Behavior

While it is normal for preschoolers to exhibit some physical and verbal aggression until they have learned more mature ways of expressing feelings, getting what they want, and settling disputes, there are things adults can do to influence them such that aggressive behavior does not develop into a predominant method of social interaction. Adults set examples for children, and children learn by observing and imitating those examples. Therefore, parents, caregivers, and teachers should not model verbally and/or physically aggressive behaviors such as calling others names, yelling at others, or punishing others' undesirable behaviors using physical force. Not only should adults avoid disciplining children physically, they should also avoid physically and/or verbally violent interactions with other adults. Social learning theorist Albert Bandura proved that children who viewed violent videos imitated what they observed and engaged in more aggressive behavior, so adults should also prevent young children's exposure to violent TV programming and video games.

Prejudice and Discrimination

Prejudice literally means prejudging, i.e. judging someone/something negatively before/without knowing anything about who/what one is judging. Prejudice gives rise to discrimination in that prejudiced ideas motivate unfair, i.e. discriminatory, behaviors toward others. Psychologist Albert Bandura, who developed social learning theory, identified the process whereby children acquire attitudes and behaviors they observe in others, which he named vicarious learning. Children commonly pick up beliefs, attitudes, and behaviors from adults around them, without applying any critical thinking to these. They are often not even aware of the attitudes and beliefs they assume in this way. Thus, they will engage in prejudicial attitudes and discriminatory behaviors without thinking through what they are doing. Though such behavior is not justified, children simply assume it is because of adults' examples. Thus, adults must carefully inspect their own beliefs and attitudes, as well as what they do and say, because these are what children will imitate.

Prejudicial Thinking

Prejudicial thinking about certain groups of people is uninformed and/or misinformed thinking. It is typically based on fear of the unknown due to lack of knowledge and/or fear due to erroneous beliefs about people. Thus, the best way to dispel prejudice is to provide information where there was none and/or to correct wrong information. When unfamiliar groups become more familiar and when wrong assumptions are corrected, people's misconceptions are replaced by reality and they become less afraid. For example, children having no experience with people from other racial, ethnic, or socioeconomic groups are likely to fear these people (as are many adults). Adults can help young children by furnishing them with many opportunities—not just isolated ones—to interact with people from diverse cultural and socioeconomic milieus. For children to experience true learning, which will supersede negative, uninformed first impressions, they must have multiple such social opportunities. School, outside classes, sports, and camp are activities affording such opportunities.

Bullying

Children who are bullied by others are victims of prejudicial thinking and discriminatory actions. Common negative effects of bullying include rage, feelings of hopelessness, anxiety, and depression. Left untreated, children with these feelings can develop suicidal ideations and actions as they grow older if bullying persists. When young, children have the additional problem of not yet knowing how to manage their negative feelings caused by others' aggression or even how to express them. Adults can give them much-needed help by assisting them in articulating their emotions openly but nonviolently. Adults must realize that young children, especially those who have experienced others' violent treatment, may not recognize that anger can be expressed in any ways other than violent ones. Based on their experience, children may internalize assumptions that they can only act out their anger through self-destructive behaviors. When adults consistently model positive, proactive ways of discussing negative emotions, children observe that more constructive behaviors are possible and learn to adopt these as more effective coping strategies.

Sex/Gender-Role Development

Various theories of development, such as psychoanalytic, behaviorist, cognitive, and social learning, have differing views of why and how children develop sexual/gender identities. To address these differences, psychologists have endeavored to produce some general conclusions about young children's self-concepts of gender. They find that during preschool ages, children gradually develop concepts of what being a girl or a boy in their culture means. These concepts become clearly articulated and shape their behaviors. Between the ages of 2 and 6, children are in the process of putting together the pieces of these gender concepts. Developing sex-appropriate behaviors and developing categories of gender roles both appear to be influenced by a combination and interaction of biological and sociological variables. Psychologists additionally conclude that children perform some mental matching process enabling them to isolate features they share in common with others, and that young children's abilities to observe, imitate, and categorize influence their later concepts of sex-appropriate behaviors. By ages 5–6, most children clearly identify with one sex or the other.

Combating Cultural Stereotypes and Discrimination

When children experience stereotyping of and discrimination against their cultural group, adults can counter these negative reflections on the group by correcting erroneous opinions they have heard. By giving children plenty of examples of positive accomplishments by members of their group, they convey cultural pride, affording children a sense of empowerment. Adults should consistently model positive, constructive, and no-violent methods of addressing prejudice for children. If prejudice proves ongoing, caregivers and teachers must assertively advocate on behalf of children and their cultures to shut down prejudicial sources. If they hear young children furthering cultural stereotypes they have absorbed, adults should immediately correct their statements and behaviors, explaining why certain words and actions harm others and are unacceptable. Extended discussions with young children are important for putting prejudice into perspective and context to help them understand it. Adults can also apply behavioral methods, such as associating prejudicial behaviors with consequences (e.g. losing a privilege or gaining work) and providing related learning activities to prevent repeated instances.

Using Historical Contexts, Correction, and Real-Life Examples to Address Prejudicial Attitudes

Because many prejudicial attitudes exist in our society on both individualized and institutionalized levels, it is all too easy for children to absorb and emulate them. When children who have been victims of prejudice learn they were attacked not as individuals, but members of a group, this does not eliminate negative effects, but can help them see it in a different perspective. Adults can place prejudice and discrimination in their historical contexts so children realize they are not lone victims but part of a larger group. Correcting false beliefs, as in Albert Ellis's Rational-Emotive Behavior Therapy and other forms of cognitive-behavioral therapy, can be applied by adults' pointing out the irrational, flawed thinking involved and supplying examples contradicting that thinking. For example, if children have been influenced to think certain groups are less intelligent or lazier than others, adults can show them examples of many members of those groups with outstanding achievements in society. They can do this through book/video biographies, personal anecdotes, and introductions to living people.

Genetic and Environmental Influences on Behavior

Young children are subject to both genetic and environmental influences upon their relative risk of displaying antisocial behaviors. Research into factors influencing early childhood behavior identifies both genetic variables and environmental ones, like corporal punishment, affecting young children's propensities toward antisocial behavior. Children experiencing more corporal punishment display greater behavior problems; children at greater genetic risk also do. However, boys at higher genetic risk for behavior problems who also experience more corporal punishment exhibit the most antisocial behavior. Therefore, both genetic risk factors and corporal punishment significantly predict preschoolers' antisocial behavior. Additionally, the nature-nurture interaction of genetic risk factors and environmental punishment is statistically significant for young boys but not young girls. Such evidence shows that environmental learning is not wholly responsible for antisocial behavior: genetic variables predispose some young children to antisocial behaviors more than others.

Behaviorist Learning Theories

Ivan Pavlov's experiments with dogs proved that when a stimulus evoking a reflexive response—drooling at the taste of meat—was repeatedly paired with an unrelated/"neutral" stimulus—a bell ringing—dogs came to associate the unrelated stimulus with the original response and drooled on hearing the bell without tasting meat. This proved generalizable to humans. Edward L. Thorndike's experiments with cats also applied to humans. Thorndike introduced the Law of Effect: we are more likely to repeat behaviors receiving desirable consequences. This set the stage for B. F. Skinner's later work. John B. Watson maintained that because inner states cannot be observed or measured, only observable outer behaviors should be used in psychology and learning. Skinner experimented with operant conditioning, wherein behaviors are trained and shaped through manipulating their antecedents/preceding stimuli and consequences/following stimuli. He expanded behaviorism into a comprehensive theory, including detailed rules for teaching new behaviors and modifying behavior (behavior modification).

Positive and Negative Reinforcement and Positive and Negative Punishment

In behaviorism, reinforcement means strengthening the probability a behavior will be repeated. Skinner used the terms positive vs. negative to mean introducing vs. removing, not good vs. bad. Therefore, positive reinforcement is introducing something rewarding immediately after a behavior. When a child's behavior is rewarded, s/he will repeat it to obtain repeated rewards: Johnny gets a treat or praise for putting away his toys; he will do it again. Negative reinforcement is rewarding by removing something unwanted: Johnny dislikes noisy crowds at preschool. One day he wakes up earlier, is taken to preschool earlier, finds it quieter and less crowded; he will want to get up and arrive earlier again. Positive punishment is introducing an aversive consequence for a behavior: Johnny refuses to put toys away; his parents then make him clean up the entire room; he is less likely to repeat the refusal. Negative punishment is removing a desirable stimulus: Johnny refuses to put away toys; his parents prohibit watching TV; he is less likely to keep refusing.

Behavioral techniques include positive reinforcement, introducing rewarding stimuli for emitting desired behaviors; negative reinforcement, removing unwanted stimuli for emitting desired behaviors; positive punishment, introducing aversive stimuli for unwanted behaviors; and negative punishment, removing desired stimuli for unwanted behaviors. Research has found positive reinforcement the most powerful of all these. One reason is that people are highly motivated by rewards. Another is that all behaviors meet needs; punishment suppresses certain behaviors, but then other behaviors must emerge to fill the same need. If a child misbehaves to get attention, even scolding/other punishment can constitute attention. But if rewarded for more appropriate behavior to get attention, like asking an available adult or peer for interaction, the child meets the attention need while replacing a maladaptive behavior with an adaptive one. Another reason is punishment's limitations: preschoolers may stop misbehaving after one teacher's punishment, but not with another teacher; punishment not applied consistently loses its effect. Also, punishment can cause resentment, anger, defiance, or fearfulness in young children.

IFSP, IEP Development and Delivery of Services and Assessment And Eligibility

Required vs. recommended information in screening

If a young child has been screened for developmental disorders or delays within the past 6 months and no changes have been observed or reported, repeat screening may be waived. Initial screenings are required. Hearing and vision screenings are mandatory in screening young children. Formal developmental measures are also required, which may include screening tests of motor skills development, cognitive development, social-emotional development, and self-help skills development. Formal screening tests of speech-language development are also required. Additional tests recommended during screening include informal measures. For example, checklists, rating scales, and inventories may be used to screen a child's behavior, mood, and performance of motor skills, cognitive skills, self-help skills, and social and emotional skills. On checklists, parents or caregivers check whether the child does or does not demonstrate listed behaviors, or assessors may complete them via parent or caregiver interviews or interviewing and observing the child. Rating scales ask parents, caregivers, and assessors to rate a child's behaviors, affect, mood, and so on, within a range of numbered and labeled descriptions. Inventories list demonstrated skills and needs. Behavioral observations and existing records and information are also used.

Differential features of developmental screenings

If a child's development is suspected of being delayed—for example, the child is not reaching developmental milestones during expected age ranges—a developmental screening may be administered. Screening tests are quickly performed and yield more general results. The hospital or doctor's office may give a questionnaire to the parent or caregiver to complete for a screening. Alternatively, a health or education professional may administer a screening test to the child. Screening tests are not intended to diagnose specific conditions or give details; they are meant to identify children who may have some problem. Screenings can overidentify or under-identify developmental delays in children. Hence, if the screening identifies a child as having developmental delay(s), the child is then referred for a developmental evaluation—a much longer, more thorough, comprehensive, in-depth assessment using multiple tests, administered by a psychologist or other highly-trained professional. Evaluation provides a profile of a child's strengths and weaknesses in all developmental domains. Determination of needs for early intervention services or treatment plans is based on evaluation results.

Developmental evaluation data

The child's social history should be obtained. This is typically done by a social worker. Details of the child's developmental progress heretofore; the family's composition, socioeconomic status, and situation; and the child's and family's health and medical histories and status should be emphasized. A physician's or nurse's medical assessment is required, including a physical examination, and if indicated, a specialist's examination. A psychologist typically assesses intellectual and cognitive development; at least one such test is generally required. At least one test of adaptive behavior is also required to assess emotional-social development. Self-help skills are evaluated; this may be included within cognitive, adaptive behavior, or programming assessments. Communication skills are typically evaluated by a speech-language pathologist. Both receptive and expressive language must be tested and comprehensively rather than simply by single-word vocabulary tests. As indicated, speech articulation is also tested. At least one test of motor skills, typically administered by a physical or occupational therapist, is required. Programming evaluation requires at least one criterion-referenced or curriculum-based measure, typically administered by an educator.

<u>Analysis of data</u>

A young child, often aged 3 to 5 years, is generally considered to have a health impairment under the following conditions: Developmental testing reveals a delay, for example, of at least 1.5 standard deviations away from the mean or average test scores used as norms for the child's age group in one or more of the five developmental areas—cognitive, emotional-social, speech-language, gross motor skills, and fine motor skills—and a physician's written statement indicates a specific type of health impairment, any developmental limits it causes, the potential necessity for medication, and medication effects. With the majority of health, medical, and physical impairments, classification of the child's disorder is based on the doctor's diagnosis. However, when attention deficit hyperactivity disorder (ADHD) is found to constitute a disabling health impairment for a child because it interferes with daily functioning, development, and early education, diagnosis is better made via a multidisciplinary team. Differential diagnosis is necessary because ADHD can be confused with or compounded by other conditions.

Data and criteria used in evaluating

Multidisciplinary professionals should be involved in differential diagnosis of ADHD due to its multifaceted nature and pervasive effects on child development. The process of evaluation depends on significant components, like the child's specific developmental history, obtained through a combination of parent or caregiver responses, and professional practitioners' findings, and on information obtained via ratings made by teachers and teachers' informal reports of problems observed with the child's behavior and pre-academic functioning within his or her natural environment. Common observational descriptions of children having ADHD include characteristics of impulsivity, inattention, distractibility, and excessive motor, physical, or vocal and verbal activity. Another general set of criteria is that, if multiple observers in different contexts report problematic behaviors by the child, if these problem behaviors started early in childhood, and if the behaviors have existed for longer than 6 months, an eventual diagnosis of ADHD is more likely. Physical examination does not directly contribute to diagnosing ADHD but is necessary to rule out other medical conditions that may mimic or resemble ADHD.

Considerations relevant to the diagnosis of attention deficit hyperactivity disorder

When the symptoms of ADHD limit a child's normal development and learning, this condition can be categorized as other health impairment. While most health impairments are diagnosed by physicians, ADHD should be diagnosed by multidisciplinary professionals. This is not only because its nature is complex and it involves psychological components such as attention, memory, impulse control, and neurologically based physical hyperactivity. It is also because ADHD can resemble other developmental disorders; it may coexist with them; and the symptoms of each often overlap. Thus, differential diagnosis is important with ADHD. When ADHD is suspected, a comprehensive assessment is indicated, including data obtained from multiple settings, including the home, and evaluations of the child's functioning in the medical, psychological, behavioral, and educational domains. It is also necessary to obtain thorough health and developmental histories of the child.

<u>Differential diagnosis of ADHD</u>

Experts have found that neurological examinations, such as EEG (electroencephalogram), CAT (computer-assisted tomography) scan, PET (positron emission tomography) scan, MRI (magnetic resonance imaging), or fMRI (functional MRI), do not help diagnose or treat ADHD and are only indicated for seizure disorders or other neurological symptoms observed through the child's history and medical and physical examinations. Also, a number of other conditions can produce symptoms similar to those caused by ADHD. For example, some medications cause side effects, including inattention and hyperactivity. Various social and emotional variables can cause a child to experience anxiety, which can have symptoms of distractibility, impulsivity, inattentiveness, or hyperactivity. Sensory impairments can cause the appearance of inattention: The child may be unable to detect sensory stimuli rather than ignoring them. Some systemic medical illnesses can also produce symptoms resembling those of ADHD. Some children with seizure disorders but not ADHD may exhibit ADHD-like symptoms of inattention or distraction, which are really minor (petit-mal or absence) seizure activity. Lead poisoning or other environmental toxicity also can produce symptoms appearing similar to those of ADHD.

Child Find process

Child Find is an ongoing process with the aim of locating, identifying, and referring young children with disabilities and their families as early as possible for service programs. This process consists of activities designed to raise public awareness and screenings and evaluations to identify and diagnose disabilities. The federal IDEA law mandates under Part B that disabled children are guaranteed early childhood special education services and under Part C that infants and toddlers at risk for developmental delays are guaranteed early intervention programs. (Eligibility guidelines vary by U.S. states.) The IDEA requires school districts to find, identify, and evaluate children with disabilities in their attendance areas. School districts have facilitated this Child Find process by establishing community informed referral networks whose members refer children who may have exceptional educational needs (EENs). Network members typically include parents, doctors, birth-to-3 programs, child care programs, Head Start programs, public health agencies, social service agencies, and any other community members with whom the young children come into contact.

Current collaborative approaches and models

Historically, the tradition was to conduct kindergarten screenings of children entering schools around age 5. However, in recent years, school districts have developed community referral networks to assist in the processes of Child Find, screening, evaluation, and referral for early intervention and early childhood special education and related services. Current models are more informal, proactive, and collaborative. Cooperative educational interagency service efforts give parents information about normal early childhood development and available community resources and offer opportunities for developmental screenings of their young children. Specific procedures are governed by individual U.S. state laws. Generally, district networks implementing current models send developmental review forms to parents to complete in advance, and then they attend a developmental screening at a community site. Parents discuss normal early childhood growth and development with program staff, while in the same room, trained professionals observe their children as they play. Children's vision and hearing are also screened. Parents can discuss their children's current development with psychologists, early childhood educators, or counselors. Thereafter, they can learn about community resources.

Elements of a comprehensive Child Find system

A comprehensive Child Find system includes at least: a definition of the target population, public awareness, referral and intake, screening and identification of young children who may be eligible for services under the IDEA (the Individuals with Disabilities Education Act), eligibility determination, tracking, and interagency coordination. Early Intervention programs provide special services for infants and toddlers from birth through 2 years old and their families. These services are designed to identify and serve the needs of children these ages having developmental disorders or delays or at risk for having them in the areas of physical, cognitive, emotional, social, communicative, and adaptive development according to the IDEA. Individual states and territories determine their respective policies for complying with IDEA provisions. Some of the services typically provided in early intervention programs include: assistive technology services and devices, audiology and hearing services, family training and counseling, educational programs, evaluative and diagnostic medical services, health services to allow the child to benefit from other services, nursing services, nutritional services, occupational therapy, physical therapy, psychological services, respite care services, speech-language services, transportation, and service coordination services.

U.S. state criteria for defining developmental delays

The IDEA Part C specifies the areas of development that states must include in defining developmental delays. However, individual states must identify the criteria they use to determine eligibility, including pertinent diagnostic instruments, procedures, and functional levels. States currently use quantitative and qualitative measures. Quantitative criteria for developmental delay include: difference between chronological age and performance level, expressed as a percentage of chronological age; performance at a given number of months below chronological age; or number of standard deviations (SDs) below mean of performance on a norm-referenced test. Qualitative criteria include: development considered atypical or delayed for established norms or observed behaviors considered atypical. At least one state differentially defines delay according to a child's age in months, with the rationale that a 25% delay, for example, is very different for a 1-year-old than a 3-year-old. Quantitative criteria for defining delay and determining eligibility vary widely among states. A 25% or 20% delay; 2 SDs below mean in 1+ areas or 1.5 SD below mean in 2+ areas are some common state criteria.

Examples of the kinds of required data

Typically, school districts track screening locations, districts involved, participants, and screening frequencies by area, numbers and ages of children screened, and referrals. For example, as identifying information, a district's data collection form may include the screening county; school district(s) or Child and Family Connection(s) (CFCs) responsible for screening and working with a screening entity; the screening date, and for cumulative reporting purposes, the screening month; the place(s) of the screening event(s); the individual in charge of each screening session, the contact person and his or her contact information; any agency or agencies or individual provider(s) that conduct the screening activities; and the agency or provider type. The total number of children screened during an event or cumulative monthly report, and number by each age, are recorded for tracking. Numbers of children referred for further evaluation, aged 0 to 3 and 3 to 5+ respectively, are recorded as are referral types and agency names. The numbers of children passing screening but referred for rescreening for various reasons (e.g., the child could not screen, parents reported variable functioning, the screener had specific concerns, etc.) may also be recorded.

Challenges and considerations for U.S. states in eligibility determination

The federal IDEA law's Part C mandates and broadly describes early intervention services for children aged 0 to 2 with developmental disabilities but assigns specific definitions and eligibility criteria to individual states. IDEA Part C requires states and jurisdictions to serve (1) children with developmental delays and (2) children with diagnosed mental or physical conditions putting them at high risk for developmental delays. States and jurisdictions also have the option to provide services to children at risk of significant developmental delays through not receiving early intervention. Defining eligible populations and establishing eligibility criteria affect types and numbers of children who need or get services, types of services rendered, and early intervention expenses, challenging state governments. While many states wanted to serve at-risk children after IDEA established its Early Intervention Program, fear of costs limited how many states included them in their definitions. Some states do not serve, but monitor, at-risk children and refer them if developmental delays appear.

Quantitative and qualitative data and testing instrumentation

Many U.S. states quantitatively express developmental delays in children aged 0 to 2 years through standard deviations below the mean on standardized, norm-referenced tests; percentage of the chronological age; or developmental age in months. However, some areas of child development are not well described by these methods. Another consideration is that traditional standardized assessment instruments may vary across developmental domains or children's ages. To address these concerns, some states also include qualitative data, like observations of atypical behaviors, along with quantitative measures to determine developmental delays. Additional considerations with using traditional testing instruments are that not enough such instruments exist for the 0 to 2 years age group; and those that do exist do not have good predictive validity. Hence, the IDEA's Part C regulations also require informed clinical opinion as a basis for determining eligibility. Such opinion is usually obtained through multidisciplinary consensus including parents, multiple data sources, and quantitative and qualitative data. Several states only identify informed clinical opinion, without separate quantitative criteria, as their eligibility criterion.

Categories of risk for developmental delays (DD)

In applying IDEA's Part C early intervention provisions for children aged 0 to 2 years, many states divide risk into established risk, biological or medical risk, and environmental risk. Established risk is a "diagnosed physical or mental condition which has a high probability of resulting in developmental delay." This includes genetic, chromosomal, or congenital disorders; severe hearing, vision, or other sensory impairments; innate metabolic disorders; congenital infections; disorders reflecting disturbed nervous system development; fetal alcohol syndrome; other disorders secondary to exposure to toxins; and severe attachment disorders. Part C makes these eligible regardless of the presence or absence of measured delay. Several states add many other conditions to this definition. Biological or medical risk includes low birth weight, chronic lung disease, intraventricular hemorrhage at birth, and failure to thrive. Because these do not always cause DD, comprehensive evaluation by multidisciplinary teams (MDTs) must determine eligibility and specific services. Environmental risk includes poverty, homelessness, parental age, education, DD, substance abuse, family social disorganization, and child abuse or neglect. Eligibility and service determination in this category require MDT evaluation as with biological or medical risk.

Availability and costs of evaluating preschool children

Even if preschoolers are not yet enrolled in the public school system, the IDEA charges school districts with providing them evaluations, eligibility determinations, and services. Parents need not pay for evaluations, which are funded by federal and state governments. If a child is determined eligible for early intervention or early childhood special education services, these are also provided by school districts at no cost to parents. In every state, parent training and information courses and community parent resource centers are funded by the federal government. For rural families, the goals of early intervention and early special education services are the same as in urban settings; however, services may be delivered differently. Organizations like the University of Montana Rural Institute and the National Rural Education Association can provide rural families with information about services. Special-needs Native American infants, toddlers, and children living on reservations are included under state lead agencies' responsibilities for providing early intervention services and state education agencies' responsibilities for special education services to preschoolers.

Tests commonly administered to premature babies

One test that physicians commonly order for premature infants is a blood gas analysis. This test yields the proportions of gases like oxygen, hydrogen, and nitrogen in the blood. Premature infants' organs are not yet fully developed, particularly their lungs and hearts. A major cause of intellectual disabilities and neurological damage is oxygen deprivation, so it is important to ensure sufficient amounts. Tests also assess the baby's blood levels of glucose, calcium, and bilirubin. Glucose is blood sugar, vital for supplying fuel to brain and body systems. Calcium is necessary for proper bone and tooth formation and also for proper conduction of key brain chemicals. Bilirubin is a yellow pigment, a by-product of used red blood cells. The liver makes bile to break down bilirubin, which is then removed from the body through fecal excretion. If the liver cannot do this job adequately, bilirubin builds up in the bloodstream, causing jaundice. It is not uncommon for premature newborns to become jaundiced; this can cause neurological damage if not resolved.

Single and multiple risk factors for developmental delays (DD)

Scientists find that developmental outcomes for children are not reliably predicted by any one risk factor or event. Developmental risk increases with increased biological, medical, or environmental risk factors. However, researchers have found some variables that afford resiliency in children to offset risk factors. These can include the child's basic temperament, the child having high self-esteem, the child having a good emotional relationship with at least one parent; and the child having experiences of successful learning. These findings indicate that assessments should include criteria for multiple biological and environmental risk factors, for cumulative biological and environmental risk factors, and for protective or resilience factors, considering all of these in the context of change occurring over time. Under the IDEA (the Individuals with Disabilities Education Act), U.S. states have the option to provide early intervention services to children considered at risk for adverse developmental outcomes as well as those already identified with them. Some states apply multiple-risk models, requiring three to five risk factors for service eligibility. Some states also determine eligibility with less DD when biological, medical, or environmental risk factors also exist.

Sources of information on early intervention and preschool special education

Military families stationed both in the United States and overseas who have young special needs children can seek information and assistance from the federally funded organization Specialized Training of Military Families (STOMP). The staff of STOMP is composed of parents having special needs children themselves, who also have been trained to work with other parents of special needs children. STOMP staff members are spouses of military personnel who thus understand the unique, specialized circumstances and needs of military families. Another government agency, the U.S. Department of Defense, includes the office of the Department of Defense Education Activity (DoDEA) and provides comprehensive guidance to military families with special needs children who are eligible to receive, or are receiving, free appropriate public education (FAPE) as mandated by the IDEA law (the Individuals with Disabilities Education Act), whether that education is located in the United States or in other countries.

Sound practices for assessing the learning progress and achievement

To plan and implement instruction, to evaluate its effectiveness, and to monitor children's progress toward program goals, ECE teachers must assess children's development and learning. Instruction and assessment should be mutual; that is, assessments evaluate what instruction is developing, and instruction develops what is being assessed. Assessment must have validity (it measures what it is meant to measure) and reliability (it can be reproduced with the same results). It should not be used for tracking, labeling, or other practices detrimental to children. It should be purposeful, strategic, and continual. Its results inform communications with children's families, instructional planning and implementation, and evaluations and improvements of programs' and teachers' effectiveness. It should focus on progress toward developmentally and educationally important goals. Programs should have systems for gathering, interpreting, and applying formative assessment results to guide classroom activity. Teachers must continually make assessments, including during all interactions with children, to improve instruction and learning.

Attributes important to assessing the progress of young children's learning

ECE assessment methods are appropriate for young children's developmental levels and experiences, acknowledge individual student differences, and accordingly permit various ways for students to demonstrate competence. Hence, appropriate ECE classroom assessment methods include clinical interviews, teacher observations of children, portfolio assessments and collections of work samples produced by children, and records of children's performance during authentic (real-life or close to it) instructional activities. Assessment tests not only children's independent achievements but also performance of tasks with needed scaffolding (temporary support), as with groups, pairs, or other assistance. Teachers incorporate information from families and children themselves about their work, along with teacher evaluations, for overall assessment. Assessments are designed for specific purposes; proven to yield valid, reliable results for those; and only used for those purposes. Major decisions for children, like enrollment or placement, are always based on multiple data sources, never one instrument. Sources include observations by and interactions with parents and family, teachers, and specialists. If screening or assessment identifies possible special needs, follow-up, evaluation, and referral as needed are made appropriately without immediate diagnosis or labeling.

Individualized Family Service Plan (IFSP) - 0 to 2 years

When a child aged from birth through 2 years has been screened, referred for comprehensive evaluation to determine whether he or she has a disability eligible for early intervention services under the IDEA law Individualized Family Service Plan, and through the evaluation results, found eligible, the next step is to develop an IFSP. This is a written document that describes in detail what early intervention services the child will be receiving. The IFSP is guided by certain principles, including that the young child's needs are closely attached to his or her family's needs and that the family is the child's most important resource. Therefore, supporting the family and building upon the family's particular strengths are the best ways to meet the needs of and support the child. The IFSP is created by a multidisciplinary team that includes the parents and is a plan for the whole family. Other interagency team members, depending on the child's needs, may include medical personnel, therapists, social workers, child development specialists, and so on.

Information included in an IFSP - 0 to 2 years

An IFSP is developed for children 0 to 2 years determined eligible through evaluation results for early intervention services. It must include: the child's current levels of functioning and needs in physical, cognitive, communication, emotional, social, and adaptive development; with parental consent, family information including the parents' and other close family members' concerns, priorities, and resources; primary effects of the IFSP expected for the child and family; specific services to be delivered; where the child will receive services in natural environments, like at home, in the community, elsewhere, or a combination; if services will not be in the natural environment, a rationale justifying this; specific service times and locations; number of sessions or days for services and session durations; whether services will be 1:1 or in groups; who will pay for the services; the name of the service coordinator managing IFSP implementation; steps supporting future transition from early intervention to other programs and services; and optionally, other services of interest to the family, for example, finances, raising children with disabilities, and so on.

Aspects of IFSPs - 0 to 2 years

When infants and toddlers are determined eligible for IDEA (the Individuals with Disabilities Education Act) services, parents and professionals from multiple, relevant disciplines develop an IFSP for services to family and child. Professionals must thoroughly explain the plan to parents, and parents must give informed, written consent before the child receives services. Every U.S. state has its own set of IFSP guidelines. The service coordinator can explain state guidelines to parents. Early intervention services range from simple to complex, including things such as prescribing eyeglasses, special instruction, home visits, counseling, and family training to help meet the child's special needs. Some services are provided in the family's home and some in hospitals, local health departments, community day care centers, clinics, or other settings. Natural environments, that is, settings where the child normally lives, plays, and learns are preferred. Personnel delivering services must be qualified. Both public and private agencies may be involved in service delivery.

Financial aspects of receiving early intervention services

The IDEA provides that, if a child has a qualifying disability, is at risk for developmental delay or disability, or is suspected of having an eligible disability, families must be given Child Find services, developmental screenings, assessment referrals, comprehensive evaluations, a developed and reviewed IFSP in which parents participate, and service coordination all at no cost to the family. Whether families pay for services other than those named above is determined by each U.S. state's individual policies. Some services can be covered by Medicaid, by private health insurance policies, or for Native American families, by Indian Health Services. Some service providers may charge fees to families on a sliding scale basis according to the family's earned income so that lower-income families can afford them. The law provides that an eligible child cannot be denied special services simply because his or her family cannot afford to pay for them; providers must make all efforts to deliver services to all babies and toddlers needing assistance and support.

Special education services - 3 to 5 years

If parents observe that their preschooler is not attaining developmental milestones within the expected age ranges or does not seem to be developing in the same way as most other children, they should seek evaluation for possible developmental delay or disability. Although 3- to 5-year-olds are likely not in elementary school yet, the elementary school in a family's school district is still the best first contact because the IDEA law (the Individuals with Disabilities Education Act) specifies that school districts must provide special education services at no family cost to eligible children, including preschoolers. Another excellent source of more information about special education is the National Dissemination Center for Children with Disabilities (NICHCY) of the U.S. Department of Education's Office of Special Education Programs. They partner with nonprofit organizations like the Academy for Educational Development (AED) to produce useful documents for families with special needs children. NICHCY supplies state resource sheets listing main contacts regarding special education services in each U.S. state. Families can obtain these sheets at NICHCY's website or by telephone.

Information sources used in the evaluation - 3 to 5 years

Under the IDEA (the Individuals with Disabilities Education Act), evaluation information sources include: physicians' reports, the child's medical history, developmental test results, current classroom observations and assessments (when applicable), completed developmental and behavioral checklists, feedback and observations from parents and all other members of the evaluation team, and any other significant records, reports, and observations regarding the child. Under the IDEA, involved in the evaluation are parents, at least one regular education teacher and special education teacher if the child has these, and any special education service provider working with the child—for children receiving early intervention services from birth through age 2 and transitioning to preschool special education, it may be an early intervention service provider; a school administrator knowledgeable about children with disabilities, special education policies, regular education curriculum, and resources available; a psychologist or educator who can interpret evaluation results and discuss indicated instruction; individuals with special expertise or knowledge regarding the child (recruited by school or parents); when appropriate, the child; and other professionals, for example, physical or occupational therapists, speech therapists, medical specialists, and so on.

Special education services - 3 to 5 years

Special education for preschoolers is education specifically designed to meet the individual needs of a child aged 3 to 5 years with a disability or developmental delay. The specialized design of this instruction can include adaptations to the content, to the teaching methods, and the way instruction is delivered to meet a disabled child's unique needs. Special education for preschoolers includes various settings, such as in the home, in classrooms, hospitals, institutions, and others. It also includes a range of related services, such as speech-language pathology services, specialized physical education instruction, early vocational training, and training in travel skills. The school district's special education system provides evaluation and services to eligible preschoolers free of charge. Evaluation's purposes are to determine whether a child has a disability under the IDEA's (the Individuals with Disabilities Education Act) definitions and determine that child's present educational needs.

Post-evaluation - 3 to 5 years

After a preschool child is evaluated, the parents and involved school personnel meet to discuss the evaluation results. Parents are included in the group that decides whether the child is eligible for special education services based on those results. For eligible children, the parents and school personnel will develop an IEP. Every child who will receive special education services must have an IEP. The main purposes of the IEP are (1) to establish reasonable educational goals for the individual child and (2) to indicate what services the school district will provide to the child. The IEP includes a statement of the child's present levels of functioning and performance. It also includes a list of more general instructional goals for the child to achieve through school and parental support along with more specific learning objectives reflecting those goals and specifying exactly what the child will be able to demonstrate, under what circumstances, how much of the time—for example, a percentage of recorded instances—and within what time period (e.g., 1 year).

Examples of Individualized Education Program (IEP) goals and objectives - 3 to 5 year

In an IEP, the goals are more global, describing a skill for the child to acquire or a task to master. The objectives are more specific articulations of achievements that will demonstrate the child's mastery of the goal. For example, if a goal is for the child to increase his or her functional communicative vocabulary, a related objective might be for the child to acquire X number of new words in X length of time; another related objective could be for the child to use the words acquired in 90% of recorded relevant situations. If the goal is for the child to demonstrate knowledge and discrimination of colors, one objective might be for the child to identify correctly a red, yellow, and blue block 95% of the time when asked to point out each color within a group of blocks. Progress toward or achievement of some objectives may be measured via formal tests; with preschoolers, many others are measured via observational data collection.

TPBA

TPBA is Transdisciplinary Play-Based Assessment. Very young children have not developed the cognitive skills needed to respond to many formal assessment instruments. For example, you would not ask a 3-year-old to conjugate verbs, add several single-digit numbers, or count more than a few concrete objects. This is true even of normally developing young children and even more so of those with developmental disabilities whose cognitive development may not be at typical age levels. However, most young children naturally engage in and enjoy playing. TPBA takes advantage of this by having trained professionals observe a young child at play. Together with parents' input, the observers can determine the child's performance levels of many motor, cognitive, adaptive, emotional, and social skills. Typically, a TPBA team collaborating or consulting with parents would include personnel such as a speech-language pathologist, a psychologist, a teacher, and a physical or occupational therapist. These specialists are most familiar with child skills across all domains of development that can be directly observed during play.

School multidisciplinary team (MDT)

While the new school or preschool is waiting for records to arrive from a transferring child's previous program, if the MDT has been informed that the child has already had an IEP developed and in place, the team should not place the child in a special education class or group in the interim, which would be premature and inappropriate without first having the prior school's records and conducting a team meeting to ascertain the child's instructional needs. Federal regulations provide that making an interim placement that is, placing the child in a regular education class or program, is more appropriate until the child's records are received and further, more detailed information is available. If the child already has an IEP, then a comprehensive evaluation was conducted to determine his or her special education eligibility. Therefore, the team should not duplicate this by performing another complete evaluation, consuming unnecessary time and resources.

Progress monitoring, updating, and revising IEPs

Once a child has been identified with a disability, determined eligible for special education and related services under the IDEA (the Individuals with Disabilities Education Act), and had an IEP developed and implemented, the child's progress must be monitored. Monitoring methods may be related to evaluation methods. For example, if a child identified with problem behaviors was initially evaluated using a behavioral checklist, school personnel can use the same checklist periodically, comparing its results to the baseline levels of frequency and severity originally obtained. If an affective disorder or disturbance was identified and instruments like the Beck Depression Inventory or Anxiety Inventory were used, these can be used again periodically;

reduced symptoms would indicate progress. If progress with IEP goals and objectives is less or greater than expected, the IEP team meets and may revise the program. This can include specifying shorter or longer times to achieve some goals and objectives; lowering or raising requirements proving too difficult or easy; resetting successive objective criteria in smaller or larger increments; changing teaching methods, content, or materials used, and so on.

Tiered service delivery models

Response to Intervention (RTI), Positive Behavior Support/Positive Behavioral Interventions and Supports (PBS/PBIS), and other service delivery models are very similar. They are generally implemented school-wide, program-wide, or classroom-wide depending on the educational program; many schools use these approaches on a school-wide basis based on the philosophy of proactively preventing learning problems by providing positive support. These models consist of tiers of gradually increasing support along a continuum. Numbers of tiers may vary, but a common feature is using three tiers. For example, the first tier is called primary intervention and implements systems that apply to all students, settings, and staff. This tier generally applies to around 80% of the students in a school, program, or classroom. The second tier is called secondary intervention and involves specialized group systems for students identified as at risk, generally involving about 15% of students. The third tier, tertiary intervention, uses specialized, individualized systems for students with intensive needs, usually about 5% of student populations.

Characteristics of Tier 2 instruction within 3-tiered service delivery models

While Tier 1 in 3-tier models addresses all students and is meant to meet typical student needs, Tier 2 is designed with additional instruction to help at-risk children to attain expected grade-level skills when they fall behind with Tier 1 instruction. Tier 2 interventions are generally supplemental instruction in small groups, with teacher-student ratios of up to 1:5, usually lasting 8 to 12 weeks and administered by special education teachers, specialists, or tutors. Programs, procedures, and teaching strategies in Tier 2 support Tier 1 instruction as well as supplementing and enhancing it. Tier 2 focuses on research evidence-based practices found effective for at-risk children. Students are introduced to Tier 2 as soon as possible after Tier 1 student progress monitoring determines they have fallen behind grade levels. This benefits many students, such as with specific learning disabilities, in bypassing lengthy referral and evaluation procedures otherwise required for special education. Monitoring showing sufficient progress dictates a return to general education classrooms; insufficient progress leads to another round of Tier 2 intervention.

4-step approach to Response to Intervention (RTI)-type tiered models

RTI models (and Positive Behavioral Support [PBS] models, which are very similar) generally use three tiers of instructional intervention. Tier 1 applies to all students, meets most student needs, and can prevent problems through proactive support. Students failing to meet grade-level expectations in Tier 1 are placed in Tier 2 to receive specialized supplemental instruction in smaller groups from a qualified specialist, special education teacher, or tutor. If this is ineffective, Tier 3 provides more intensive support, individualized to each student, in even smaller groups. Some educators recommend a 4-step process in a protocol treatment approach to RTI: (1) screening, involving Tier 1 or all students—responsibility is shared by general and special education teachers; (2) implementing general education and monitoring responses to it involves Tier 1—general education departments and teachers are responsible for this; (3) implementing supplementary, diagnostic instructional trials and monitoring responses involves Tier 2—responsibility is shared by general and special education teachers; (4) designating and classifying disability, special intensive instructional placement, and monitoring thereof affect Tier 3—special education professionals are responsible.

Features of Tier 1 instruction within 3-tier service delivery models

In 3-tiered service delivery models, Tier 1 targets all students for support to meet the needs of the general student population and prevent problems before they occur. In Tier 1, general education teachers deliver core instructional programs that are based on solid research evidence to students. While this entails reading, writing, and mathematics for school-age students, for preschoolers it involves pre-academic skills like phonological awareness, alphabetic awareness, vocabulary development, counting skills using concrete objects, categorizing objects, and adaptive skills development for functioning independently in daily life. Student progress is monitored using measurements based on the given curriculum. The results of student progress monitoring are analyzed to identify students who are not making sufficient progress and are therefore at risk for developmental delays or learning problems. Students thus identified as at risk would qualify for Tier 2 intervention.

Features of Tier 3 instruction within Response to Intervention (RTI)

Children who fall behind in general Tier 1 instruction designed to support all or most students are placed in Tier 2, where supplemental instruction is given, providing additional support to children at risk for developmental delays, disorders, or learning problems. When progress monitoring finds a student is not making adequate progress toward grade levels after two rounds of Tier 2 intervention, or whose progress is severely limited in 1 round of Tier 2, Tier 3 intervention is indicated. Tier 3 involves instruction customized for the individual child; provides much more intensive, sustained support; and depending on the student's needs, can have much longer durations than Tier 2 interventions. Typically, instruction is in smaller groups with teacher-student ratios of no more than 1:3. Progress monitoring is closer and more ongoing in Tier 3. If a child meets the program's established benchmarks as determined by monitoring or testing, he or she may be exited to Tier 1. However, if the student then fails without such intensive support, he or she may be returned to Tier 2 or Tier 3.

Premack principle

The Premack principle is a principle derived from behaviorism or learning theory. It involves encouraging a child to engage in a behavior less desirable to him or her by making a behavior more desirable or rewarding to the child contingent upon demonstrating the less desired behavior. Behaviorism has established that people (and animals) are more likely to repeat any behavior that receives a reward, or reinforcement, immediately after it occurs. Adults are more likely to repeat work tasks when they are paid money for them; children are more likely to eat their vegetables when they receive dessert for doing so. For example, if Johnny loves to play with finger paints but will only tolerate wearing the headphones that are an important part of his educational programming (and do not cause discomfort) for 1 to 2 minutes at a time, contingent reinforcement could be used to increase this time by letting him have finger paints only after progressively longer periods wearing the headphones—2 minutes, then 3, then 5, and so on.

Activity-based intervention

Activity-based intervention is (1) child directed, (2) embeds intervention across varied activities, (3) utilizes naturally and logically occurring antecedents (events coming before a desired behavior) and consequences (events immediately following a desired behavior), and (4) focuses on developing functional skills. For example, if a young child demonstrates particular interest in balloons, activity-based intervention using balloons in activities fulfills component (1) of being child directed. The teacher might elicit the child's requests for balloons, give directions for the child to follow in painting or decorating balloons, teach words related to balloons and have the child use them, and offer the child games to play with balloons. This fulfills component (2) of embedding intervention across varied activities. Component (3) of natural and logical antecedents and consequences is met by using balloons, which are naturally motivating and rewarding to this child. The activities named all develop functional skills (4): requesting desired objects, following directions, fine motor skills, vocabulary development and application, and learning and following (game) rules.

Cumulative and delayed influences

Both positive and negative experiences children have early in life exert significant accumulating effects on their development. For example, some children's preschool social interactions promote confidence and social skills, facilitating making friends later, improving both their social competencies and academic performance. When other children do not develop basic social skills early on, peers reject or ignore them, putting them at higher risk for dropout, delinquency, or mental health issues later. Children's early neurological development is enhanced by receiving ample, varied, rich environmental stimuli, furthering formation of more neural connections, which then promote additional development and learning. Children deprived of such early stimulation have less ability to develop and learn through future experiences, triggering cumulative disadvantages. The earlier the intervention and support, the more effective they are. For example, it is much easier and cheaper to prevent reading problems than remediate them. Research indicates a child's first three years are the optimal time for developing spoken language. Giving children necessary stimuli and supports at optimal times most consistently produces

Developmental principle of movement from simpler to more complex abilities

Increasing complexity is a principle throughout child development observed in nearly all domains including motor and physical, linguistic, cognitive, and social skills. Neurological development enables growing children to use their expanding memories and organizational abilities to combine simpler routines they have learned into more complex strategies. Even preschoolers understand some abstract concepts, such as that addition creates more while subtraction creates fewer and the one-to-one principle in counting things. However, children proceed in general from more concrete to more abstract thought as they grow. Children also progress from infancy's complete dependence to learning control and internalizing it, and adults play important parts in helping them. When babies are aroused and adults soothe them, this helps them learn to self-soothe. When preschool teachers provide scaffolding and support for dramatic role-plays, help young children learn how to express their feelings, and involve them in planning and decision making, they help them develop emotional self-regulation, to maintain focused attention, and to manage strong feelings.

Constructivist and interactionist orientations inform multiple, varied teaching methods

Constructivism states that young children build their comprehension and knowledge of reality through their experiences with the environment and interactions with family, peers, older children, teachers, and media. Through manipulating concrete objects and learning abstract concepts, children form hypotheses regarding the world and test these via interacting with things, people, and their own thinking processes. They observe events, reflect on their discoveries, imagine possibilities, ask questions, and form answers. Such owning of knowledge by children affords deeper comprehension and superior generalization and application of learning to different contexts. Variation in children's learning needs dictates variation in teaching methods. In both play and structured activities, teachers having wide ranges of strategies can choose the best one for each particular situation, context, learning goal, and individual child needs at the moment. This includes providing greater support, even during play or exploration, to children needing it. It also encompasses teacher demonstration and modeling, providing challenges, specific instruction, and directions, and organizing classrooms and planning to further education goals through opportunities presented in child- and teacher-initiated activities.

Vygotsky's Zone of Proximal Development (ZPD) and Bruner's scaffolding

What Vygotsky termed the ZPD is the area wherein children best learn skills just beyond their current mastery levels and accomplish learning tasks which they could not achieve alone through guidance and support from adults and from other children with slightly higher skill levels. Scaffolding is Bruner's related term for support that adults provide to learning children as needed and gradually withdraw as the child's competence increases until the child can complete a task or skill independently. When achieving autonomy in this manner, children can also generalize, applying skills learned to various new contexts. An important consideration for educators to maintaining children's motivation and persistence is enabling their success at new tasks more often than not. Most children give up trying after repeatedly failing. Another educator consideration is repeatedly giving children opportunities for practicing and consolidating new concepts and skills. This allows the mastery children need to apply and generalize learning. Educators need knowledge of child developmental sequences, plus close observation of individual children's thought processes, to provide challenges without frustration.

Contributing to creating a caring learning community for young children

Children learn about themselves and their environments through observation of and participation in the learning community. By demonstrating that each member of the community values and is valued by other members, educators help children learn to establish constructive relationships with others. They also help them learn to value each individual and to recognize and respect all individual and group differences. Because a significant context wherein children develop and learn is relationships with adults and peers, educators can give them various opportunities to play with others, have conversations and discussions with peers and adults, and collaborate on projects and investigations to promote development and learning. By assigning young children to small groups, educators can give them opportunities to learn and practice social interaction; cooperation in problem solving, sharing and building upon each other's ideas; and expanding their thinking. Such interactions support young children's construction of their understandings of reality through their interactions with other members of the learning community.

Planning environments, schedules, and activities

By offering richly varied ideas, challenges, and materials, ECE teachers can provide young children with firsthand activities that give them creatively and intellectually stimulating experiences that invite children's ongoing, active engagement, exploration, and investigation. During periods of child-initiated or child-chosen activity, teachers can help and guide children not yet able to put such activities to good use or enjoy them. They can also support children more able to choose by giving them opportunities to make meaningful choices and decisions. Effective ECE teachers organize daily and weekly schedules to afford children substantial time periods for uninterrupted play, exploration, investigation, and social interaction with peers and adults. ECE teachers should also arrange experiences and interactions and provide materials for young children that allow them fully to push the boundaries of their imaginations and of their linguistic, self-regulatory, and interactional abilities to practice the skills that they have newly developed.

Assuring the full participation, development, and learning

ECE teachers can encourage young children to select and plan their own learning activities, which helps them develop initiative. Teachers can ask children questions, pose problems, and make suggestions and comments to stimulate their thinking and expand their learning. To expand the scope of children's interests and thoughts, teachers can introduce stimulating ideas, problems, hypotheses, or problems, and experiences novel to them. In adjusting activity complexity for children's knowledge and skill levels, teachers increase challenges commensurately with children's increasing understanding and competency. Providing experiences with genuine challenge and success is a way teachers can enhance children's motivation, persistence, risk taking, confidence, and competence as learners. Intensive interviews, extended conversation and discourse, and similar strategies encouraging children to revisit and reflect upon their experiences are ways teachers can further children's conceptual understanding. ECE teachers should also give specific feedback (e.g., "You got the same total both times you counted those buttons!") rather than generic praises (e.g., "Good job!").

Making the learning experiences responsive and accessible

In making learning responsive and accessible to all children's needs, ECE teachers must include those learning English as a new language, those from diverse cultures, those having disabilities, and those in impoverished and otherwise difficult living situations. To do this, teachers use a wide range of materials, equipment, teaching strategies, and experiences to address individual differences in children's previous experiences, developmental levels, abilities, skills, interests, and needs. They include each child's home language and culture into the learning community, such that the child's home and family ties are supported and the community realizes and values each culture and language's unique contributions. They include all children in all activities and model and encourage children's behaviors and peer interactions to be inclusive. ECE teachers can meet the needs of children with disabilities using their own strategies, plus consulting as needed with family and indicated specialists, and ensure children receive necessary adaptations or modifications and specialized services to succeed in learning.

Planning and Managing the Learning Environment

School readiness and achievement

Socioeconomic factors and their implications

Typically, children from less educated or more impoverished families are found to begin school with lower levels of basic skills in language, reading, and mathematics. Children from the lowest socioeconomic group begin kindergarten with scores on cognitive measures averaging 60% lower than the most affluent socioeconomic group. African-American children have 21% lower average math achievement, and Hispanic children 19% lower, than white children. This is mainly because of the socioeconomic status of these ethnic groups. Additionally, entrenched inequities in communities and hence in schools make these early gaps in achievement more likely to increase with time than to decrease. Concern about achievement gaps among U.S. demographic groups is contained within a larger concern about competing in a global economy: Comparing standardized test scores shows that America's students have not consistently exceeded or matched student achievements in other industrialized countries. Such concern has fueled the accountability and standards movement, as exemplified by the 2001 No Child Left Behind act.

Achievement gaps

Research finds that, in comparing standardized measures of academic achievement, low-income Hispanic and African-American children fall behind their peers significantly and encounter more difficulties in school settings throughout the school years. Children's early access to quality schools and programs differs dramatically across socioeconomic and ethnic groups, as do their early educational experiences. Disparity between minority children's home cultures and school cultures is a factor. Also, young children's exposure to language is basic to literacy development, cognitive development, and learning; the home linguistic experiences of many low-income children are substantially less rich than those of middle-class children. Children in low-income families hear dramatically fewer words and are involved in fewer extended conversations with parents and other family members. One example of the results of these differences is that significant socioeconomic disparities in children's vocabulary knowledge are found by the time they are 3 years old.

Interplay of nature and nurture

Early childhood development and learning are the outcome of the interactions between biological influences and environmental experiences. These interactions are ongoing and dynamic in nature. For example, a child may be genetically predisposed for strong, healthy development, but environmental deprivation such as malnutrition in early childhood can impede fulfillment of that biological potential. On the other hand, a child may be diagnosed with an organic condition known to have adverse influences on development and learning; however, systematically applying interventions individualized for that child can mitigate such effects and promote the optimal possible outcomes. Also, children's interactions with adults and other children, and vice versa, reciprocally influence and are influenced by children's basic temperaments, such as extraversion or introversion. Because of the strength of the influences of both biological and experiential factors and their interactions, early childhood teachers need to hold and communicate high expectations for each child and to access their own funds of knowledge, persistence, and creativity in seeking different methods that enable each individual child's success.

Considerations related to the social and cultural contexts

Growing children are strongly affected by multiple, interacting social and cultural contexts, including their families, educational settings, communities, and the larger society. The latter's biases, for example, sexism, racism, and related discrimination and negative stereotypes, influence all children, including those with supportive, loving families living in healthy, solid communities. Although cultural aspects in education are frequently represented as considerations for diverse, minority, and immigrant children and families, every individual is a member of, and thus influenced by, a culture. Each culture individually and characteristically organizes and views child development and behavior. Therefore, early childhood teachers must comprehend how family and sociocultural settings influence children's developing abilities and learning and recognize children's resulting varied expressions of their developmental accomplishments. Educators' sensitivity to their own cultural experiences and how these form their viewpoints is crucial, as is considering multiple perspectives, for their decision making regarding children's development and education.

Social influences promoting optimal emotional and social development

Relationships that are secure, warm, consistent, and nurturing, afforded to babies and young children by responsive adults are required for children to develop language, communication skills, emotional self-regulation, empathy, cooperation, cultural socialization, identity formation, and peer relationships. Children and adults who know one another well learn to anticipate one another's behaviors and cues. They become attuned to each other and develop trust. The attachments they form with parents and caregivers prepare them for all other relationships with children and adults. Just as trusting relationships with parents are the foundations for later interactions, positive relationships between teachers and young children also contribute to children's emotional development, social skills, and learning and achievements. Children develop high self-esteem, strong senses of self-efficacy (belief in one's ability to perform given tasks or skills), social skills for establishing connections and friendships with others, and skills for cooperation and conflict resolution through nurturing relationships with adults. Moreover, adults' positive modeling and support help children feel confident and secure in attempting new experiences and skills, furthering learning.

Implications of globalization

As our economy becomes more global, societies also receive more multicultural influences. As they grow, young children move from learning within their families to within increasingly larger social circles and within their communities and, eventually, to learning to interact easily with others from both similar and different backgrounds. Children do have inherent capacities for learning to operate within multiple social and cultural settings and to change their uses of language and behaviors accordingly for each context. However, the realization of these capacities is a complex process. It happens gradually rather than quickly; children do not develop these abilities independently but need support from adults. Many educational experts believe that children should acquire languages and cultures in addition to native ones rather than in place of them. For example, while some advocate replacing immigrant children's native languages with English in America, these experts point out the importance of continuing fluency in native family and community languages while additionally gaining English proficiency. The same applies to native English-speaking children when acquiring new languages.

Functions and types of play

Playing has been observed in all young humans and animals. Various types of play are beneficial for physical, cognitive, emotional, and social development and learning in all species. Human children develop their physical abilities and their appreciation of the outdoors and nature, practice developing skills, make sense of their environments, express their emotions and control them, interact socially with others, and develop their abilities to represent reality symbolically and to solve problems. Researchers find correlations between playing and basic abilities including self-regulation, memory, spoken language, social skills, and school success. Play includes physical play, playing with objects, pretend and dramatic play, constructive play, and playing games involving rules. From birth, children act upon their environments for the enjoyment of observing cause and effect; for example, repeatedly tossing a bottle out of the crib. Children who have had experiences observing others' make-believe behaviors will begin imitating these around age 2, for example, pretending to drink from a seashell.

Benefits of developing play abilities

By the time they are 3 to 5 years old, children expand rudimentary make-believe, representing objects with other objects, to more developed play involving planning plots, acting out roles, and interacting in these roles. As play is highly motivating, children adhere to their roles and scenario or game rules, helping them develop self-regulation and impulse control. Dramatic play also develops children's skills in planning, cooperating, and coordinating actions with others. Research finds this play cognitively, emotionally, and socially beneficial to children. One educational trend counter to these benefits is more overt adult direction in using media and activities in general: Researchers observe that children's richly imaginative, socially interactive play consequently appears to be decreasing. Adults must actively support children's early imaginative play to establish bases for later, more mature dramatic play promoting overall development. They should also use established methods for encouraging children's sustained involvement in higher-level play. Playing does not interfere with academic achievement; rather, it is found to support the requisite abilities for scholastic learning and success.

Getting to know each individual child and his or her family

By establishing personal, positive relationships with each child and his or her family, ECE teachers gain better appreciations of the child's specific needs, abilities, and interests and his or her family's child-rearing practices, goals, expectations, and values. Teachers should use what they learn from conversations with each child and family—using community translators or interpreters as needed for other languages, including sign language—to inform their planning and actions. To monitor and further young children's progress, teachers should be using a variety of methods for collecting information about each child's development and learning on an ongoing basis. ECE teachers should also be vigilant in watching for any signs in any individual child of excessive stress, or of traumatic events taking place in any child's life. When they are aware of these signs, teachers can often learn more about the events or situations they signify. They can then utilize strategies designed to relieve and minimize stress and to support young children in developing resilient responses to environmental challenges.

Effective 2-way relationships

ECE teachers and the families of the children they teach should be mutually sharing with one another their knowledge about the individual child and also sharing their respective understandings of child development and learning. They should do this sharing as a part of their daily communications, as well as during planned conferences and meetings. ECE teachers should also support the children's families in whichever ways they find are best for enhancing the families' abilities and proficiency in making decisions for the child and family. Before a child enters an ECE program, the program's practitioners should engage the child's family as an important source of information about the child and should involve them in educational planning for their child. Once the child is enrolled in the program, program practitioners should also continue to engage the family in planning and progress assessment as an ongoing practice. ECE programs and practitioners should additionally provide children's families with connections to a range of services according to family concerns, needs, priorities, and identified resources.

Establishing mutual relationships with young children's families

ECE teachers must know not only general principles of early childhood development and specific characteristics of their individual students; they must also know children's living contexts. The younger the children, the more teachers must obtain this knowledge through relationships they develop with children's families. Reciprocal relationships require cooperation, shared responsibility, mutual respect, and negotiation of any conflicts—all for achieving goals for children shared by teachers and families. Teachers create and sustain frequent, regular, bilateral communication with families for collaborative partnerships. This includes nonnative English-speaking families: Teachers use the child's home language if able or recruit volunteer translators. Families should participate in the programs' decisions about their children's caregiving and instruction. Families must be welcome in programs and be offered multiple opportunities to participate. Teachers recognize, respect, and respond to family goals and choices for children while maintaining responsibility for practices supporting children's development and learning.

Dr. Murray Bowen's family systems theory

Psychiatrist Bowen took knowledge about the human species as the result of evolution and knowledge from research into families and integrated these two areas through the application of systems theory. A central assumption of Bowen's theory is that human relationship systems are regulated by an emotional system that developed over billions of years of evolution. While humans use language, have higher-order thinking processes, and have a psychology and culture that are complex, they nevertheless perform all the same functions that other life forms do. Family systems theory holds that most of human behavior is influenced by the emotional system and that this emotional system is the main impetus that causes clinical problems to develop. Dr. Bowen maintains that new and more efficacious choices for solving problems within a person's family, social, and work systems can be discovered through attaining knowledge of how the emotional system functions in each of these domains. Bowen sees the family as an emotional unit, describing family interactions in terms of systems.

Characterizes the emotional nature of families

According to Bowen's family systems theory, families by nature involve intense emotional connections among their members. Though some people feel distance or disaffection from family members, this is found to be more subjective than objective. In reality, family members have such profound impacts upon one another's feelings, thoughts, and actions that they may be said to live within the same emotional skin. They react to one another's expectations, needs, and distress and recruit one another's attention, support, and approval. The reactive and interconnected nature of families causes their members' functioning to be interdependent. When one member's functioning changes, the other members' functioning ensues reciprocally. While individual families vary in their degrees of interdependence, this dynamic always exists to some extent. Bowen assumes that emotional interdependency evolved to support familial cooperation and cohesion, which are necessary for sheltering, feeding, and protecting family members.

Family emotional interdependence

Bowen proposed that, because families must stick together and cooperate to nurture and protect their members, families' characteristic emotional interdependence probably evolved to reinforce family unification and teamwork. However, he also found that, when tension within a family increases, it can intensify emotional interdependence processes, resulting in problems. Due to emotional connection, anxiety in one or more family members becomes infectious, spreading to other members. This makes their emotional interconnectedness less comforting and more stressful. Eventually, one or more family members feel isolated, out of control, or overwhelmed. Those who develop these negative feelings are the same members who make the most accommodations in efforts to reduce the tension of other members. Like all family systems processes, this involves mutual interactions. For instance, if some family members have unrealistic expectations of another member, the latter reacts by taking excessive responsibility or blame for their distress. Members who accommodate the most "absorb" the family's anxiety and, hence, are those most at risk for depression, physical illness, substance abuse, or infidelity.

Differentiation of self

Social groups, including families, influence their members' feelings, thoughts, and actions. However, the amount of pressure to conform varies among groups, and individuals' vulnerability to group pressures varies. These variations reflect different levels in differentiation of self. When an individual's sense of self is less developed, others influence his or her behavior more, and he or she tries more—actively or passively—to control others' behavior. Bowen believes the basic raw materials of self are innate, but family relationships influence how much sense of differentiated self an individual develops. Those with poorly differentiated selves may become chameleons, agreeing with others to please them, or bullies, pressuring others to agree with them. Either form is equally threatened by disagreement. Extreme rebels disagree, but habitually or indiscriminately, and are also poorly differentiated. Those with well-differentiated selves realistically acknowledge dependence on others but can be objective during conflict, rejection, or criticism, separating fact from emotion. They can agree or disagree, resisting pressure, retaining independent thought, and being neither wimpy nor pushy. What they decide, say, and do are consistent.

Nuclear family emotional system

According to Bowen, clinical symptoms and problems develop during times of protracted, increased family tension. Stressors, family adaptations to stress, and family connections with social networks or extended family determine tension levels. The nuclear family emotional system comprises four basic relationship patterns determining where family problems appear according to which patterns are most active. Greater tension likely increases symptom severity and produces symptoms in several members. The patterns are: (1) marital conflict—both spouses externalize their anxiety to the marriage, and each focuses on the other's faults, tries to control the other, and resists the other's attempts at control; (2) dysfunction in one spouse—one spouse pressures the other, who yields, and escalating tension exacerbates the subordinate spouse's anxiety; (3) impairment of one or more children—parents externalize anxieties on the child or children, worrying overly, and the more they focus on the child, the more the child reciprocally focuses on them, overreacting to parental expectations, needs, and attitudes, which undermines the child's differentiation from family; (4) emotional distance—consistently associated with #1 through #3, members withdraw emotionally to reduce relationship intensity, risking isolation.

Bowen's interconnected concepts

Triangles

Triangles or 3-person relationship systems are the smallest stable systems and hence molecules, building blocks of larger systems. Two-person systems, or dyads, are unstable, withstanding less tension before requiring third persons. Because tension can shift among three relationships, triangles tolerate more tension. Despite greater stability, triangles also generate one odd person out, increasing tension. Excessive tension for one triangle spreads to a series of interconnected triangles. Behaviors in triangles indicate individuals' attempts to preserve emotional attachments to significant others, their responses to excessive intensity in attachments, and their taking sides in others' conflicts. There are always two insiders excluding one outsider trying to become an insider with one of them, with individual roles alternating when whoever is most uncomfortable maneuvers for change. With moderate tension, usually one side has conflict and two have harmony. With high tension, if two insiders conflict, one replaces the current outsider to let him or her fight with the other instead, seeking to regain insider status once conflict and tension abate. Two parents' intense focus on a child's problem(s) can cause the child's rebellion, depression, or illness.

Ramifications of having greater or lesser differentiation of self

People with good differentiation of self recognize their realistic dependence on others but can independently make decisions important to family and society based on careful thought and principles they have developed rather than on momentary emotional reactions. They can support or reject others' viewpoints objectively, without subjective extremes of unquestioning allegiance or enmity. People with poorer differentiation of self either try to please by agreeing with others, or bully others to agree with them, or try to simulate a self through extreme rebellion but rebel against everybody or everything routinely rather than based on personal principles or individual choices. Differentiation of self exists in humans to all varying extents within the range between strong and weak differentiation. Hence, the intensity of emotional interdependence in families and other social groups varies according to its members' levels of differentiation of self. More intensely interdependent groups are less able to adapt to stressful occurrences without exacerbating chronic anxiety. This causes them to develop greater proportions of the most severe problems in society.

Bowen's Family projection process

The main way that parents pass their emotional problems to their child or children is described in Bowen's family systems theory by the family projection process, which can impair children's functioning and raise their risk for clinical symptoms. Problems from parents affecting children's lives most are relationship sensitivities, for example, blaming self or others, difficulties with others' expectations, excessive need for attention and approval, feeling responsible for others' happiness, feeling others are responsible for their own happiness and not tolerating anxiety, and acting not thoughtfully but impulsively to relieve momentary anxiety. Relatively intense projection processes cause children to develop relationship sensitivities stronger than those of their parents. These sensitivities promote behaviors that exacerbate chronic anxiety in relationship systems, increasing susceptibility to clinical symptoms. The intensity of the family projection process is related to the degree of a parent's emotional involvement with a child but not to the amount of time a parent spends with a child.

<u>Influence of family projection process</u>

Bowen's family projection process, whereby parents transmit their problems to children, proceeds in three steps:

1. The parent focuses on a child because of fear that something is wrong with the child.
2. The parent construes the child's behavior as a confirmation of the parental fear.
3. The parent then treats the child as though he or she really has something wrong.

These steps are also described as scanning, diagnosing, and treating. They start early in a child's life and are perpetuated. The child's development and behavior are influenced by parental perceptions and fears, so the child eventually embodies these. The projection process becomes a self-fulfilling prophecy: Parents try to "fix" problems they believe the child has. For example, if parents see their child as having low self-esteem, they constantly try to give affirmations; the child becomes dependent on parental affirmations for self-esteem. While parents frequently feel they have slighted the child with problems, they actually devote more time and energy to worrying about that child than siblings.

Bowen's concept of the multigenerational transmission process

Multigenerational transmission is the process whereby small variations between parents and children in differentiation of self accumulate over time to larger variations among family generations. Through relationships, information causing variations is transferred across generations. This transfer is both consciously taught and learned and unconsciously, automatically programmed through emotional responses and behaviors. Through genetics, relationships, and their interactions, information forms the individual self. While differentiation levels are similar in parents and children due to human children's long dependency duration, at least one sibling often develops somewhat more self-differentiation and one less than others because of the relationship patterns inherent in nuclear family emotional systems. Grown children choose mates with self-differentiation levels matching theirs; one of their children will be more or less self-differentiated than they are and grow up to marry someone with similar self-differentiation. As this process repeats, successive generations show greater disparity. This explains greater variation within multigenerational families in marital stability, reproduction, health, longevity, education, and occupational outcomes: Relative differentiation of self influences all these.

<u>Emotional cutoff</u>

Emotional cutoff, that is, decreasing or completely cutting off emotional contact with family members, is a way people manage unresolved family emotional issues. Some people move away and rarely visit their families; others stay there but avoid confronting sensitive matters. While cutoff may preserve an appearance of better relationships, hidden problems remain unresolved. Cutoff decreases tension in original-family interactions; however, an individual may consequently overemphasize his or her new relationships' importance, potentially pressuring his or her spouse, children, and friends to meet his or her needs or making excessive efforts to meet their expectations and to protect these relationships. New relationships normally start out smoothly, but entrenched patterns of the original family's dynamics eventually surface, creating tension. People who are emotionally cut off may attempt to bring their intimate relationships stability by turning work and social relationships into substitute "families."

<u>Affects on the child's relationship with parents</u>

The family projection process depicts how parents pass on their emotional imbalances to their children. By worrying something is wrong with a child and trying to correct it, parents unwittingly cause the child to reflect parental fears and perceptions in his or her behavior. For example, if parents worry a child lacks confidence and continually try to encourage him or her, the child comes to depend on parental encouragement—an external factor—for confidence, instead of developing it internally. Siblings less embroiled in this process have more realistic and mature relationships with parents; they develop into less reactive, needy, more goal-directed individuals. Mothers, as primary caretakers, are usually more likely to become overly emotionally involved with one or more children. In terms of Bowen's triangles, fathers usually are on the outside, with mother and the targeted child (or children) on the inside. These positions shift during times when the mother-child relationship experiences increased tension. Both parents are unsure relative to the child; however, typically one parent feigns sureness with the other's complicity.

High vs. low levels of differentiation of self

Through the multigenerational transmission process, some children develop slightly higher or lower levels of differentiation of self than their parents and marry spouses with levels similar to theirs; some of their children do likewise; eventually, these differences become magnified over generations. Thus, small differences between parents and children become more marked differences among a family's multiple generations. These differences affect overall life functioning, including health, life span, reproduction, marriage stability, education, and work. Individuals with high differentiation of self typically have nuclear families with great stability and make many contributions to society. Those with poor differentiation of self have disorganized personal lives and are overly dependent on others' support. Multigenerational transmission significantly implies that the origins of both the most exemplary human achievements and the most serious human difficulties go back generations. The process programs not only individuals' levels of self but also their interactions with others. An individual programmed by family for intense attachments and dependency will probably choose a spouse who also attaches intensely but is directive and controlling.

Examples of three general forms that unresolved family attachments can take

Individuals form different types of attachments to their original families. Some parts of their attachments are always unresolved. Unresolved attachments can appear in many different forms, including these three examples:

1. An individual regresses to feeling childlike when visiting his or her parents, expecting parents to make decisions for him or her that he or she normally makes independently.
2. An individual experiences guilt when around his or her parents, feeling that he or she must solve the parents' problems, resolve their conflicts, or alleviate their distress.
3. An individual feels that his or her parents do not appear to approve of or understand him or her, and consequently has an enraged reaction.

The real source of unresolved attachment is both the parents' and the adult child's immaturity. However, it is typical for individuals experiencing unresolved attachment to blame either themselves or other people for the problems occurring. Although everybody has some amount of unresolved attachment to his or her original family, those with higher differentiation of self have far more resolution than those with lower differentiation of self.

Examples of emotional cutoff to manage unresolved attachments to their original families

All grown children have unresolved attachments to their families of origin to some extent. Adult children may move away from their original families and seldom visit as a form of emotional cutoff. When they do visit, they may hope interactions will be better and look forward to this. However, according to Bowen's family systems theory, nuclear family emotional systems are characterized by certain patterns of interactions. These patterns become so habitual that individuals repeat them automatically; they are reactivated when adult children visit their original families, usually within a short time. In some families, these patterns cause interactions to devolve into obvious fighting. In others, relations seem harmonious on the surface, but strong emotions lurk just beneath. Even short visits can exhaust all members. Parents become so reactive that they are relieved when a highly emotionally cutoff adult child departs or stays away; siblings are often enraged at him or her for upsetting their parents. Families do not desire such interactions; however, all members are so sensitive that their contact cannot be comfortable.

Probabilities of divorce differ according to sibling position in the original family

Older brothers of younger sisters marrying younger sisters of older brothers are less likely to divorce than older brothers of brothers marrying older sisters of sisters. This is because, in the former situation, each spouse is used to living with the opposite sex, and each duplicates his or her rank in the original family. But in the latter, neither spouse grew up with an opposite-sex sibling, and neither married into a complementary rank position. The older brother of a brother and older sister of a sister may clash over control. Two youngest children marrying may clash over who gets to be more dependent. Differences among individuals with the same sibling positions are explained partly by differentiation of self. An oldest child who feels anxiety rather than comfort regarding leadership or responsibility may develop indecision and reactivity to expectations; the younger sibling may become the functional oldest in the family system. Anxiously focused youngest children may become especially helpless and demanding. Conversely, two more mature youngest children may have a very successful marriage.

Bowen's concept of societal emotional process

Bowen's theory both describes family dynamics and also applies to occupational and social nonfamily groups. The societal emotional process depicts how the influences of emotional systems on behavior extend to the level of society, causing alternately progressive and regressive eras. While cultural influences significantly affect societal functioning, they do not adequately explain these fluctuations in societal adaptations to challenges. While treating families with juvenile delinquents, Dr. Bowen discovered that society's responses to them mirrored families' responses. In trying to give delinquent children unconditional love, families tried but failed to control them. Children sensed parents' uncertainty, resisted their attempts at control, and ignored their punishments. Bowen found that, after World War II, society started regressing, worsening in the 1950s and quickly escalating in the 1960s. Societal institutions including schools, governments, and the juvenile court system, reflected parental behaviors regarding delinquents. He described this regression as driven by need to relieve existing anxiety instead of acting according to principles and long-term perspectives.

Siblings' positions in families affect individual development and behavior

Neo-Freudian psychiatrist Alfred Adler first proposed that a child's birth order influenced his or her personality. Later, psychologist Walter Toman researched the position of siblings within a family and its effect on personality and behavior development. Murray Bowen incorporated Toman's findings into his family systems theory as he found them so consistent with his own thinking. They both believed that people develop similar significant traits in common with others growing up in the same sibling position. For example, oldest children tend to lead, while youngest children tend to follow. Youngest children who like being in charge typically demonstrate different leadership styles from oldest siblings. Positions are not considered better or worse but complementary: Oldest-child bosses may work best with youngest-child assistants. Toman found sibling position affects spouses' probability of divorcing. An older brother of a younger sister has less chance of divorcing when marrying another younger sister with an older brother. An older brother of a brother who marries an older sister of a sister has more chance of divorce.

Sibling order's influence on relationships

Toman and Bowen both found certain characteristics and variations in individuals' personalities, behaviors, and relationships according to their positions among siblings in their original families. Not only birth order but also individual sibling roles affect development. For example, sometimes the chronologically oldest sibling is uncomfortable with a leadership role, and a younger sibling assumes it, becoming the functional oldest. When a youngest child who is very mature marries another mature youngest child, they are at much lower risk of divorcing than couples wherein one or both spouses were immature youngest children. Middle children function showing characteristics of two sibling positions. A girl with an older brother and a younger sister typically demonstrates some characteristics of a younger sister of a brother and some of an older sister of a sister. Another significant factor is the sibling positions of an individual's parents. The oldest child of parents who were both the youngest children in their respective families meets with different parental expectations than one whose parents were both oldest children.

Symptoms of societal regression

According to Bowen's description of the societal emotional process, societies reflect the same interactional patterns observed within families on a larger level. Societies go through progressive and regressive periods. In progressive times, people take actions based on principles and considerations for the long-term future; in regressive times, people instead take actions reactively to alleviate their current anxieties. Symptoms of societal regression include increasing divorce rates, climbing crime and violence rates, more racial polarization, rising bankruptcy rates, drug abuse epidemics, more litigious behavior, and more attention to rights than to responsibilities, and leadership's decision making becoming less principled. Recent regressive signs appear related to factors including the population explosion, natural resource depletion, and a sense of decreasing frontiers. Bowen predicted that, as in families, societal regression continues until taking the easy way out in difficult matters results in consequences worse than those of making long-term decisions. He predicted human society living in greater harmony with nature by the mid-21st century.

Lev Vygotsky and the Zone of Proximal Development

Vygotsky identified an area or range of skills wherein a learner can complete a task s/he could not yet complete independently, given some help. He termed this area the Zone of Proximal Development. Vygotsky found if a child is given assistance, guidance, or support from someone who knows more—especially another child just slightly more advanced in knowledge and/or skills—the first child can not only succeed at a task s/he is still unable to do alone; but that child also learns best through accomplishing something just slightly beyond his/her limits of expertise to do alone. Jerome Bruner coined the term "scaffolding" to describe temporary support that others give learners for achieving tasks. Scaffolding is closely related to the ZPD in that only the amount of support needed is given, and it allows the learner to accomplish things s/he could not complete autonomously. Scaffolding is gradually withdrawn as the child's skills develop, until the child reaches the level of expertise needed to complete the task on his/her own.

Montessori Method

Sections of the Montessori Method of Early Childhood Instruction

The Practical Life area of Montessori classes helps children develop care for self, others, and the environment. Children learn many daily skills, including buttoning, pouring liquids, preparing meals, and cleaning up after meals and activities. The Sensorial area gives young children experience with learning through all five senses. They participate in activities like ordering colors from lightest to darkest; sorting objects from roughest to smoothest texture; and sorting items from biggest to smallest/longest to shortest. They learn to match similar tastes, textures, and sounds. The Language Arts area encourages young children to express themselves in words, and they learn to identify letters, match them with corresponding phonemes (speech sounds), and manually trace their shapes as preparation for learning reading, spelling, grammar, and writing. In the Mathematics and Geometry area, children learn to recognize numbers, count, add, subtract, multiply, divide, and use the decimal system via hands-on learning with concrete materials. In the Cultural Subjects area, children learn science, art, music, movement, time, history, geography, and zoology.

Aspects of the Philosophy of the Montessori Method as a Curriculum Approach

Maria Montessori's method emphasizes children's engagement in self-directed activities, with teachers using clinical observations to act as children's guides. In introducing and teaching concepts, the Montessori Method also employs self-correcting ("autodidactic") equipment. This method focuses on the significance and interrelatedness of all life forms, and the need for every individual to find his/her place in the world and to find meaningful work. Children in Montessori schools learn complex math skills and gain knowledge about diverse cultures and languages. Montessori philosophy puts emphasis on adapting learning environments to individual children's developmental levels. The Montessori Method also believes in teaching both practical skills and abstract concepts through the medium of physical activities. Montessori teachers observe and identify children's movements into sensitive periods when they are best prepared to receive individual lessons in subjects of interest to them that they can grasp readily. Children's senses of autonomy and self-esteem are encouraged in Montessori programs. Montessori instructors also strive to engage parents in their children's education.

General Practices in the Montessori Method

What Montessori calls "work" refers to developmentally appropriate learning materials. These are set out so each student can see the choices available. Children can select items from each of Montessori's five sections: Practical Life, Sensorial, Language Arts, Mathematics and Geometry, and Cultural Subjects. When a child is done with a work, s/he replaces it for another child to use and selects another work. Teachers work one on one with children and in groups; however, the majority of interactions are among children, as Montessori stresses self-directed activity. Not only teachers but also older children help younger ones in learning new skills, so Montessori classes usually incorporate 2- or 3-year age ranges. Depending on students' ages and the individual school, Montessori schooldays are generally half-days, e.g. 9 a.m.–noon or 12:30 p.m. Most Montessori schools also offer afternoon and/or early evening options. Children wanting to "do it myself" benefit from Montessori, as do special-needs children. Individualized attention, independence, and hands-on learning are emphasized. Montessori schools prefer culturally diverse students and teach about diverse cultures.

Schedules of Reinforcement in Behaviorism

Continuous schedules of presenting rewards or punishments are fixed. Fixed ratio schedules involve introducing reinforcement after a set number of instances of the targeted behavior. For example, when asking a preschooler to put away materials, a teacher might present punishment for noncompliance only after making three consecutive requests. The disadvantage is, even young children know they can get away with ignoring the first two requests, only complying just before the third. Fixed interval schedules introduce reinforcement after set time periods. Again, the disadvantages are, even multiply disabled infants quickly learn when to expect reinforcement, rather than associating it with how long they have engaged in a desired behavior; young children only change their behavior immediately before the teacher will observe and reward it. Variable ratio and variable interval schedules apply reinforcement following irregular numbers of responses or irregular time periods, respectively. The advantage of variable schedules is, since children cannot predict when they will receive reinforcements, they are more likely to repeat/continue desired behaviors more and for longer times.

Bank Street Curriculum Approach to Early Childhood Education

Lucy Sprague Mitchell founded the Bank Street Curriculum, applying theoretical concepts from Jean Piaget, Erik Erikson, John Dewey, and others. Bank Street is called a Developmental Interaction Approach. It emphasizes children's rich, direct interactions with wide varieties of ideas, materials, and people in their environments. The Bank Street method gives young children opportunities for physical, cognitive, emotional, and social development through engagement in various types of child care programs. Typically, multiple subjects are included and taught to groups. Children can learn through a variety of methods and at different developmental levels. By interacting directly with their geographical, social, and political environments, children are prepared for lifelong learning through this curriculum. Using blocks, solving puzzles, going on field trips, and doing practical lab work are among the numerous learning experiences Bank Street offers. Its philosophy is that school can simultaneously be stimulating, satisfying, and sensible. School is a significant part of children's lives, where they inquire about and experiment with the environment and share ideas with other children as they mature.

Classroom Characteristics for 5- to 6-Year-Olds

The Bank Street Developmental Interaction Approach to teaching recommends that children at the oldest early childhood ages of 5–6 years should have classrooms that are efficient, organized, conducive to working, and designed to afford them sensory and motor learning experiences. Classrooms should include rich varieties of appealing colors, which tend to energize children's imaginations and activity and encourage them to interact with the surroundings and participate in the environment. "Interest corners" in classrooms are advocated by the Bank Street approach. These are places where children can display their art works, use language, and depict social life experiences. This approach also recommends having multipurpose tables in the classroom that children can use for writing, drawing, and other classroom activities. The Bank Street Developmental Interaction Approach also points out the importance of libraries in schools, not just for supporting classroom content, but for providing materials for children's extracurricular reading.

Requirements and Roles of Classrooms and Teachers

The Bank Street Developmental Interaction Approach requires educators to create well-designed classrooms: this curriculum approach finds children are enabled to develop discipline by growing up in such controlled environments. Teachers are considered to be extremely significant figures in their young students' lives. The Bank Street Approach requires that teachers always treat children with respect, to enable children to develop strong senses of self-respect. Teachers' having faith in their students and believing in their ability to succeed are found to have great impacts on young children's performance and their motivation to excel in school and in life. The Bank Street Curriculum emphasizes the importance of providing transitions from one type of activity to another. It also stresses changing the learning subjects at regular time intervals. This facilitates children's gaining a sense of direction and taking responsibility for what they do. Bank Street views these practices as helping children develop internal self-control, affording them discipline for dealing with the external world.

Froebel's Educational Theory Regarding Learning and Teaching

Froebel, 19th-century inventor of Kindergarten, developed an influential educational theory. He found that observation, discovery, play, and free, self-directed activity facilitated children's learning. He observed that drawing/art activities develop higher level cognitive skills and that virtues are taught through children's games. He also found nature, songs, fables, stories, poems, and crafts effective learning media. He attributed reading and writing development to children's self-expression needs. Froebel recommended activities to develop children's motor skills and stimulate their imaginations. He believed in equal rather than authoritarian teacher-student relationships, and advocated family involvement/collaboration. He pointed out the critical nature of sensory experiences, and the value of life experiences for self-expression. He believed teachers should support students' discovery learning rather than prescribing what to learn. Like Piaget, Dewey, and Montessori, Froebel embraced constructivist learning, i.e. children construct meaning and reality through their interactions with the environment. He stressed the role of parents, particularly mothers, in children's educational processes.

Froebel's Famous Achievement

Friedrich Froebel (1782–1852) invented the original concept and practice of Kindergarten. His theory of education had widespread influences, including using play-based instruction with young children. Froebel's educational theory emphasized the unity of humanity, nature, and God. Froebel believed the success of the individual dictates the success of the race, and that school's role is to direct students' will. He believed nature is the heart of all learning. He felt unity, individuality, and diversity were important values achieved through education. Froebel said education's goals include developing self-control and spirituality. He recommended curricula include math, language, design, art, health, hygiene, and physical education. He noted school's role in social development. According to Froebel, schools should impart meaning to life experiences; show students relationships among external, previously unrelated knowledge; and associate facts with principles. Froebel felt human potential is defined through individual accomplishments. He believed humans generally are productive and creative, attaining completeness and harmony via maturation.

Salient Aspects Regarding Society, Educational Opportunity, and Consensus

Friedrich Froebel originated the concept and practice of Kindergarten (German for "child's garden") in 1837. His educational theory had great influence on early childhood education. Froebel's theory addressed society's role in education. He saw education as defined by the "law of divine unity," which stated that everything is connected and humanity, nature, and God are unified. Froebel believed all developments are by God's plan; he found the social institution of religion an important part of children's education. He emphasized parental and sibling involvement in child education. He theorized that culture is changed not by acquiring ideas, but by the productivity, work, and actions of the individual. Froebel believed all children deserve respect and individual attention; should develop their individual potentials; and can learn, irrespective of social class or religion, providing they are developmentally ready for given specific content. Regarding consensus, Froebel's view was religious: he believed God's supreme plan determined social and moral order. He felt people should share common experiences and learn unity, while also respecting diversity and individuality.

Siegfried Engelmann's Contributions to Early Childhood Education

Engelmann (b. 1931) cofounded the Bereiter-Engelmann Program with Carl Bereiter with funding from the U.S. Office of Education. This project demonstrated the ability of intensive instruction to enhance cognitive skills in disadvantaged preschool-aged children, establishing the Bereiter-Engelmann Preschool Program. Bereiter and Engelmann also conducted experiments reexamining Piaget's theory of cognitive development, specifically concerning the ability to conserve liquid volume. They showed, contrary to Piaget's contention that this ability depended solely on a child's cognitive-developmental stage, it could be taught. Engelmann researched curriculum and instruction, including preschoolers with Down syndrome and children from impoverished backgrounds, establishing the philosophy and methodology of Direct Instruction. He designed numerous reading, math, spelling, language, and writing instruction programs, and also achievement tests, videos, and games. Engelmann worked with Project Head Start and Project Follow Through. The former included his and Wesley Becker's comparison of their Engelmann-Becker model of early childhood instruction with other models in teaching disadvantaged children. The latter is often considered the biggest controlled study ever comparing teaching models and methods.

Engelmann's Methods and Features of His Curricula

In the 1960s, Siegfried Engelmann noted a lack of research into how young children learn. Wanting to find out what kinds of teaching effected retention, and what the extent was of individual differences among young learners, Engelmann conducted research, as Piaget had done, using his own children and those of colleagues and neighbors. With a previous advertising background, Engelmann formed focus groups of preschool children to test-market teaching methods. Main features of the curricula Engelmann developed included emphasizing phonics and computation early in young children's instruction; using a precise logical sequence to teach new skills; teaching new skills in small, separate, "child-sized" pieces; correcting learners' errors immediately; adhering strictly to designated teaching schedules; constantly reviewing to integrate new learning with previously attained knowledge; and scrupulous measurement techniques for assessing skills mastery. To demonstrate the results of his methods for teaching math, Engelmann sent movies he made of these to educational institutions. They showed that with his methods, toddlers could master upper-elementary-grade-level computations, and even simple linear equations.

Direct Instruction Method of Teaching Children

Direct Instruction (DI) is a behavioral method of teaching. Therefore, learner errors receive immediate corrective feedback, and correct responses receive immediate, obvious positive reinforcement. DI has a fast pace—10–14 learner responses per minute overall—affording more attention and less boredom; reciprocal teacher-student feedback; immediate indications of learner problems to teachers; and natural reinforcement of teacher activities. DI thus promotes more mutual student and teacher learning than traditional "one-way" methods. Children are instructed in small groups according to ability levels. Their attention is teacher-focused. Teacher presentations follow scripts designed to give instruction the proper sequence, including prewritten prompts and questions developed through field-testing with real students. These optimized prepared lessons allow teachers to attend to extra instructional and motivational aspects of learning. Cued by teachers, who control the pace and give all learners with varying response rates chances for practice, children respond actively in groups and individually. Small groups are typically seated in semicircles close to teachers, who use visual aids like blackboards and overhead projectors.

- 103 -

Project Follow Through

In 1967, President Lyndon B. Johnson declared his War on Poverty. This initiative included Project Follow Through, funded by the U.S. Office of Education and Office of Economic Opportunity. Research had previously found that Project Head Start, which offered early educational interventions to disadvantaged preschoolers, had definite positive impacts; but these were often short-lived. Project Follow Through was intended to discover how to maintain Head Start's benefits. Siegfried Engelmann and Wesley Becker, who had developed the Engelmann-Becker instructional model, invited others to propose various other teaching models in communities selected to participate in Project Follow Through. The researchers asked parents in each community to choose from among the models provided. The proponents of each model were given funds to train teachers and furnish curriculum. Models found to enhance disadvantaged children's school achievement were to be promoted nationally. Engelmann's Direct Instruction model showed positive results surpassing all other models. However, the U.S. Office of Education did not adopt this or other models found best.

Approaches to Remedial or Compensatory Education

A huge comparative study of curriculum and instruction methods, Project Follow Through incorporated three main approaches: Affective, Basic Skills, and Cognitive. Affective approaches used in Project Follow Through included the Bank Street, Responsive Education, and Open Education models. These teaching models aim to enhance school achievement by emphasizing experiences that raise children's self-esteem, which is believed to facilitate their acquisition of basic skills and higher-order problem-solving skills. Basic Skills approaches included the Southwest Labs, Behavior Analysis, and Direct Instruction models. These models find that mastering basic skills facilitates higher-order cognitive and problem-solving skills, and higher self-esteem. Cognitive approaches included the Parent Education, TEEM, and Cognitively Oriented Curriculum models. These models focus on teaching higher-order problem-solving and thinking skills as the optimal avenue to enhancing school achievement, and to improving lower-order basic skills and self-esteem. Affective and Cognitive models have become popular in most schools of education. Basic Skills approaches are less popular, but are congruent with other, very effective methods of specialized instruction.

Contributions of Constance Kamii to Early Childhood Education

Professor of early childhood education Constance Kamii, of Japanese ancestry, was born in Geneva, Switzerland. She attended elementary school in both Switzerland and Japan, completing secondary school and higher education degrees in the United States. She studied extensively with Jean Piaget, also of Geneva. She worked with the Perry Preschool Project in the 1960s, fueling her subsequent interest in theoretically grounded instruction. Kamii believes in basing early childhood educational goals and objectives upon scientific theory of children's cognitive, social, and moral development; and moreover that Piaget's theory of cognitive development is the sole explanation for child development from birth to adolescence. She has done much curriculum research in the U.S., and published a number of books, on how to apply Piaget's theory practically in early childhood classrooms. Kamii agrees with Piaget that education's overall, long-term goal is developing children's intellectual, social, and moral autonomy. Kamii has said, "A classroom cannot foster the development of autonomy in the intellectual realm while suppressing it in the social and moral realms."

Theoretical Orientation, Philosophy, and Approach of the Kamii-DeVries Approach

Constance Kamii and Rhetta DeVries formulated the Kamii-DeVries Constructivist Perspective model of preschool education. It is closely based upon Piaget's theory of child cognitive development and on the Constructivist theory to which Piaget and others subscribed, which dictates that children construct their own realities through their interactions with the environment. Piaget's particular constructivism included the principle that through their interacting with the world within a logical-mathematical structure, children's intelligence, knowledge, personalities, and morality develop. The Kamii-DeVries approach finds that children learn via performing mental actions, which Piaget called operations, through the vehicle of physical activities. This model favors using teachers experienced in traditional preschool education, who employ a child-centered approach, and establish active learning settings, are in touch with children's thoughts, respond to children from children's perspectives, and facilitate children's extension of their ideas. The Kamii-DeVries model has recently been applied to learning assessments using technology (2003) and to using constructivism in teaching physics to preschoolers (2011).

High/Scope Curriculum

David Weikart and colleagues developed the High/Scope Curriculum in the 1960s and 1970s, testing it in the Perry Preschool and Head Start Projects, among others. The High/Scope philosophy is based on Piaget's Constructivist principles that active learning is optimal for young children; that they need to become involved actively with materials, ideas, people, and events; and that children and teachers learn together in the instructional environment. Weikart and colleagues' early research focused on economically disadvantaged children, but the High/Scope approach has since been extended to all young children and all kinds of preschool settings. This model recommends dividing classrooms into well-furnished, separate "interest areas," and regular daily class routines affording children time to plan, implement, and reflect upon what they learn, and to participate in large and small group activities. Teachers establish socially supportive atmospheres; plan group learning activities; organize settings and set daily routines; encourage purposeful child activities, problem-solving, and verbal reflection; and interpret child behaviors according to High/Scope's key child development experiences.

High/Scope Curriculum's Key Experiences for Preschoolers

The High/Scope Curriculum, developed by David P. Weikart and colleagues, takes a constructivist approach influenced by Piaget's theory, advocating active learning. The High/Scope curriculum model identified a total of 58 "key experiences" it finds critical for preschool child development and learning. These key experiences are subdivided into ten main categories: (1) Creative representation, which includes recognizing symbolic use, imitating, and playing roles; (2) Language and literacy, which include speaking, describing, scribbling, and narrating/dictating stories; (3) Initiative and social relations, including solving problems, making decisions and choices, and building relationships; (4) Movement, including activities like running, bending, stretching, and dancing; (5) Music, which includes singing, listening to music, and playing musical instruments; (6) Classification, which includes sorting objects, matching objects or pictures, and describing object shapes; (7) Seriation, or arranging things in prescribed orders (e.g. by size or number); (8) Numbers, which for preschoolers focuses on counting; (9) Space, which involves activities like filling and emptying containers; and (10) Time, including concepts of starting, sequencing, and stopping actions.

<u>Technology Use, School Day Durations and Settings, and Targets for Its Application</u>

The High/Scope Curriculum frequently incorporates computers as regular program components, including developmentally appropriate software, for children to access when they choose. School days may be full-day or part-day, determined by each individual program. Flexible hours accommodate individual family needs and situations. High/Scope programs work in both child care and preschool settings. High/Scope was originally designed to enhance educational outcomes for young children considered at-risk due to socioeconomically disadvantaged, urban backgrounds, and was compatible with Project Head Start. This model of early childhood curriculum and instruction advocates individualizing teaching to each child's developmental level and pace of learning. As such, the High/Scope approach is found to be effective for children who have learning disabilities, and also for children with developmental delays. It works well with all children needing individual attention. High/Scope is less amenable to highly structured settings that use more adult-directed instruction.

Head Start Program

Head Start was begun in 1964, extended by the Head Start Act of 1981, and revised in its 2007 reauthorization. It is a program of the U.S. Department of Health and Human Services designed to give low-income families and their young children comprehensive services of health, nutrition, education, and parental involvement. While Head Start was initially intended to "catch up" low-income children over the summer to reach kindergarten readiness, it soon became obvious that a six-week preschool program was inadequate to compensate for having lived in poverty for one's first five years. Hence the Head Start Program was expanded and modified over the years with the aim of remediating the effects of system-wide poverty upon child educational outcomes. Currently, Head Start gives local public, private, nonprofit, and for-profit agencies grants for delivering comprehensive child development services to promote disadvantaged children's school readiness by improving their cognitive and social development. It particularly emphasizes developing early reading and math abilities preschoolers will need for school success.

<u>Genesis and Rationale of the Head Start Program</u>

The Early Head Start program developed as an outgrowth of the original Head Start Program. Head Start initially aimed to remediate the deprivation of poor preschool-aged children by providing educational services over the summer to help them attain school readiness by kindergarten. Because educators and researchers soon discovered the summer program was insufficient to make up for poor children's lack of preparation, Head Start was expanded to become more comprehensive. Head Start was established in 1964 and expanded by the Head Start Act in 1981. After research had accumulated considerable evidence of how important children's earliest years are to their ensuing growth and development, the U.S. Department of Health and Human Services Administration for Children and Families' Office of Head Start established the Early Head Start Program in 1995. Early Head Start works to improve prenatal health; improve infant and toddler development; and enhance healthy family functioning. It serves children from 0–3 years. Like the original program, Early Head Start stresses parental engagement in children's growth, development, and learning.

Emergent Literacy Theory

<u>Emergent Literacy Versus Reading Readiness</u>

Historically, early childhood educators viewed "reading readiness" as a time during young children's literacy development when they were ready to start learning to read and write, and taught literacy accordingly. However, in the late 20th and early 20th centuries, research has found that children have innate learning capacities and that skills emerge under the proper conditions. Educational researchers came to view language as developing gradually within a child rather than a child's being ready to read at a certain time. Thus, the term "emergent" came to replace "readiness," while "literacy" replaced "reading" as referring to all of language's interrelated aspects of listening, speaking, writing, and viewing, as well as reading. Traditional views of literacy were based only on children's reading and writing in ways similar to those of adults. However, more recently, the theory of emergent literacy has evolved through the findings of research into the early preschool reading of young children and their and their families' associated characteristics.

Emergent Literacy Theory's Principles About How Young Children Learn to Read and Write

Through extensive research, emergent literacy theorists have found that: (1) Young children develop literacy through being actively involved in reading and rereading their favorite storybooks. When preschoolers "reread" storybooks, they have not memorized them; rather, theorists find this activity to exemplify young children's reconstruction of a book's meaning. Similarly, young children's invented spellings are examples of their efforts to reconstruct what they know of written language; they can inform us about a child's familiarity with specific phonetic components. (2) Adults' reading to children, no matter how young, is crucial to literacy development. It helps children gain a "feel" for the character, flow, and patterns of written/printed language, and an overall sense of what reading feels like and entails. It fosters positive attitudes toward reading in children, strongly motivating them to read when they begin school. Being read to also helps children develop print awareness and formulate concepts of books and reading. (3) Influenced by Piaget and Vygotsky, emergent literacy theory views reading and writing as developmental processes having successive stages.

Perspective Regarding Instructional Models

The emergent literacy theoretical perspective yields an instructional model for the learning and teaching of reading and writing in young children that is founded on building instruction from the child's knowledge. Emergent literacy theory's assumption is that young children already know a lot about language and literacy by the time they enter school. This theory furthermore regards even 2- and 3-year-olds as having information about how the reading and writing processes function, and as having already formed particular ideas about what written/printed language is. From this perspective, emergent literacy theory then dictates that teaching should build upon what a child already knows and should support the child's further literacy development. Researchers conclude that teachers should furnish open-ended activities allowing children to show what they already know about literacy; to apply that knowledge; and to build upon it. From the emergent literacy perspective, teachers take the role of creating a learning environment with conditions that are conducive to children's learning in ways that are ideally self-motivated, self-generated, and self-regulated.

How Babies and Young Children Learn to Read and Write

(1) According to the theory of emergent literacy, even infants encounter written language. Two- and three-year-old's commonly can identify logos, labels, and signs in their homes and communities. Also, young children's scribbles show features/appearances of their language's specific writing system even before they can write. For example, Egyptian children's scribbles look more like Egyptian writing; American children's scribbles look more like English writing. (2) Young children learn to read and write concurrently, not sequentially; the two abilities are closely interrelated. Moreover, though with speech, receptive language comprehension seems easier/sooner to develop than expressive language production, this does not apply to reading and writing: first learning activities involving writing are found easier for preschoolers than those involving reading. (3) Research finds that form follows function, not the opposite: young children's

literacy learning is mostly through meaningful, functional, purposeful/goal-directed real-life activities. Literacy comprises not isolated, abstract skills learned for their own sake, but rather authentic skills applied to accomplish real-life purposes, the way children observe adults using literacy.

Developmentally Inappropriate Kindergarten and Preschool Literacy Practices

Research finds some preschools are like play centers, but not optimal for literacy because their curricula exclude natural reading and writing activities. Researchers have also identified a trend in many kindergartens to ensure children's "reading readiness" by providing highly academic programs, influencing preschool curricula to get children "ready" for such kindergartens. Influenced and even pressured by kindergarten programs' academic expectations, parents have also come to expect preschools to prepare their children for kindergarten. However, experts find applying elementary-school programs to kindergartens and preschools developmentally inappropriate. Formal instruction in reading and writing and worksheets are not suitable for younger children. Instead, research finds print-rich preschool environments both developmentally appropriate and more effective. For example, when researchers changed classrooms from having a "book corner" to having a centrally located table with books plus paper, pencils, envelopes, and stamps, children spent 3 to 10 times more time on direct reading and writing activities. Children are found to take naturally to these activities without prior formal reading and writing lessons.

Planning a Play-Based Curriculum

To plan a curriculum based on children's natural play with building blocks (Hoisington, 2008), a teacher can first arrange the environment to stimulate further such play. Then s/he can furnish materials for children to make plans/blueprints for and records and models of buildings they construct. The teacher can make time during the day for children to reflect upon and discuss their individual and group building efforts. Teachers can also utilize teaching strategies that encourage children to reflect on and consider in more depth the scientific principles related to their results. A teacher can provide building materials of varied sizes, shapes, textures, and weights, and props to add realism, triggering more complex structures and creative, dramatic, emotional, and social development. Teachers can take photos of children's structures as documents for discussions, stimulating language and vocabulary development. Supplying additional materials to support and stick together blocks extends play-based learning. Active teacher participation by offering observations and asking open-ended questions promotes children's standards-based learning of scientific, mathematical, and linguistic concepts, processes, and patterns.

Supporting and Integrating Standards-Based Learning in Scientific, Mathematical, and Linguistic Domains

When children play at building with blocks, for example, they investigate material properties such as various block shapes, sizes, and weights and the stability of carpet vs. hard floor as bases. They explore cause-and-effect relationships; make conclusions regarding the results of their trial-and-error experiments; draw generalizations about observed patterns; and form theories about what does and does not work to build high towers. Ultimately, they construct their knowledge of how reality functions. Teachers support this by introducing relevant learning standards in the play context meaningful to children. For example, math standards including spatial awareness, geometry, number, operations, patterns, and measurement can be supported through planning play. By encouraging and guiding children's discussion and documentation of their play constructions, and supplying nonfictional and fictional books about building, a teacher also integrates learning goals and objectives for language and literacy development. Teachers can plan activities specifically to extend learning in these domains, like counting blocks;

- 108 -

comparison/contrast; matching; sorting; sequencing; phonological awareness; alphabetic awareness; print awareness; book appreciation; listening, comprehension, speech, and communication.

Using Thematic Teaching Units

To develop a thematic teaching unit, a teacher designs a collection of related activities around certain themes or topics that crosses several curriculum areas or domains. Thematic units create learning environments for young children that promote all children's active engagement, as well as their process learning. By studying topics children find relevant to their own lives, thematic units build upon children's preexisting knowledge and current interests, and also help them relate information to their own life experiences. Varied curriculum content can be more easily integrated through thematic units, in ways that young children can understand and apply meaningfully. Children's diverse individual learning styles are also accommodated through thematic units. Such units involve children physically in learning; teach them factual information in greater depth; teach them learning process-related skills, i.e. "learning how to learn"; holistically integrate learning; encourage cohesion in groups; meet children's individual needs; and provide motivation to both children and their teachers.

Project Approach

The Project Approach (Katz and Chard, 1989) entails having young children choose a topic interesting to them, studying this topic, researching it, and solving problems and questions as they emerge. This gives children greater practice with creative thinking and problem-solving skills, which supports greater success in all academic and social areas. For example, if a class of preschoolers shows interest in the field of medicine, their teacher can plan a field trip to a local hospital to introduce a project studying medicine in depth. During the trip, the teacher can write down/record children's considerations and questions, and then use these as guidelines to plan and conduct relevant activities that will further stimulate the children's curiosity and imagination. Throughout this or any other in-depth project, the teacher can integrate specific skills for reading, writing, math, science, social studies, and creative thinking. This affords dual benefits: enabling both children's skills advancement, and their gaining knowledge they recognize is required and applies in their own lives. Children become life-long learners with this recognition.

Integrated Curriculum and Early Childhood Education

An integrated curriculum organizes early childhood education to transcend the boundaries between the various domains and subject content areas. It unites different curriculum elements through meaningful connections to allow study of wider areas of knowledge. It treats learning holistically and mirrors the interactive nature of reality. The principle that learning consists of series of interconnections is the foundation for teaching through use of an integrated curriculum. Benefits of integrated curricula include an organized planning mechanism; greater flexibility; and the ability to teach many skills and concepts effectively, include more varied content, and enable children to learn most naturally. By identifying themes children find most interesting, teachers can construct webs of assorted themes, which can provide the majority of their curriculum. Research has proven the effectiveness of integrated teaching units for both children and their teachers. Teachers can also integrate new content into existing teaching units they have identified as effective. Integrated units enable teachers to ensure children are learning pertinent knowledge and applying it to real-life situations.

Skills, Topics, Strategies, and Benefits Related to Creating Thematically-Based Teaching Units

EC teachers can incorporate many skills into units organized by theme. This includes state governments' educational standards/benchmarks for various skills. Teachers can base units on topics of interest to young children, e.g. building construction, space travel, movie-making, dinosaurs, vacations, nursery rhymes, fairy tales, pets, wildlife, camping, the ocean, and studies of particular authors and book themes. Beginning with a topic that motivates the children is best; related activities and skills will naturally follow. In planning units, teachers should establish connections among content areas like literacy, physical activity, dramatic play, art, music, math, science, and social studies. Making these connections permits children's learning through their strongest/favored modalities and supports learning through meaningful experiences, which is how they learn best. Theme-based approaches effectively address individual differences and modality-related strengths, as represented in Gardner's theory of Multiple Intelligences. Thematic approaches facilitate creating motivational learning centers and hands-on learning activities, and are also compatible with creating portfolio assessments and performance-based assessments. Teachers can encompass skill and conceptual benchmarks for specific age/developmental levels within engaging themes.

Guidelines for Indoor and Outdoor Space Use

Indoor and outdoor EC learning environments should be safe, clean, and attractive. They should include at least 35' square indoors and 75' square outdoors of usable play space per child. Staff must have access to prepare spaces before children's arrival. Gyms/other larger indoor spaces can substitute if outdoor spaces are smaller. The youngest children should be given separate outdoor times/places. Outdoor scheduling should ensure enough room, plus prevent altercations/competition among different age groups. Teachers can assess if enough space exists by observing children's interactions and engagement in activities. Children's products and other visuals should be displayed at child's-eye level. Spaces should be arranged to allow individual, small-group, and large-group activity. Space organization should create clear pathways enabling children to move easily among activities without overly disturbing others, should promote positive social interactions and behaviors; and activities in each area should not distract children in other areas.

Arrangement of Learning Environments

Arranging Indoor Learning Environments According to Curricular Activities

EC experts indicate that rooms should be organized to enable various activities, but not necessarily to limit activities to certain areas. For example, mathematical and scientific preschool activities may occur in multiple parts of a classroom, though the room should still be laid out to facilitate their occurrence. Sufficient space for infants to crawl and toddlers to toddle are necessary, as are both hard and carpeted floors. Bolted-down/heavy, sturdy furniture is needed for infants and toddlers to use for pulling up, balancing, and cruising. Art and cooking activities should be positioned near sinks/water sources for cleanup. Designating separate areas for activities like block-building, book-reading, musical activities, and dramatic play facilitates engaging in each of these. To allow ongoing project work and other age-appropriate activities, school-aged children should have separate areas. Materials should be appropriate for each age group and varied. Equipment/materials for sensory stimulation, manipulation, construction, active play, dramatic play, and books, recordings, and art supplies, all arranged for easy, independent child access and rotated for variety, are needed.

<u>Arranging Learning Environments to Children's Personal, Privacy, and Sensory Needs</u>

In any EC learning environment, the indoor space should include easily identifiable places where children and adults can store their personal belongings. Since EC involves children in groups for long time periods, they should be given indoor and outdoor areas allowing solitude and privacy while still easily permitting adult supervision. Playhouses and tunnels can be used outdoors, small interior rooms and partitions indoors. Environments should include softness in various forms like grass outdoors; carpet, pillows, and soft chairs indoors; adult laps to sit in and be cuddled; and soft play materials like clay, Play-Doh, finger paints, water, and sand. While noise is predictable, even desirable in EC environments, undue noise causing fatigue and stress should be controlled by noise-absorbing elements like rugs/carpets, drapes, acoustical ceilings and other building materials. Outdoor play areas supplied/arranged by school/community playgrounds should be separated from roadways and other hazards by fencing and/or natural barriers. Awnings can substitute for hills, and inclines/ramps for shade, when these are not naturally available. Surfaces and equipment should be varied.

Principles Related to Early Childhood Behavior Management

Repetition and consistency are two major elements for managing young children's behavior. Adults must always follow and enforce whichever rules they designate. They must also remember that they will need to repeat their rules over and over to make them effective. Behaviorism has shown it is more powerful to reward good behaviors than punish bad behaviors. Consistently rewarding desired behaviors enables young children to make the association between behavior and reward. Functional behavior analysis can inform adults: knowing the function of a behavior is necessary to changing it. For example, if a toddler throws a tantrum out of frustration, providing support/scaffolding for a difficult task, breaking it down to more manageable increments via task analysis, and giving encouragement would be appropriate strategies; but if the tantrum was a bid for attention, adults would only reinforce/strengthen tantrum recurrence by paying attention. Feeling valued and loved within a positive relationship greatly supports young children's compliance with rules. The "10:1 Rule" prescribes at least 10 positive comments per 1 negative comment/correction.

Including Families in Children's Education

First, ECE personnel can make sure that communication between the school/program and family is reciprocal and regular. EC educators should promote and support the enhancement and application of parenting skills. They should also acknowledge that parents have an integral part in supporting children's learning. All school personnel should make parents feel welcome in school, and moreover should seek parents' help and support. When school administrators, teachers, and other staff make educational decisions that affect the children and their families, they should always be sure that the children's parents are involved in these decisions. In addition, educational personnel should not just work on children's educational goals, learning objectives, and curricular and instructional planning and design on their own, keeping the school or program isolated; they should make use of all available community resources. Instead of trying to educate young children within a school bubble, educators who collaborate with their communities realize benefits of stronger families, schools, and child learning.

Managing the Normal Behavior of Young Children

Before reacting to young children's behaviors, adults should make sure children understand the situation. They should state rules simply and clearly; repeat them frequently for a long time for young children to remember and follow them; and state and enforce rules very consistently to avoid confusion. Adults should tell children clearly what they expect of them. They should never assume they need do nothing when children follow rules; they should consistently give rewards for compliance. Adults should also explain to young children why they are/are not receiving rewards by citing the rule they did/did not follow. Adults can arrange the environment to promote success. For example, if a child throws things that break windows, adults can remove such objects and substitute softer/more lightweight items. Organization is also important. Adults should begin with a simple, easy-to-implement plan and adhere to it. They should record children's progress; analyzing the records shows what does/does not work and why, enabling new/revised plans.

Family, Community, and Professional Relationships

Elements of U.S. federal legislation passed in 1997, 2001, and 2004

The 1990 Individuals with Disabilities Education Act (IDEA) was reauthorized in 1997 and numbered Public Law 108-446. It provided more access for children with disabilities to the general education curriculum and extended collaborative opportunities for teachers, other professionals, and families of children with disabilities. No Child Left Behind (NCLB, 2001, now the Every Student Succeeds Act, ESSA 2015), the reauthorization of the Elementary and Secondary Education Act (ESEA), stressed accountability for outcomes by identifying schools and districts needing improvement and assuring teacher quality. It required school performance data to include disabled students' standardized test scores. NCLB emphasized giving teachers and administrators better research information and schools more resources, parents more information about their children's progress and the school's performance, and more local flexibility and control in utilizing federal education funds and in improving teacher qualifications, for example, through alternative certifications. And, 2004's IDEA reauthorization, Individuals with Disabilities Education Improvement Act (IDEIA), covers better alignment of NCLB with IDEA, appropriately identifying students needing special education, ensuring reasonable discipline while protecting special needs students defining highly qualified teachers, reducing paperwork, and increasing cooperation to decrease litigation.

Litigations challenging school funding

As of June 2010, the 13 U.S. states of Alaska, California, Colorado, Connecticut, Florida, Illinois, Kansas, New Jersey, North Carolina, Rhode Island, South Carolina, South Dakota, and Washington had litigations in process to challenge the constitutionality of government funding for K–12 education. They included cases that had recently been filed and cases wherein a remedy was ordered and that remedy was still in the process of being implemented. The five U.S. states of Delaware, Hawaii, Mississippi, Nevada, and Utah had never had a lawsuit challenging the constitutionality of school funding as of June 2010. The remaining 32 U.S. states did not currently have a lawsuit as of that date. In U.S. history, lawsuits challenging state practices of funding public schools have been brought in 45 of the 50 U.S. states.

America's history of court litigations over school funding issues

The first court decision in educational financing litigation was in 1819 Massachusetts. In modern times, school funding cases included a 1971 California and a 1973 New Jersey case in the U.S. Supreme Court. The U.S. Supreme Court ruled in Rodriguez v. San Antonio (1973) that education was not a basic U.S. constitutional right; however, the plaintiffs then won their case in the Texas state courts, setting precedent for plaintiffs thereafter to use state courts and state constitutions. In the 1970s and 1980s, equity suits in Colorado, Georgia, and other states were won by defendants in about ⅔ of the cases. In Connecticut, Washington, and West Virginia, plaintiffs won some cases. But, plaintiffs have won about ⅔ of school funding decisions since 1989, including in New Hampshire and Vermont and landmark Kentucky and Montana cases, although plaintiffs lost equity cases in Maine, Nebraska, and Wisconsin. Shifting legal strategy from equity to adequacy in education increased victories. In Idaho and South Carolina, previous cases wherein defendants won were even reversed or differentiated.

<u>Failed and successful legal strategies</u>

A 1973 Texas case challenging the constitutionality of state school funding was taken to the U.S. Supreme Court: In Rodriguez v. San Antonio, the federal Supreme Court ruled that education was not a fundamental right under the U.S. Constitution. However, the plaintiffs subsequently won this after they filed it in the Texas state courts. This established a legal precedent in that later plaintiffs have directed most claims to state courts, citing the provisions of state constitutions. One strategy was to cite constitutional equal protection clauses. However, when equal protection or equity claims were unsuccessful, another strategy was to claim the right to an adequate education rather than an equal right to education under state law. When litigation failed, some have claimed state financing discrimination under Title VI of the U.S. Civil Rights Act and, in Alaska, under the post-Civil War antidiscrimination statute; however, U.S. Supreme Court rulings have recently prohibited this. Alternative strategies have included amending state constitutions, as in Florida and Oregon.

Daily practices and standards to avoid legal and ethical problems

1. Lawful standards that EC educators can use to measure their practices include: being consistent; following the written policies and procedures; retaining objectivity and acting reasonably; documenting and reporting the facts; eschewing discrimination against protected students; and exercising due process, for example, giving parents notice of new policies, inviting their input, and observing their right to a hearing if they dispute their child's evaluation, classification, or placement.
2. EC educators should document who, what, when, and where but not why. In other words, they should stick to the facts, avoiding opinions, commentaries, and moral judgments. As is stated and practiced in Head Start programs, "If it isn't documented, it didn't happen." Simple, concise documentation is best.
3. EC teachers can write parent handbooks, staff handbooks, job descriptions, and reports of new procedures. They need not be expert writers. When EC educators write down policies and publicize them, and the readers sign them or have requested them, this constitutes giving notice.

Core values of the NAEYC's Code of Ethical Conduct

The National Association for the Education of Young Children (NAEYC) states that it is committed to the following core values, founded in the history of early childhood care and education: the appreciation of childhood as a valuable, unique stage of human life, basing its work on knowledge of child development and learning; appreciation and support for the bonds between children and their families; the realization that children receive the best understanding and support within the context of their families, cultures (including ethnicity, racial identity, socioeconomic status, family structure, language, religious beliefs and practices, and political beliefs and views), communities, and society; showing respect for each individual's worth, dignity, and unique character, including children, their family members, and educators' colleagues; showing respect for diversity among children, their families, and educators' colleagues; and the recognition that both children and adults realize their full potentials within the contexts of relationships based upon trust and respect.

Section I, Ethical Responsibilities to Children

The first principle, taking precedence over all others, is not to harm children physically, mentally, or emotionally. Other principles address positive environments providing cognitive stimulation and supporting each child's culture, language, ethnicity, and family structure; not discriminating for or against children; involving everyone with relevant knowledge in decisions for children while protecting information confidentiality; using appropriate, multiple sources of assessment

- 114 -

information; building individual relationships with each child, making individualized educational adaptations, and collaborating with families and specialists; familiarity with risk factors for child neglect and abuse and following state laws and community procedures protecting against these; reporting reasonable cause to suspect child abuse or neglect, following up regarding actions taken, and informing parents or guardians; assisting others suspecting child abuse or neglect in taking appropriate protective action; and being ethically responsible to protect children or inform parents or others who can protect them when becoming aware of situations or practices endangering children's safety, health, or well-being.

Legal changes to the Americans with Disabilities Act (ADA)

The ADA Amendments Act (ADAAA, 2009) overrules prior Supreme Court decisions narrowly interpreting the ADA. This qualifies many more conditions as disabilities.

1. Physical or mental impairments substantially limiting one or more life activities now include immune system functioning; normal cell growth; brain, and neurological, respiratory, circulatory, endocrine, reproductive, digestive, bowel, and bladder functions, added to the existing activities of eating, sleeping, thinking, communicating, concentrating, lifting, and bending.
2. Impairments include physical (deaf, blind, or wheelchair-bound); conditions (AIDS, diabetes, or epilepsy); mental illnesses and ADHD; record of impairment, for example, cancer in remission and regarded as impaired.
3. Reasonable accommodations mean adaptations or modifications enabling persons with disabilities to have equal opportunities. The ADA describes this regarding equal employment opportunities, but it could also be interpreted relative to equal educational opportunities.
4. Reasonable accommodations that would cause undue hardship, for example, financial, are not required.

Preliteracy skills predictive of later reading and writing proficiency

Recent research has found strong evidence that phonological awareness, alphabetic knowledge, and print awareness in young children significantly predict their reading and writing proficiency when they are older. About 10 to 15 years ago, many teachers of preschoolers did not view teaching preliteracy skills as being a part of their jobs or even as being appropriate. Because of more recent research findings, though, it has become apparent that giving young children familiarity and practice with recognizing, differentiating, breaking down, and combining speech sounds, with the letters of the alphabet and their correspondence to and symbolic representation of speech sounds and with printed texts and how they are used, are important prekindergarten foundations for later literacy. Though many early childhood classrooms still need considerable improvements in their treatment of early literacy, at least the profession of ECE now realizes that providing such literacy foundations is an important aspect of preschool children's learning experience.

Relation to elementary school reading and writing success

Research finds that young children's vocabulary knowledge and other spoken language elements significantly predict their later reading comprehension. Although young children with limited vocabularies may learn basic decoding skills, they are nonetheless likely to have problems by grade 3 or 4, when they must read about different subjects in more advanced texts. Deficient comprehension caused by deficient vocabulary inhibits success across the curriculum. This difficulty is compounded for students hearing little or no English at home. Early childhood education (ECE) programs beginning proactive vocabulary development early can mitigate achievement gaps for these students. EC teachers should engage children in linguistic interactions throughout their days. For example, they can read to small groups of children and then engage them in discussions about the stories. Recent research has discovered that extended discourse, that is, conversations between children and adults on any given topic, continued across multiple sessions or instances, is particularly beneficial to young children's language development.

Current status of teaching numeracy skills

Typically, prekindergarten teaching currently addresses math very little. One reason for this oversight is that ECE teachers are frequently missing preparation, skills, and self-confidence to give more attention to math in their curriculums. This omission is not trivial: Research has found that preschool children's knowledge of numbers and numerical sequences strongly predicts their mathematics success in higher grades. Not only does early numeracy predict success in later math learning; moreover, it also predicts success in later student literacy. Educational professionals and researchers find the curriculum and teaching practices used in ECE will require substantial strengthening to incorporate sufficient numeracy (and literacy) concepts. They observe that methods exist to teach young children foundational numeracy and literacy skills in developmentally appropriate and engaging ways but have not yet been included in most ECE programs. Doing so would improve children's school readiness and achievement, reduce achievement gaps within the U.S. population, and improve overall U.S. student performance relative to that of other developed nations.

Effective practices

Researchers have investigated a number of ECE practices that predict children's success. These include strong curriculum content; teachers adhering carefully to established learning sequences in literacy, math, sciences, physical education, and so on; and focusing on developing children's emotional self-regulation, focused attention, and engagement in learning. Some additional practices that are familiar specifically to educators in the ECE field that afford positive outcomes for young children include relationship-based learning and teaching; establishing partnerships with children's families; adapting instruction for children from diverse linguistic, cultural, ethnic, religious, and socioeconomic backgrounds; individualizing instruction for specific children; providing children with active learning experiences; making learning activities meaningful to children; and having classes with smaller sizes. Educational researchers recommend extending these beneficial practices to elementary grades on a widespread basis. Also, some recent pilot projects emerging nationwide involve schools encompassing pre-K through grade 3, exploring ways to enhance alignment, continuity, and cohesion. Researchers are studying some of these programs to learn more about connecting EC and elementary education.

Areas of knowledge to make decisions

ECE teachers should consider the areas of knowledge about: child development and learning, each individual child, and cultural and social contexts in which children live.

1. Teachers' knowledge of child development and learning enables them to predict generally what children typically can and cannot do at specific ages, how they behave, and optimal teaching approaches and strategies and to know individual children in an age or developmental group are always the same in some ways but differ in others. This knowledge informs decisions regarding materials, environments, activities, and interactions.

2. Knowing each child as an individual allows teachers to address diagnosed and undiagnosed special learning needs; learning styles; personalities; strengths, interests, and preferences; prior experience and knowledge; background and living circumstances; and variations across contexts, domains, disciplines, and time.
3. Knowing children's cultural and social contexts helps teachers understand what makes sense to them; how they use language, show respect, and interact with friends versus new acquaintances; and rules for dressing, personal space, time, and so on, informing how teachers shape children's learning environments.

Principle that informs teachers' design of curriculum, learning environments, learning experiences, and teaching interactions

Individual children develop and learn at individually diverse rates; and different domains of individual development vary within the individual child. Patterns and schedules vary to some extent around norms; and each child is unique. Contributing variables include individual child temperaments, personalities, aptitudes and abilities, and how their experiences are influenced by familial, social, and cultural contexts. While chronological age indicates general developmental levels, within these, each child can differ greatly. Teachers often must deploy added resources and actions to assure optimal learning and development in children with special abilities or needs and when children's background experiences do not prepare them for certain educational settings. Thus, teachers should individualize curricular, teaching, and interactional decisions insofar as they can. Inflexibly expecting performance based on group norms does not account for knowledge of true developmental and learning variations. Nonetheless, teachers must maintain high expectations of all children and must supply resources and utilize methods to aid them in fulfilling those expectations.

Principles related to developmentally appropriate practice

One general principle in ECE is that all domains, for example, physical, cognitive, emotional, or social, are significant and are closely interrelated. Child development in one domain influences and is influenced by development and influences in other domains. For example, motor development in infants and toddlers affords greater environmental exploration; hence, motor development influences their cognitive development and psychosocial development of a sense of autonomy. Language development affects young children's ability to engage in social interactions; ensuing social experiences further influence additional language development, showing the reciprocal interrelation of linguistic and social development.

Another principle is that many areas of child growth and development follow a fairly predictable, stable order; more advanced skills and knowledge build upon those attained earlier. For example, learning to count is a foundation for later understanding numbers and then learning math. While many changes are predictable, the ways they manifest and their associated meanings can vary greatly across various cultural and linguistic contexts. Knowing developmental sequences informs practices in curriculum development and teaching.

Control physical and psychological conditions

ECE practitioners can protect learning children's health and safety by supporting their physical needs for sensory stimulation, physical activity, rest, nourishment, and fresh air and outdoor activity. They can balance children's daily schedules between physical activity and rest and give them opportunities to interact with nature. Psychologically, ECE practitioners should make children feel safe, secure, comfortable, and relaxed in their learning experiences and interactions with other learning community members rather than causing feelings of fear, worry, disengagement, or excessive stress. ECE teachers should promote children's interest and enjoyment in learning. By organizing the environment and creating orderly schedules and routines, ECE teachers give young children stability and structure that are conducive to learning. Dynamically varying aspects of the environment provide variety, while such teacher-created stability and structure still maintain the overall learning situation's comprehensibility and predictability from young children's perspectives. ECE teachers can additionally maintain optimally positive psychological, emotional, and social learning climates by assuring that children's home languages and cultures are represented in their classrooms' daily activities and interactions.

Scaffolding

Scaffolding is support that adults lend to youngsters while they learn a skill they have not yet mastered—just enough to enable them to perform it and gradually withdrawn as they gain proficiency until they can do it independently. Three general principles related to scaffolding are: (1) teachers realize that any single child's scaffolding needs vary through time and that skills and hence support needs vary among children and respond accordingly; (2) scaffolding can have varied forms, for example, modeling a skill, providing a cue, giving a hint, or modifying or adapting activities and materials; scaffolding can be given in varied settings, for example, planned learning activities, outdoor activities, play situations, and daily routines; (3) teachers can model a skill to provide scaffolding directly, or the teacher can plan for peers, such as learning buddies, to model it.

Planning and implementing relative to program curriculum goals

ECE teachers are responsible for knowing what their program's learning goals are and how their program's curriculum is designed for attaining these goals. They implement their program's curriculum by teaching young children using practices that fit the general developmental sequences wherein children learn certain skills and concepts that build upon children's prior knowledge, understanding, and experience and, additionally, which are most responsive to the abilities and needs of the individual children that they are teaching.

ECE teachers plan learning experiences for young children that are effective in implementing a comprehensive curriculum. One aim in teaching such a comprehensive curriculum is to help young children to achieve the most important learning goals across the physical, cognitive, social, and emotional domains. Another objective is to teach preschoolers basic skills that will prepare them for later school success across all academic disciplines, for example, language literacy, including English as a second language, math, sciences, arts and music, social studies, health, and physical education.

Planning curriculum and collaborating with educators

Although practitioners of infant and toddler caregiving may not refer to a part of their work as curriculum planning, they nevertheless do fulfill this function. They do this by identifying the experiences and routines that will nurture children's development and learning and enable children to reach the identified developmental and learning goals and then developing plans for systematically providing children with these experiences and routines. Early childhood and preschool education teachers do not work in isolation. Instead, they collaborate with caregivers and teachers working with children younger than their own students and with teachers working with students in higher grades than theirs. Caregivers and teachers share information about individual children as they progress through grade levels, about groups and classes, and about general developmental levels and transitions. They collaboratively strive to achieve greater continuity and connection across age and grade levels, at the same time preserving the appropriateness and integrity of instructional practices within each level.

Appropriate curriculum planning

ECE teachers must know and clearly express their young students' developmental and learning goals. They take into account what young children should understand, know, and be able to do in the physical, cognitive, emotional, and social domains of development and the preparation and readiness they need for future learning and performance across the school disciplines in elementary and higher grades. ECE teachers should familiarize themselves thoroughly with any state mandates or standards that exist for their schools or programs. They should also provide additional goals not sufficiently addressed by these standards. In addition, regardless of where learning goals may have originated, both teachers and administrators in ECE make sure that they clearly define these goals and communicate them to young students' families and other stakeholders in the children's education and that all stakeholders understand these goals and their definitions.

Planning curriculum and educational activities

All students learn best when they are given concepts, language, and skills that relate to something familiar and important to them. This includes young children. Not only is learning facilitated through connections with prior knowledge and interests; it is also facilitated through meaningful interconnections among the new things learned, which give them more coherence.

1. ECE teachers' curriculum planning integrates children's learning, both within each of the domains—physical, cognitive, emotional, and social—and also across them. They do the same regarding readiness for school disciplines.
2. ECE teachers use children's individual interests in curriculum planning and promoting motivation and attention. Teachers also introduce children to new experiences and topics they are likely to be interested in based on their identified interests. Developing and expanding children's interests are especially important for preschoolers just learning to focus their attention.
3. ECE teachers plan logically ordered curriculum experiences that permit focusing in depth on each content area for sustained periods rather than shallowly skimming over too many areas.

Future issues critical to the field of early childhood education (ECE)

In recent years, social changes have affected the ECE field. There is a shortage of quality infant and child care. More immigration has increased issues of English as a second language (ESL), home languages and cultures, and school cultures. Many more special needs children are in EC settings today. America has a shortage of well-qualified teachers. The EC field, particularly child care, is underfunded and rapidly losing well-prepared administrative and teaching personnel. Future projections are for substantially increasing demands for early child education and care, dramatically increasing cultural and linguistic diversity, and more poverty in families with young children. The largest demographic change predicted for future decades affecting young children is more ESL children in America. Another significant factor today is increased political and public awareness of the impact of the EC period upon children's futures. EC educators identify challenges including increasing all child achievement, decreasing learning gaps, improving preschool and elementary education and connecting them better, and increasing recognition of teachers' knowledge and decision making as crucial to effective education.

Movement for accountability policy and learning standards

The movement for school accountability in educating all American children has not only affected public education beginning with kindergarten; it has also influenced preschool education. By 2007, greater than ¾ of U.S. states had established early learning standards, and the other ¼ were developing these. The Head Start program has established a child outcomes framework that defines educational expectations in eight domains of learning. U.S. public policy statements and national reports espouse widespread efforts to improve early childhood teaching and learning for the purpose of developing greater school readiness; these efforts include creating standards-based curricula and assessment for early childhood learning. The issues of enabling all children's success and eliminating learning gaps are not new but are receiving more attention in the current context of accountability. Emerging scientific evidence and innovative teaching practices are being used to guide the ECE field regarding what skills and knowledge teachers must particularly cultivate in young children and how they can do this.

Purpose and method of the No Child Left Behind law

NCLB created a national policy in America to make schools accountable for eradicating achievement gaps that persist among diverse child groups. The law's purpose was to assure equality in education. It requires disaggregated, separate reporting of standardized achievement test scores of English language learners, special education students, racial and ethnic minorities, and economically disadvantaged students. It also requires annual gains in achievement be made in each of these groups. The aim is to keep schools responsible for effective instruction of all students. However, much controversy surrounds whether schools can attain the intended outcomes. Also, criticisms include that accountability legislation has unintentional, undesirable effects like restricting curriculum, excessive testing, and inappropriate testing methods. Although the public may not support the accountability movement's methods, the majority does support its goals for uniformly high achievement. Educators such as the National Association for the Education of Young Children (NAEYC) see this attitude as a demand for educators to enhance student achievement and close gaps wasting children's potential and harming their future prospects.

Separation between preschool and elementary education

America's preschool and elementary education have long been separate in their infrastructures, traditions, values, and funding sources. The American educational establishment has not viewed preschool as a complete component of public education, largely because preschool is not required and often not publicly funded. Additionally, the sponsorship, delivery systems, and teacher credentials in preschool programs vary widely. Many such programs began to provide child care for working parents. However, recently the educational potentials and aims of preschools have gained more recognition. This awareness adds to a softening of boundaries between preschool and elementary education. Educators now call for increased collaboration and continuity between the two. Accountability laws mandating third-grade standardized testing put greater pressure on K–2 teachers, who then rely on preschool educators to prepare children for K–2. Also contributing is an increase in state-funded prekindergarten, now serving more than a million 3- and 4-year-olds; additional millions are in child care and Head Start programs meeting state pre-K requirements and receiving state pre-K funding.

Statistics related to government funding

Head Start now serves more than 900,000 children nationally and is required at the state level to coordinate with public school systems. At least 300,000 children receive preschool education and services funded by Title I monies. Approximately 35% of 4-year-olds in America are in publicly funded prekindergarten programs. Because there are not enough affordable yet high-quality programs for children below age 5, and workers in such programs typically receive low pay, proponents expect advantages from having public funding provide educational services to more 4-year-olds and possibly even 3-year-olds. Advocates also see an advantage of better connection between preschool and elementary education programs in that they can learn from each other, affording more continuity and congruence from pre-K through grade 3. Disadvantages anticipated by preschool educators include excessive influence on early childhood by public K–12 schools pressured for accountability by high-stakes testing. Already seeing adverse effects on K–3 students, educators fear these extending to younger children. Early childhood education generally supports early learning standards in principle but in practice may doubt their adverse consequences.

Less effective vs. more effective ways of aligning preschool and elementary educational standards

Educators find preschool-elementary standards alignment crucial for their effectiveness. Some note that what they call downward mapping, that is, taking standards for older children and simplifying them for younger children, is not realistic and hence not effective. They recommend that early learning standards should be developed on the bases of research-based and practice-based evidence about children from diverse backgrounds at specific ages and developmental stages and about sequences, processes, variations, and long-term outcomes of early development and learning. Currently, though educators are discussing the establishment of a framework for national standards, this does not yet exist, and individual state standards vary without alignment. Accordingly, textbook and curriculum publishers striving to be competitive in the market attempt to address all state standards. Teachers, feeling pressure to cover these myriad topics, touch only fleetingly and shallowly upon each. This sacrifices in-depth knowledge and concentration on and mastery of fewer, more central learning goals.

Government accountability

Accountability and standards have caused U.S. states and education stakeholders to define what knowledge and abilities children should have at respective grade levels and demand rapid progress in achievement across all student groups. Therefore, many administrators and policy makers prefer strategies and tools meant to expedite these results, including curricula, lessons, and schedules that are "teacher-proofed." In some state and district publicly-funded early childhood (EC) settings, teachers report much less freedom than before, or none, to decide on curricula, assessments, or even how they use class time. The question emerges regarding the balance between how much teacher independence is optimal for child learning and how much direction and support of teachers' practices furthers this end. Many school administrators lack early childhood education (ECE) backgrounds and cannot judge best EC practices. ECE teachers have this specialized knowledge and daily classroom interaction with children. However, due to no standards for entry-level ECE credentials, diverse program settings and conditions, low pay, and high turnover, many EC teachers also lack current preparation in some parts of the curriculum.

Aspects of early learning standards

The Good Start, Grow Smart legislation passed in 2002 mandated early learning standards for language, literacy, and mathematics, so such standards are fairly recent. Some U.S. states have applied these standards comprehensively across developmental and learning domains; others concentrate mainly on the legally mandated areas, especially literacy. When a state does not develop comprehensive standards, the ensuing curriculum will also be less comprehensive. Any alignment between preschool and elementary education would probably be restricted to those few curriculum elements named by the standards. In addition to narrowing the scope of curriculum, many state standards overestimate or underestimate young children's abilities by adhering to shallow learning objectives rather than addressing desired child abilities and knowledge and aligning with age and grade, developmental levels, developmental sequences, and learning characteristics. Predominantly English-language assessments are also of concern because they prohibit demonstration of significant knowledge by English-as-a-second-language (ESL_ English-language-learner (ELL) students.

Adverse effects upon teaching practices

Because current learning standards vary among U.S. states with no nationalized standards, publishers of curriculum materials try to address all state standards, resulting in too many standards that teachers feel they must cover. This becomes overwhelming to both teachers and children. Additional adverse effects upon preschool, kindergarten, and first-grade teaching practices include too much whole-class and group lecturing, teaching separate objectives in a fragmented or unconnected manner, and forcing teachers to adhere to rigid schedules with tight paces. Another result is that, in these practices, schools sacrifice important experiences for children in problem solving, peer collaboration, emotional and social development, physical and outdoor activities, arts activities, and rich play activities. Professional educators are concerned that high-pressure teaching environments prevent children from developing senses of self-efficacy, competence, choice-making ability, love of learning, and the expansiveness and joy of childhood learning. Many educators aver that preschool-primary collaboration is not meant to teach elementary school skills earlier but to assure that younger children develop optimally and learn the basic skills they will need for future school learning.

Accountability pressures and standards limiting teacher autonomy

Due to the complexity of learning and teaching processes, all of a teacher's decisions and actions cannot be directed in advance. When programs or administrators gravitate toward practices expediting accountability pressures and standards, teachers lose autonomy to decide on curriculum, assessments, and even disposition of classroom time. Good teachers must be allowed to apply their knowledge, expertise, and judgment to decisions benefiting their students. However, autonomy does not dictate isolation: Teachers must also be given supports, tools, and resources to make solid instructional choices. A school or program's proven curriculum framework is a good basis for guiding curriculum development. Teachers can then apply their skills and experience in adapting curriculum optimally for their students. Teachers should be given professional development associated with curriculum frameworks and collaborative opportunities. Curricular direction helps teachers choose effective learning strategies, experiences, and materials to meet learning goals. Not having to create entire curricula, they can concentrate on instructional decisions. Many ECE personnel are insufficiently prepared; addressing this is informed by recent research into critical teaching factors.

Areas and ways research can inform best practices in the field

Recent research findings show hope for decreasing learning barriers and gaps and increasing all children's performance. More knowledge has been discovered regarding which competencies in physical, cognitive, emotional, social, and academic areas enable young children's meeting their full potentials for development and learning. These findings help decide curriculum sequences and content for all children but particularly to help children entering school with lower basic skills levels, including children of poverty, children of color, and English language learners. Research is also helping EC educators to assure early intervention for children with learning disabilities. Research confirms the superior effectiveness of earlier, sometimes intensive, intervention over reactive or remedial (too little, too late) approaches. For instance, the comprehensive, 2-generation Early Head Start program for children up to age 3 and their families has been proven by research to enhance cognitive, linguistic, emotional, and social development. While such high-quality infant and toddler services in America are scarce, they produce enduring positive effects on child development, learning, and emotional self-regulation.

20th- and 21st-century court cases improving educational opportunities

The landmark 1998 New Jersey Supreme Court case of Abbott v. Burke, regarding school funding, resulted in the first court-ordered early childhood education (ECE) program. The court ordered New Jersey to establish full-day preschool programs for all 3- and 4-year-olds in disadvantaged school districts. By 2003, these programs served more than 36,000 children. In Hoke County v. State (2000), the North Carolina trial court ordered funding of prekindergarten programs for all 4-year-olds considered at risk. In Montoy v. State (2003), the District Court of Shawnee County, Kansas, found the state school funding system unconstitutional, approving Kansas educators' testimony recommending a comprehensive preschool program to be part of their state's plans to improve educational outcomes for students presenting the greatest challenges. The Arkansas Supreme Court ruled in 2002 that the state's school finance system was unconstitutional. In 2004, this court appointed two special masters to evaluate Arkansas compliance with that 2002 ruling. The special masters' report stated Arkansas could not offer the constitutional standard of "substantially equal educational opportunity" without providing disadvantaged children preschool programs.

Trends in early childhood education (ECE)

Before World War II, ECE made slow progress toward unification, and progress was not measured. However, after World War II, influences such as many new job opportunities for women have furthered more global unifying of ECE programs. The advent of Head Start and Early Head Start provided models for making use of the most critical time in child development and have been important parts of the unification process. Today, the majority of ECE school settings are centralized on the basis of teachers', learning assistants', and administrators' educational qualifications in the ECE field. To become ECE educators, candidates must pass tests to obtain degrees, certifications, and licensure, required by both federal and state governments. ECE learning is based on existing scientific research measures and on children's learning capacities. However, ECE teachers have varied educational backgrounds, including philosophy, mathematics, music, psychology, social sciences, literature, and the arts. Teacher requirements include a bachelor's degree from an accredited university or college, licensure or certification from a state board of education, and passing a national accreditation body's educational requirements.

Government policies represent educational practices

ECE practitioners have crucial influences in the formation of our future citizens and democracy. As such, ethically they are responsible for practicing in accordance with professional standards. However, full implementation of these standards and practices depends upon public funds and policies that are supportive of an ECE system founded on providing all young children with high-quality, developmentally appropriate learning experiences. Educators call for progress on both sides—more developmentally appropriate practices by ECE professionals and more policies created and funds dedicated to support of these practices. Federal, state, and local policies need to reflect developmentally appropriate practice, including these at the very least: standards of early learning for young children with associated curricula and assessments; a comprehensive system governing compensation and professional development; a system for rating ECE program quality, informing families, policy makers, and the public regarding program quality, and improving program quality; coordinated, comprehensive services for young children; focus on program evaluation; and more public funding for quality, affordable programs in all settings.

Origins of the IDEA law

Public Law 94-142, the Education for All Handicapped Children Act/Education for the Handicapped Act (EHA), passed in 1975; and Public Law 99-457, the EHA Amendments, passed in 1986, provided foundations that were expanded by new 1990 legislation. As a result, EHA was renamed the Individuals with Disabilities Education Act (IDEA). The IDEA's six main principles follow:

1. Publicly funded education cannot exclude any student because of the student's disability.
2. The rights of students with disabilities and of their parents are assured by the protection of due process procedures.
3. The parents of students with disabilities are encouraged to participate in their children's educations.
4. The assessment of all students must be fair and unbiased.
5. All students must be given a free, appropriate public education (FAPE), and it must be provided in the least restrictive environment (LRE) where the student and other students can learn and succeed.
6. Information related to students with disabilities and their families must be kept confidential.

Purposes and key points of the legislation for Section 504

In 1973, Section 504 of the Rehabilitation Act, also called Public Law 93-112, was enacted to ensure individuals with disabilities equal access to federally financed programs and to promote their participation in them. A child must have a physical or mental impairment that substantially limits a major life activity to be eligible for a free, appropriate public education (FAPE) under Section 504. This law stimulated motivation to educate students with disabilities, contributing to the passage of the Education for All Handicapped Children Act, also called Public Law 94-142, in 1975. This law provides that all children with disabilities must receive a FAPE provided in the least restrictive environment possible and individualized. Its procedural safeguards mandate due process. The 1986's EHA amendments, or Public Law 99-457 extended special education to disabled preschoolers aged 3 to 5 years; services to infants and toddlers are at each U.S. state's discretion. And 1990's Americans with Disabilities Act (ADA) requires access for disabled people to public buildings and facilities, transportation, and communication but does not cover educational services.

Required and Recommended Information in Screening for Developmental Disorders

If a young child has been screened for developmental disorders or delays within the past 6 months and no changes have been observed or reported, repeat screening may be waived. Initial screenings are required. Hearing and vision screenings are mandatory in screening young children. Formal developmental measures are also required, which may include screening tests of motor skills development, cognitive development, social-emotional development, and self-help skills development. Formal screening tests of speech-language development are also required. Additional tests recommended during screening include informal measures. For example, checklists, rating scales, and inventories may be used to screen a child's behavior, mood, and performance of motor skills, cognitive skills, self-help skills, and social and emotional skills. On checklists, parents or caregivers check whether the child does or does not demonstrate listed behaviors, or assessors may complete them via parent or caregiver interviews or interviewing and observing the child. Rating scales ask parents, caregivers, and assessors to rate a child's behaviors, affect, mood, and so on, within a range of numbered and labeled descriptions. Inventories list demonstrated skills and needs. Behavioral observations and existing records and information are also used.

Features of Developmental Screenings and Evaluations

If a child's development is suspected of being delayed—for example, the child is not reaching developmental milestones during expected age ranges—a developmental screening may be administered. Screening tests are quickly performed and yield more general results. The hospital or doctor's office may give a questionnaire to the parent or caregiver to complete for a screening. Alternatively, a health or education professional may administer a screening test to the child. Screening tests are not intended to diagnose specific conditions or give details; they are meant to identify children who may have some problem. Screenings can overidentify or under-identify developmental delays in children. Hence, if the screening identifies a child as having developmental delay(s), the child is then referred for a developmental evaluation—a much longer, more thorough, comprehensive, in-depth assessment using multiple tests, administered by a psychologist or other highly-trained professional. Evaluation provides a profile of a child's strengths and weaknesses in all developmental domains. Determination of needs for early intervention services or treatment plans is based on evaluation results.

Developmental Evaluation Data Types

The child's social history should be obtained. This is typically done by a social worker. Details of the child's developmental progress heretofore; the family's composition, socioeconomic status, and situation; and the child's and family's health and medical histories and status should be emphasized. A physician's or nurse's medical assessment is required, including a physical examination, and if indicated, a specialist's examination. A psychologist typically assesses intellectual and cognitive development; at least one such test is generally required. At least one test of adaptive behavior is also required to assess emotional-social development. Self-help skills are evaluated; this may be included within cognitive, adaptive behavior, or programming assessments. Communication skills are typically evaluated by a speech-language pathologist. Both receptive and expressive language must be tested and comprehensively rather than simply by single-word vocabulary tests. As indicated, speech articulation is also tested. At least one test of motor skills, typically administered by a physical or occupational therapist, is required. Programming evaluation requires at least one criterion-referenced or curriculum-based measure, typically administered by an educator.

Behavioral Variations and Characteristics of ADHD

While the chief symptoms associated with ADHD are inattentiveness, impulsive behavior, distractibility, and excessive physical activity, there is considerable variation among individual children having ADHD. For example, the degree of severity of this condition can vary widely from one child to the next. In addition, each child can vary in how much he or she exhibits each of these primary characteristics. Some children might not appear to behave very impulsively but show severe deficits in attention. Some may focus better, but only for short periods, and are very easily distracted. Some display very disruptive behavior, while others do not but may daydream excessively, not attending to programming. In general, children who have ADHD can show deficits in following rules and directions. Also, when their developmental skills are evaluated or observed, they are likely to demonstrate inconsistencies in performance over time. To identify or select

- 125 -

specific intervention methods and strategies, professionals should use a comprehensive evaluation to obtain information about the child's specific behaviors in his or her natural environment that need remediation.

Child Find

Child Find is an ongoing process with the aim of locating, identifying, and referring young children with disabilities and their families as early as possible for service programs. This process consists of activities designed to raise public awareness and screenings and evaluations to identify and diagnose disabilities. The federal IDEA law mandates under Part B that disabled children are guaranteed early childhood special education services and under Part C that infants and toddlers at risk for developmental delays are guaranteed early intervention programs. (Eligibility guidelines vary by U.S. states.) The IDEA requires school districts to find, identify, and evaluate children with disabilities in their attendance areas. School districts have facilitated this Child Find process by establishing community informed referral networks whose members refer children who may have exceptional educational needs (EENs). Network members typically include parents, doctors, birth-to-3 programs, child care programs, Head Start programs, public health agencies, social service agencies, and any other community members with whom the young children come into contact.

Current Collaborative Approaches and Models of Screening

Historically, the tradition was to conduct kindergarten screenings of children entering schools around age 5. However, in recent years, school districts have developed community referral networks to assist in the processes of Child Find, screening, evaluation, and referral for early intervention and early childhood special education and related services. Current models are more informal, proactive, and collaborative. Cooperative educational interagency service efforts give parents information about normal early childhood development and available community resources and offer opportunities for developmental screenings of their young children. Specific procedures are governed by individual U.S. state laws. Generally, district networks implementing current models send developmental review forms to parents to complete in advance, and then they attend a developmental screening at a community site. Parents discuss normal early childhood growth and development with program staff, while in the same room, trained professionals observe their children as they play. Children's vision and hearing are also screened. Parents can discuss their children's current development with psychologists, early childhood educators, or counselors. Thereafter, they can learn about community resources.

Defining Developmental Delays in Infants and Toddlers

The IDEA Part C specifies the areas of development that states must include in defining developmental delays. However, individual states must identify the criteria they use to determine eligibility, including pertinent diagnostic instruments, procedures, and functional levels. States currently use quantitative and qualitative measures. Quantitative criteria for developmental delay include: difference between chronological age and performance level, expressed as a percentage of chronological age; performance at a given number of months below chronological age; or number of standard deviations (SDs) below mean of performance on a norm-referenced test. Qualitative criteria include: development considered atypical or delayed for established norms or observed behaviors considered atypical. At least one state differentially defines delay according to a child's age in months, with the rationale that a 25% delay, for example, is very different for a 1-year-old than a 3-year-old. Quantitative criteria for defining delay and determining eligibility vary widely among states. A 25% or 20% delay; 2 SDs below mean in 1+ areas or 1.5 SD below mean in 2+ areas are some common state criteria.

Single and Multiple Risk Factors in Infants and Toddlers for Developmental Delays

Scientists find that developmental outcomes for children are not reliably predicted by any one risk factor or event. Developmental risk increases with increased biological, medical, or environmental risk factors. However, researchers have found some variables that afford resiliency in children to offset risk factors. These can include the child's basic temperament, the child having high self-esteem, the child having a good emotional relationship with at least one parent; and the child having experiences of successful learning. These findings indicate that assessments should include criteria for multiple biological and environmental risk factors, for cumulative biological and environmental risk factors, and for protective or resilience factors, considering all of these in the context of change occurring over time. Under the IDEA (the Individuals with Disabilities Education Act), U.S. states have the option to provide early intervention services to children considered at risk for adverse developmental outcomes as well as those already identified with them. Some states apply multiple-risk models, requiring three to five risk factors for service eligibility. Some states also determine eligibility with less DD when biological, medical, or environmental risk factors also exist.

Information Sources on Early Intervention and Preschool Special Education Services

Military families stationed both in the United States and overseas who have young special needs children can seek information and assistance from the federally funded organization Specialized Training of Military Families (STOMP). The staff of STOMP is composed of parents having special needs children themselves, who also have been trained to work with other parents of special needs children. STOMP staff members are spouses of military personnel who thus understand the unique, specialized circumstances and needs of military families. Another government agency, the U.S. Department of Defense, includes the office of the Department of Defense Education Activity (DoDEA) and provides comprehensive guidance to military families with special needs children who are eligible to receive, or are receiving, free appropriate public education (FAPE) as mandated by the IDEA law (the Individuals with Disabilities Education Act), whether that education is located in the United States or in other countries.

Providing Special Education Services for Preschoolers

If parents observe that their preschooler is not attaining developmental milestones within the expected age ranges or does not seem to be developing in the same way as most other children, they should seek evaluation for possible developmental delay or disability. Although 3- to 5-year-olds are likely not in elementary school yet, the elementary school in a family's school district is still the best first contact because the IDEA law (the Individuals with Disabilities Education Act) specifies that school districts must provide special education services at no family cost to eligible children, including preschoolers. Another excellent source of more information about special education is the National Dissemination Center for Children with Disabilities (NICHCY) of the U.S. Department of Education's Office of Special Education Programs. They partner with nonprofit organizations like the Academy for Educational Development (AED) to produce useful documents for families with special needs children. NICHCY supplies state resource sheets listing main contacts regarding special education services in each U.S. state. Families can obtain these sheets at NICHCY's website or by telephone.

Information Sources for Evaluation to Determine Developmental Disability

Under the IDEA (the Individuals with Disabilities Education Act), evaluation information sources include: physicians' reports, the child's medical history, developmental test results, current classroom observations and assessments (when applicable), completed developmental and behavioral checklists, feedback and observations from parents and all other members of the evaluation team, and any other significant records, reports, and observations regarding the child. Under the IDEA, involved in the evaluation are parents, at least one regular education teacher and special education teacher if the child has these, and any special education service provider working with the child—for children receiving early intervention services from birth through age 2 and transitioning to preschool special education, it may be an early intervention service provider; a school administrator knowledgeable about children with disabilities, special education policies, regular education curriculum, and resources available; a psychologist or educator who can interpret evaluation results and discuss indicated instruction; individuals with special expertise or knowledge regarding the child (recruited by school or parents); when appropriate, the child; and other professionals, for example, physical or occupational therapists, speech therapists, medical specialists, and so on.

Special Education Services for Preschool Children

Special education for preschoolers is education specifically designed to meet the individual needs of a child aged 3 to 5 years with a disability or developmental delay. The specialized design of this instruction can include adaptations to the content, to the teaching methods, and the way instruction is delivered to meet a disabled child's unique needs. Special education for preschoolers includes various settings, such as in the home, in classrooms, hospitals, institutions, and others. It also includes a range of related services, such as speech-language pathology services, specialized physical education instruction, early vocational training, and training in travel skills. The school district's special education system provides evaluation and services to eligible preschoolers free of charge. Evaluation's purposes are to determine whether a child has a disability under the IDEA's (the Individuals with Disabilities Education Act) definitions and determine that child's present educational needs.

Post-Evaluation and the Individualized Education Program

After a preschool child is evaluated, the parents and involved school personnel meet to discuss the evaluation results. Parents are included in the group that decides whether the child is eligible for special education services based on those results. For eligible children, the parents and school personnel will develop an IEP. Every child who will receive special education services must have an IEP. The main purposes of the IEP are (1) to establish reasonable educational goals for the individual child and (2) to indicate what services the school district will provide to the child. The IEP includes a statement of the child's present levels of functioning and performance. It also includes a list of more general instructional goals for the child to achieve through school and parental support along with more specific learning objectives reflecting those goals and specifying exactly what the child will be able to demonstrate, under what circumstances, how much of the time—for example, a percentage of recorded instances—and within what time period (e.g., 1 year).

Individualized Education Program Goals and Objectives

In an IEP, the goals are more global, describing a skill for the child to acquire or a task to master. The objectives are more specific articulations of achievements that will demonstrate the child's mastery of the goal. For example, if a goal is for the child to increase his or her functional communicative vocabulary, a related objective might be for the child to acquire X number of new words in X length of time; another related objective could be for the child to use the words acquired in 90% of recorded relevant situations. If the goal is for the child to demonstrate knowledge and discrimination of colors, one objective might be for the child to identify correctly a red, yellow, and blue block 95% of the time when asked to point out each color within a group of blocks. Progress toward or achievement of some objectives may be measured via formal tests; with preschoolers, many others are measured via observational data collection.

Progress Monitoring, Updating, and Revising IEPs

Once a child has been identified with a disability, determined eligible for special education and related services under the IDEA (the Individuals with Disabilities Education Act), and had an IEP developed and implemented, the child's progress must be monitored. Monitoring methods may be related to evaluation methods. For example, if a child identified with problem behaviors was initially evaluated using a behavioral checklist, school personnel can use the same checklist periodically, comparing its results to the baseline levels of frequency and severity originally obtained. If an affective disorder or disturbance was identified and instruments like the Beck Depression Inventory or Anxiety Inventory were used, these can be used again periodically; reduced symptoms would indicate progress. If progress with IEP goals and objectives is less or greater than expected, the IEP team meets and may revise the program. This can include specifying shorter or longer times to achieve some goals and objectives; lowering or raising requirements proving too difficult or easy; resetting successive objective criteria in smaller or larger increments; changing teaching methods, content, or materials used, and so on.

Informal Assessment Instruments

EC teachers assess pre-K children's performance in individual, small-group, and whole-class activities throughout the day using informal tools that are teacher-made, school/program/district-furnished, or procured by school systems from commercial educational resources. For classroom observations, teachers might complete a form based on their observations during class story or circle time, organized using three themes per day, each targeting different skills—social-emotional, math, alphabet knowledge, oral language, or emergent writing. They note the names of children demonstrating the specified skill and those who might need follow-up, and provide needed one on one interventions daily. For individual observations, teachers might fill out a chart divided into domains like physical development; oral language development; math; emergent reading; emergent writing; science and health; fine arts; technology and media; social studies; social-emotional development; and approaches to learning, noting one child's strengths and needs in each area per chart. In addition to guided observation records, teachers complete checklists; keep anecdotal and running records; and assemble portfolio assessments of children's work. Tracking children's progress informs responsive instructional planning.

Screening Versus Assessment Instruments

A variety of screening and assessment instruments exist for EC measurement. Some key areas where they differ include which developmental domains are measured by an instrument; for which applications an instrument is meant to be used; to which age ranges an instrument applies; the methods by which a test or tool is administered; the requirements for scoring and interpreting a test, scale, or checklist; whether an instrument is appropriate for use with ethnically diverse populations; and whether a tool is statistically found to have good validity and reliability. EC program administrators should choose instruments that can measure the developmental areas pertinent to their program; support their program's established goals; and include all EC ages served in their program. Instruments' administration, scoring, and interpretation methods should be congruent with program personnel's skills. Test/measure administration should involve realistic time durations. Instruments/tools should be appropriate to use with ethnically diverse and non-

English-speaking children and families. Tests should also be proven psychometrically accurate and dependable enough.

Typical Applications of Screening and Assessment Instruments

The ways in which screening and assessment instruments applicable to ECE are used include a wide range of variations. For example, ECE programs typically need to identify children who might have developmental disorders or delays. Screening instruments are used to identify those children showing signs of possible problems who need assessments, not to diagnose problems. Assessment instruments are used to develop and/or confirm diagnoses of developmental disorders or delays. Assessment tools are also used to help educators and therapists plan curricular and treatment programs. Another important function of assessment instruments is to determine a child's eligibility for a given program. In addition, once children are placed in ECE programs, assessment tools can be used to monitor their progress and other changes occurring through time. Moreover, program administrators can use assessment instruments to evaluate children's achievement of the learning outcomes that define their program goals—and by extension, the teachers' effectiveness in furthering children's achievement of those outcomes.

Formal Assessment Instruments

Formal assessment instruments are typically standardized tests, administered to groups. They give norms for age groups/developmental levels for comparison. They are designed to avoid administrator bias and capture children's responses only. Their data can be scaled and be reported in aggregate to school/program administrators and policymakers. The Scholastic Early Childhood Inventory (SECI) is a formal one on one instrument to assess children's progress in four domains found to predict kindergarten readiness: phonological awareness, oral language development, alphabet knowledge, and mathematics. Other instruments measuring multiple developmental domains include the Assessment, Evaluation and Programming System (0–6 years) for planning intervention; the Bayley Scale for Infant Development (1–42 months) for assessing developmental delays; the Brigance Diagnostic Inventory of Early Development (0–7 years) for planning instruction; the Developmental Profile II (0–6 years) to assess special needs and support IEP development; the Early Coping Inventory (4–36 months) and Early Learning Accomplishment Profile (0–36 months), both for planning interventions; and the Infant-Toddler Developmental Assessment (0–42 months) to screen for developmental delays.

Screening and Assessment Instruments Measuring Development

The available screening and assessment instruments for EC development cover a wide range in scope and areas of focus. Some measures are comprehensive, assessing young children's progress in many developmental domains including sensory, motor, physical, cognitive, linguistic, emotional, and social. Some other instruments focus exclusively on only one domain, such as language development or emotional-social development. Some instruments even focus within a domain upon only one of its facets, e.g. upon attachment or temperament within the domain of emotional-social development. In addition, some tools measure risk and resiliency factors influencing developmental delays and disorders. Programs like Head Start that promote general EC development should select comprehensive assessment instruments. Outreach programs targeting better identification of children having untreated and/or undetected mental health problems should choose instruments assessing social-emotional development. Clinics treating children with regulatory disorders might select an instrument measuring temperament. Prevention programs helping multiple-needs families access supports and services could use a measure for risk and resiliency factors. Multifaceted EC programs often benefit most from using several instruments in combination.

Age Ranges Included in Various Screening and Assessment Instruments

An important consideration for screening and assessment in early childhood is that EC development is very dynamic and occurs rapidly. Hence screening and assessment instruments must be sensitive to such frequent and pronounced developmental changes. Some instruments target specific age ranges like 0–36 months. Others cover wider ranges, e.g. children aged 2–16 years. The latter may have internal means of application to smaller age ranges; for example, sections respectively for 3–6-month-old babies, 7–12-month-olds, and 12–18-month-olds. Or they indicate different scoring and interpretation criteria by age; for example, some screening tools specify different numbers of test items depending on the child's age to indicate a need for assessment. Choosing screening and assessment instruments covering the entire age range served in an ECE program is advantageous—not only because they can be used with all child ages in the program, but also because they can be administered and readministered at the beginning and end of programs and/or in between, to compare and monitor changes, which is difficult with separate, age-specific tests.

Features of Paper-and-Pencil Reports

The most common form of paper-and-pencil report about infants and young children are questionnaires. Parents, caregivers, and teachers read printed questions or statements and respond by selecting Yes or No to a question or a number/level on a Likert-type scale showing the degree to which they agree with a statement. For self-administration, instruments must contain questions/statements written on reading levels accessible to the respondents and in their native languages. Alternatively, some questionnaires or surveys can be read to the respondent by an interviewer trained in or familiar with administration of the chosen instrument. Such self-reporting instruments usually take fewer than 20 minutes to finish, and ECE program personnel need comparatively little training to administer them. However, employees may need further training to score and/or interpret responses, or already-trained specialists may score and interpret them in some cases. ECE schools/programs/agencies can obtain some self-reporting instruments free of charge; other tools' publishers charge for response forms; and others charge only for initially obtaining their materials, allowing purchasers to reproduce them thereafter.

Features of Formal and Informal Observations

Some instruments require EC staff to watch a child's behavior and/or interactions with parents/caregivers and/or peers. Formal observations involve watching activities structured for the screening/assessment instrument. Informal observations involve watching a child's activities in natural settings like at home or in preschool during play times. Formal observation tools typically require staff to be trained to administer them. The trained observers' findings can include records of which developmentally normal behaviors a child has attained, incidences of problem behaviors noted, descriptions and evaluations of the quality of a child's social interactions with other people, and other observations of the child's behaviors that can inform screening and assessment. Observational screening and assessment instruments usually take more than 20 minutes for administration. Publishers of observational tests typically charge EC programs to order single-use recording forms; some allow them to purchase templates and then reproduce the forms.

Scoring and Interpretation of Various Screening and Assessment Instruments

Some instruments are fairly simple to score and interpret, needing little training of EC personnel. For example, paper-and-pencil questionnaires/surveys often only need the numbers/points for each item response added up for a total score; or a group of scores is obtained by summing values within sections. Interpreting some screening scores can be as simple as noting whether a child's score surpasses a designated cut-off value that signals assessment is needed. Such screenings can be scored and interpreted right after administration, and readily shared with parents and other stakeholders. Assessment instruments using more complicated scoring and interpretation include such procedures as weighting item values; reversing point values for certain items; converting raw scores into standardized scores or percentages; and referring to tables giving national norms for comparison. Standardized tests, including preschool IQ scales, commonly involve such methods. Assessors often need considerable training; advanced psychometric education and experience; thorough knowledge of EC development; and additional time to score and interpret these tests. Results may be discussed in separately scheduled meetings.

Interview Features

In EC programs conducting assessments, personnel usually conduct interviews with a child's parents, teachers, and/or caregivers. Interviews can be made in structured formats, i.e. the administrator reads prescribed questions as written to the interviewee, or semi-structured formats, wherein the administrator uses his/her judgment to add more questions to the written ones until s/he determines that the information provided is complete enough. Interview questions vary, covering subjects of parental concern, the child's identified areas of strengths and accomplishments, the child's identified areas of deficits or needs, the interactions between parents and child, and the child's behavior. Interviews can be brief, but usually they are longer than paper-and-pencil self-reporting questionnaires, surveys, or checklists. EC personnel frequently need to be trained to administer published interview-based instruments. Publishers typically charge schools/programs/agencies for ordering multiple, single-use response forms, or they may require a one-time order and allow them to reproduce the forms from their initial purchase to use for multiple administrations.

Features of Screening and Assessment Tools Using Structured Tasks

Screening and assessment instruments that use structured tasks involve a list of behaviors and/or skills that a child is expected to attain by a certain age range or developmental level. The administrators must present various activities or tasks to a child, and then record the details of the child's performance of each activity or task. Instruments using structured tasks require EC staff training for administration. They take over 20 minutes to complete. EC programs/schools/agencies must buy testing equipment/materials and single-use recording forms. Because paper-and-pencil questionnaires/surveys are easy to administer; apply across various settings, e.g. preschools, pediatricians' waiting rooms, homes, etc.; cost comparatively little; require minimal administrator training; and are frequently short, they are appropriate for screening use. While formal/informal observational tools, structured/semistructured interview tools, and structured-task tools take more training, time, and expense, they also provide more detailed information, making them useful for determining diagnoses and/or developing individualized care/instruction plans. Instruments using multiple methods, e.g. collecting data from various settings and respondents, yield the most comprehensive information.

Test-Retest Reliability

Test-retest reliability is how consistent/stable an instrument's results are across administrations. An instrument with good test-retest reliability yields the same results when administered twice or more to the same child within a short time. For example, the same assessor gives a child the same test twice within a few days or weeks, comparing the results. The more similar the results between/among administrations, the higher the test-retest reliability. This implies the instrument measures an attribute/construct that is stable over a short time. Due to the inherent rapidity and dynamism of EC development, we expect significant developmental changes over years and months; but over only weeks or days, we expect little or no substantial change. Therefore, instruments whose results are not stable over a short time are less utile for EC screening/assessment. For example, a child's scoring with "typical development" on one administration but "possible delay/disorder" a week later means the instrument does not define the child's developmental needs, and thus is not reliable.

Inter-Rater Reliability of Screening and Assessment Instruments

Inter-rater reliability is how consistent/stable an instrument's results are across different individual administrators/raters. Good inter-rater reliability means the instrument will give the same/similar results for the same child, at the same time, in the same setting, when administered by different people. This shows that the instrument measures a quality/construct that remains stable regardless of who administers the test. Significant differences among different raters' results present problems, especially with instruments using unstructured interviews, observations, or structured tasks. For example, if one rater scores a child as possibly having a developmental delay or disorder while another rater using the same test scores the same child as within the range of normal development, the instrument does not identify the child's true developmental needs and is unreliable. When different assessors (like parent vs. teacher) observe a child in different settings, though, like home vs. preschool, and/or at different times, varying results are expected and not necessarily indicative of inter-rater unreliability because children's behaviors can vary by setting.

Internal Consistency Regarding Test Instruments

A testing instrument is said to have internal consistency when its individual items correlate strongly with each other and with the total test score. This means that all of the individual items (questions, stimuli, tasks, etc.) measure parts of the same construct that the test is intended to measure. A test with low internal consistency could be measuring additional attributes that the authors did not define or mean for the test to measure. Children with disparate developmental needs could thus receive similar scores, based on different test items. With comprehensive screening and assessment instruments that cover multiple domains of development, EC educators should look for internal consistency within each subscale of the test or within each domain tested. However, they should not necessarily expect internal consistency among the different domains or at the level of the test's full-scale/overall score. For example, they should not expect high correlation between a test's subscale measuring a child's language skills development and its subscale measuring a child's gross motor skills development.

Internal Consistency and Screening and Assessment Instruments

Whether a test's individual items contribute to measuring the construct the test is supposed to measure is internal consistency. It is determined by how much the test's individual items correlate with one another and with the overall score. A test with high internal consistency more accurately measures the specific content area/developmental domain/construct it means to measure. A test with low internal consistency poses problems when children who might have very different needs get the same score. For example, if a test meant to measure aggression has low internal consistency, its individual items are not correlated with one another or the overall score, implying it tests more than one construct. Two children given this test could score beyond the cutoff level indicating diagnosis or assessment need, but their scores could be due to completely different individual test items. Since individual test items do not correlate, the two children might have markedly different needs. Furthermore, those needs may not be related to aggression, since the test probably unintentionally measures additional constructs.

Concurrent Validity Regarding Screening and Assessment Instruments

When a screening or assessment instrument yields results comparable to those of another instrument whose validity has been previously established, it has good concurrent validity. Since the test used for comparison was already found valid, users have confidence in its results. Therefore, their confidence is warranted in another test showing high concurrent validity with the established test. For example, the Stanford-Binet Intelligence Scales and the Wechsler Preschool and Primary Scales of Intelligence (WPPSI) are both well-established IQ tests with demonstrated statistical validity and reliability. So if EC educators have found or been given a new instrument for measuring intelligence, they are likely to find that its authors have compared the test's results to the results obtained by the Stanford-Binet and/or WPPSI. Educators who have confidence in the Stanford-Binet and/or the WPPSI are then justified in having comparable confidence in the new test if its results were found similar to those of the established tests, indicating its high concurrent validity.

Content Validity Regarding Screening and Assessment Instruments

Whether a test instrument measures the entire content area it purports to measure is known as content validity. It determines whether a test can yield accurate and fair measures of the totality of the construct that the assessor wants to test. For example, if a screening instrument is intended to measure social-emotional development in a young child, it should include individual test items covering the range of this domain's important components. A screening test that covers a child's interactions with caregivers but not with peers; screens attention but not initiation of play; or screens for social skills but not communication skills would not address all elements of social-emotional development and thus not have good content validity. EC educators can use instruments with high content validity to generalize with more confidence about how a child's test performance predicts his/her levels of functioning in real life. By contrast, if a test has low content validity, generalizations about the tested child's development can exceed the test's scope and be inaccurate and/or unrealistic.

Predictive Validity in Screening and Assessment Instruments

A screening/assessment instrument's prediction of a child's behavior in real life is predictive validity. For example, an instrument screening for social-emotional disorders in preschool children might predict tantrum and/or oppositional behaviors in kindergarten. In another example, you would expect a screening instrument for social-emotional disorders to differentiate between children with normal/typical social-emotional development and those with mental health disorders. If a screening tool identifies a child with a potential mental health disorder and has high predictive validity, a complete clinical diagnostic evaluation of the screened child would diagnose a mental health disorder. Sensitivity is the instrument's accuracy—here, in identifying developmental disorders/delays, if it correctly identifies 9 of 10 children really having disorders/delays, it has 90 percent sensitivity. Specificity conversely would be accuracy in identifying children without disorders/delays. Despite high sensitivity and specificity, screeners yield some errors. False-positives over-identify delays/disorders where none exist; false-negatives under-identify existing delays/disorders. Unnecessary concern is a consequence of false-positives; lack of prevention/early intervention/treatment is a more serious consequence of false-negatives.

Norm-Referenced Versus Criterion-Referenced Tests

Norm-referenced tests compare a child's test results to those of a comparison group of other children in the same age group, grade, or developmental level. This comparison group is called a normative or standardization sample. Norm-referenced tests show how an individual child's performance compares to that of the general population of children. Criterion-referenced tests compare a child's test results to a predetermined standard of performance for the child's age group/grade/level. They show how an individual child's performance compares to standards established by educational experts. Norm-referenced tests are useful for determining whether a child is similar to the "average" child and identifying children performing significantly above or below average. Criterion-referenced tests are good for measuring the extent to which an individual child has mastered areas or domains of development and for monitoring changes over time in the child's levels of mastery.

Establishing and Maintaining Good Communication with Parents

When teachers send home a letter to parents explaining classroom practices and giving contact information at the beginning of the school year, parents perceive them as approachable and available. When a teacher calls each parent/guardian during school's first two weeks, parents appreciate and enjoy conversations. Calls also make it easier for teachers to contact parents later in the year regarding child issues if needed. Experts find it effective to mail postcards home, addressed to children or parents. Establishing simple class websites including teacher contact information facilitates parental access. Teachers' printing business cards and attaching them to their first parent letters conveys professionalism. Teachers using Internet/e-mail/print to publish weekly/monthly class newsletters informally keep parents apprised of children's instruction and teach parents to expect communication. Teachers can send parents invitations to visit prior to school/program Open Houses: teachers are perceived as more approachable when more parents are comfortable in classrooms. Having children write appreciation letters to parents for Open Houses encourages children to invite parents; parents also perceive teacher appreciation by association.

Applying Assessment Results to Planning Instruction for Individuals and Groups

ECE settings should provide organized outlines of developmentally appropriate guidelines for their children, including when and how to introduce and reinforce guidelines at each learning stage. These outlines are foundations for anecdotal observations and authentic assessments tracking developmental progress. ECE programs supply opportunities and activities to develop each discrete skill, including copious review and practice young children require for retention. Teachers should plan learning experiences meaningfully promoting developing identified guidelines and addressing children's interests. ECE settings should have organized progress-tracking systems following developmental sequences. These help teachers determine whether a child can move to the next level or prior skills that need additional reinforcement. Tracking systems should be easy to maintain and immediately give teachers basic information regarding each child's level of functioning for planning activities and discussions. Teachers should then create "ready reference" charts/graphs of assessment and monitoring results, giving an idea of the class/group's general functioning level, to inform activity/lesson planning and additional support needed for individual children—one on one for those below class/group level, enriched for those above it.

IDEA Law

Public Law 94-142, the Education for All Handicapped Children Act/Education for the Handicapped Act (EHA), passed in 1975; and Public Law 99-457, the EHA Amendments, passed in 1986, provided foundations that were expanded by new 1990 legislation. As a result, EHA was renamed the Individuals with Disabilities Education Act (IDEA). The IDEA's six main principles follow:

1. Publicly funded education cannot exclude any student because of the student's disability.
2. The rights of students with disabilities and of their parents are assured by the protection of due process procedures.
3. The parents of students with disabilities are encouraged to participate in their children's educations.
4. The assessment of all students must be fair and unbiased.
5. All students must be given a free, appropriate public education (FAPE), and it must be provided in the least restrictive environment (LRE) where the student and other students can learn and succeed.
6. Information related to students with disabilities and their families must be kept confidential.

Section 504, EHA, EHA Amendments, and ADA

In 1973, Section 504 of the Rehabilitation Act, also called Public Law 93-112, was enacted to ensure individuals with disabilities equal access to federally financed programs and to promote their participation in them. A child must have a physical or mental impairment that substantially limits a major life activity to be eligible for a free, appropriate public education (FAPE) under Section 504. This law stimulated motivation to educate students with disabilities, contributing to the passage of the Education for All Handicapped Children Act, also called Public Law 94-142, in 1975. This law provides that all children with disabilities must receive a FAPE provided in the least restrictive environment possible and individualized. Its procedural safeguards mandate due process. The 1986's EHA amendments, or Public Law 99-457 extended special education to disabled preschoolers aged 3 to 5 years; services to infants and toddlers are at each U.S. state's discretion. And 1990's Americans with Disabilities Act (ADA) requires access for disabled people to public buildings and facilities, transportation, and communication but does not cover educational services.

U.S. Federal Legislation Passed in 1997, 2001, and 2004

The 1990 Individuals with Disabilities Education Act (IDEA) was reauthorized in 1997 and numbered Public Law 108-446. It provided more access for children with disabilities to the general education curriculum and extended collaborative opportunities for teachers, other professionals, and families of children with disabilities. No Child Left Behind (NCLB, 2001, now the Every Student Succeeds Act, ESSA 2015), the reauthorization of the Elementary and Secondary Education Act (ESEA), stressed accountability for outcomes by identifying schools and districts needing improvement and assuring teacher quality. It required school performance data to include disabled students' standardized test scores. NCLB emphasized giving teachers and administrators better research information and schools more resources, parents more information about their children's progress and the school's performance, and more local flexibility and control in utilizing federal education funds and in improving teacher qualifications, for example, through alternative certifications. And, 2004's IDEA reauthorization, Individuals with Disabilities Education Improvement Act (IDEIA), covers better alignment of NCLB with IDEA, appropriately identifying students needing special education, ensuring reasonable discipline while protecting special needs students defining highly qualified teachers, reducing paperwork, and increasing cooperation to decrease litigation.

Recent Legal Changes to the Americans with Disabilities Act

The ADA Amendments Act (ADAAA, 2009) overrules prior Supreme Court decisions narrowly interpreting the ADA. This qualifies many more conditions as disabilities.

- Physical or mental impairments substantially limiting one or more life activities now include immune system functioning; normal cell growth; brain, and neurological, respiratory, circulatory, endocrine, reproductive, digestive, bowel, and bladder functions, added to the existing activities of eating, sleeping, thinking, communicating, concentrating, lifting, and bending.
- Impairments include physical (deaf, blind, or wheelchair-bound); conditions (AIDS, diabetes, or epilepsy); mental illnesses and ADHD; record of impairment, for example, cancer in remission and regarded as impaired.
- Reasonable accommodations mean adaptations or modifications enabling persons with disabilities to have equal opportunities. The ADA describes this regarding equal employment opportunities, but it could also be interpreted relative to equal educational opportunities.
- Reasonable accommodations that would cause undue hardship, for example, financial, are not required.

Legal Responsibilities of EC Professionals

Historically, special education was introduced with the purpose of separating special-needs children from their normally developing peers. However, since 1991, the IDEA legislation has established the necessity of inclusion in normal care and educational environments, including EC settings, for children with disabilities. EC professionals know excluding any child is illegal. Another example of legal responsibilities is the "mandated reporter" status of caregivers/teachers/other adults working with children and families. They are legally required to report suspected child abuse and neglect; the law penalizes them for not reporting. For example, an EC teacher sees injuries to a child. S/he knows the mother has a new boyfriend, displays a fearful attitude, and responds evasively to teacher questions. Later, the child tells the teacher the boyfriend hurt him/her. The teacher pities the mother, realizing she needs the boyfriend financially and emotionally, and reporting suspected abuse could make the mother lose her children or their home. Regardless, the teacher must report suspicions by law, which was enacted for stopping violence against children.

Attributes Indicating EC Educators' Professionalism and Professional Responsibility

While care and instruction of young children are delivered through a variety of program types, EC educators share common general goals. They appreciate EC as a unique period in life. They work to educate holistically, considering the mind, feelings, and body of the whole child. The educational goals they develop are designed to support each child's fulfilling his/her individual potential within relationship contexts. EC professionals realize children are inseparable from their social milieus of family, society, and culture; they work to relate to and understand children in these contexts, while also appreciating and supporting family ties. They apply their knowledge of child development, teaching according to how children learn and what they need, and apply research in the field to differentiating common assumptions and myths from valid scientific findings. They have appropriate behavioral expectations for children at each developmental stage. EC professionals realize the significance of confidentiality: they never gossip or tell families personal information about other families. Lifelong learners, they set their own professional goals, pursuing ongoing professional development.

Interactions with Adults in the Learning Environment

Regarding teachers' roles, much of the focus is on observing children and their behaviors, helping children manage peer interactions, and giving children opportunities for developing peer-group social skills. Too often a similar emphasis is not accorded to teachers' reflecting on their interactions and behaviors with other adults; learning to collaborate with other adults; and developing skills for conflict resolution and managing disagreements with other adults. Some experts say teachers should work diligently and deliberately to make adult interactions integral parts of daily classroom activity. For group ECE settings to attain their goals, adults must make and implement plans collaboratively. However, mandatory staff meetings are commonly occupied with curricular and administrative requirements; beyond these, little or no attention or time is applied to nurturing adult-adult relationships. Adults interact during in-service trainings and professional development experiences, but outside of daily classroom settings. Nevertheless, these experiences can be used as foundations for better adult-adult communication within ECE contexts. Conscious efforts to develop adult-adult relationships benefiting children's growth, development, and learning are necessary.

Conditions Enabling and Supporting Positive Interactions Among Adults Within the ECE Setting

Adults engage in positive interactions with each other within ECE programs when they make time to share their anecdotal records and observations of their young students, and collaboratively plan instruction based on their collective contributions. When adults share information and communicate with one another about the children and their families with whom they work, they interact positively together. When EC educators engage in problem-solving activities and dialogues, these help them identify which learning goals and experiences they can make more effective for the children and how they can do this. Adults within ECE settings should engage in reciprocal exchanging of ideas about the EC learning environment and about how to share responsibilities for performing instructional tasks, rearranging classrooms as needed, setting up class projects, taking care of class pets and plants, and other such daily duties.

Adult-Adult Interactions Not Addressed in Research, Theoretical Literature, and Professional Development

ECE research contains little work addressing adults' cooperation and collaborative expertise with each other and the influences of these on children. However, the High/Scope curriculum model, The Creative Curriculum, and similar curriculum models and approaches do address adult-adult interactions by stressing how important teamwork is in planning lessons and sharing responsibilities and information. In addition, some educational experts have written about power struggles and other interactional dynamics in adult-adult relationships that can impede employee performance in a variety of settings. Professional development and training programs rarely include adult conflict-resolution techniques, instruction in working collaboratively, or adult learning principles. Hence educators must consider how their adult-adult interactions can support children's development of competence, capability, and confidence. Sharing instructional goals, planning learning experiences that support goals, and sharing responsibilities as a team for implementing projects establishes climates of safety and trust for children.

Applying Quality Time to EC Educators' Interactions with Adults

Educators have noted that attitudes and things we commonly say to children, e.g. "Your actions speak louder than your words" would equally benefit us addressing our own behaviors as adults.

Applying the same principles we teach children to interactions among adults in the learning community can positively influence those interactions, which in turn affects adult-child/teacher-student interactions and overall classroom atmospheres. Without such atmospheres conducive to trust and honesty in adult relationships, educators can fall prey to misunderstandings and internalizing negative attitudes, which influence not only coworker interactions but moreover classroom climates. One solution is for adults in ECE to establish occasions affording "quality adult time." Psychotherapist and psychological theorist Virginia Satir, pioneer of family therapy, found interpersonal dynamics influenced by positive adult-adult communication. Trust-building, mutual colleague support, and sharing experiences/feelings—related or unrelated to classrooms—promote adult relationships that benefit teacher-learner relationships and thus enhance young children's development and learning.

Regulations Regarding the Confidentiality of Records

In EC settings, records kept about children and their families must be treated with strict confidentiality. EC centers/programs/preschools/agencies should limit access to student records to children's immediate family members; only those employees authorized; and agencies having legal authority to access records. Confidentiality of records and restricted access to them in all centers/programs/preschools/agencies that receive federal funding are mandated by the Family Educational Rights and Privacy Act (FERPA). Moreover, with the ongoing trend toward educational inclusion, many EC settings serve children with disabilities, whose student records are additionally subject to regulations under the federal Individuals with Disabilities Education Act (IDEA), and also to the special education laws of their respective U.S. states. An exception to the laws regarding records confidentiality is mandated reporting by EC personnel of suspected child abuse and neglect. Laws applying to child abuse and neglect supersede FERPA regulations. Legally, EC employees are both required to report suspected abuse and neglect of children, and immune from liability for releasing child records information relevant to their reporting.

Quality Care and Economic Considerations

To furnish and sustain quality care in EC settings is always challenging to care providers. It is even more so during difficult economic times. Many EC centers must face decisions whether to downsize the services they offer or to go out of business. When administrators choose to remain in operation, they encounter equally difficult decisions regarding how to reduce services, but not at the expense of quality. A legal issue related to such economic considerations is that EC personnel are often placed at legal risk when service quality is compromised. While EC employers, employees, young children's parents, and educational researchers are all interested in and pursue a definition of quality care, no single operational definition has been attained. However, EC professionals with ample work experience in EC centers have contributed various definitions. The consensus of their contributions includes the following common elements: a nurturing environment; employees trained in EC development and methods; age-appropriate curricula; sufficient space, equipment, and materials; safety and good maintenance of physical environments; and good parent-teacher communication.

Medical Care and Treatment Emphasized in Legal Regulations

The child care licensing regulations of each U.S. state government mostly govern children's medical care and treatment in EC settings. Overall, state regulations emphasize four areas of medical care and treatment: (1) Health requirements for all employees, such as having no communicable diseases; passing a TB test; having no health conditions preventing active child care; and maintaining accurate employee as well as child health records; (2) Administration by staff of medication to children being served in EC settings; (3) Management by EC staff of emergencies due to illness, injury, and accidents; and (4) Treatment of nonemergency minor illnesses, injuries, and accidents occurring to children in EC settings. To protect children's health and safety, EC programs/schools/centers must maintain written policies and procedures for emergency and nonemergency care. To protect personnel from litigation, they must adhere scrupulously to written policies and procedures. Litigation for damages/injury is likely when not following procedures. Not reporting suspected/observed child abuse/neglect and not completing accident reports also invite lawsuits.

Administration of Medication Guidelines

The administration of medication to children in EC settings has been subject to much controversy due to obvious issues of dangers and liability. EC centers/programs must write their policies and procedures to include their state government's licensing requirements for medical care and treatment, which they must follow closely. Experts recommend that parent and doctor permission be required for administering any prescription and nonprescription medications to children. EC settings should keep on file written parental consent for each medication, and review these records regularly for changes. They should also post separate charts, easily accessible to staff, with each child's name, medication, dosage, administration time, and teacher initials. These provide documentation of teachers following parent directions and can prevent mistakes. Staff should label all medications with the drug name, child's name, doctor's name and contact information, and administration instructions. EC centers seasonally and frequently contain many children simultaneously recovering from a variety of illnesses; labeling prevents giving children the wrong medication. Empty drug containers should be returned to parents.

Transportation from EC Locations and Emergency Medical Treatment by EC Employees

For a child's non-life-threatening medical emergencies, EC personnel should request transportation by the child's parents. However, if parents cannot transport the child, or in a more severe emergency, EC administrators should call an ambulance. In life-threatening emergencies that preclude waiting for an ambulance, EC administrators must designate the vehicle and responsible employee for transporting the child to the hospital; this information should be posted in the facility's emergency procedures. Administrators should keep the number of staff involved in emergency medical treatment to a minimum. Those employees they designate for involvement should be willing to take on the responsibility and should have current first aid training. The administrators can include a clause in these employees' job descriptions providing for their transporting children in the event of an emergency. The EC facility may also pay for additional or separate liability insurance coverage of the employees they designate as responsible for providing necessary emergency medical treatment.

Child Custody Issues Involving EC Facilities

EC facilities are affected by two types of issues involving child custody: (1) Parents are pursuing legal and/or physical custody of the child but they are not living together; and (2) State authorities have removed a child from the parents' legal and physical custody. Parents frequently demand the right to visit with and/or take the child home on occasion. Two types of custody are: legal custody, defined as an individual's or agency's right to make decisions on a child's behalf regarding the child's place of residence, medical treatment, and education; and physical custody, defined as an individual's or agency's right and responsibility to provide a child with immediate care, and a household or care facility for the present and immediate future. Physical custody does not include all of the rights of full legal custody. It is serious for a child to be in the middle of a custody battle between divorcing parents or between parents and foster parents; therefore EC facilities need the most concise, clear-cut guidelines possible.

Emergency Medical Treatment and First Aid Recommendations

EC programs and preschools must write specific, detailed procedures regarding emergency treatment and keep these on file. Children's parents, EC administrators, and EC staff need to be informed regarding what will occur in the event of a child's serious illness or injury. EC settings must also keep written, signed parental consent forms on file, as well as parent contact information, parental physician and hospital preferences, and health insurance information. EC staff should have current, regularly updated first aid training. First aid equipment should be stored in locations accessible to personnel, who should be frequently reminded of these locations. Lists of each staff member's first aid responsibilities and training should be posted, also accessibly. Licensing regulations require EC facilities to notify parents of emergencies; not doing so is subject to legal action. In non-life-threatening emergencies, staff should ask parents to furnish transportation and medical treatment. For grave emergencies, parental consent forms should be filed and updated semi-annually, including physician and hospital names, ambulance service, and other transportation procedures.

Non-Emergency Medical Illnesses

EC programs must keep procedures for, and reports on, non-emergency medical treatment of children on file just as they do for emergency procedures and reporting. Staff must contact and notify a sick child's parents, who decide if the child should leave the center/preschool. If so, parents should transport their child. Parental consent forms should authorize a doctor or nurse to provide routine medical treatment. EC centers/preschools should have sick children wait to be picked up in a location that is separate from other children and activities, but closely supervised by staff. For children with allergies, diabetes, and other chronic medical conditions, EC centers/preschools should not only keep this information on file in records, but also post it accessibly at all times for staff reference. Instructions for any special treatment should be included. For any health impairment(s) a child has that could potentially involve emergency treatment, directions for staff should be visibly posted, including specific employees designated to administer treatment. This protects children from harm and caregivers/educators from legal liability.

Custody Status

It is recommended that during a child's enrollment, EC programs procure a signed, dated document clarifying the child's custody status, including names, contact information, and relationships of all individuals authorized to pick up the child. Copies of any separation agreement/court decree should also be filed. Any time EC staff do not recognize an individual coming to pick up a child, they should ask the person to produce photo identification, which they should closely inspect. EC program administrators cannot make decisions regarding who has legal or physical custody of a child they serve. When a parent or other adult enrolls a child in an EC program, that adult is asked to list other persons to be contacted in the event of an emergency. EC administrators are advised to present all parents/guardians with a statement that the EC center will only release their child to someone the enrolling parent/adult listed on the emergency form as authorized to pick up the child.

Picking Up Children

Non-Custodial or Non-Authorized Adults Attempting to Pick Up Children

EC centers should always have up-to-date documentation on file of a child's custodial arrangements, signed and dated by the enrolling adult. If an adult not authorized to pick up the child attempts to do so, an EC administrator should inform that adult of the center's policies and procedures regarding custody. They may even show the unauthorized adult their copy of the custodial court order if needed. If the unauthorized adult then departs, the administrator must notify the enrolling adult of the incident; file a written report of it; meet with the custodial adult to clarify custody arrangements anew; document this meeting, including its date and signatures; and file the document in the child's record. If the unauthorized adult refuses to leave and makes a scene or threatens/displays violence, the EC administrator should call the police if needed. The EC center's having a procedure in place for protecting children against emotionally upsetting scenes and/or violent adult behavior is crucial to the children's safety and well-being.

Legal Responsibilities When Children Are Not Picked Up Timely

If a child is not picked up on time from an EC center at the end of its defined day, the EC center has the legal responsibility for the child's welfare as long as the child is on the premises. In the event that a child is left at the EC center for a long time and the parent/authorized adult has not notified the center why and/or when the child will be picked up, EC personnel are advised that keeping the child at the center is less likely to incur legal liability than for the child to stay at an EC staff member's home, for example. If the child has to be removed, it is important for EC staff to inform the police of this and where they are taking the child. If parents are chronically tardy picking up children, EC staff should review the child's information and/or inquire further of parents to ascertain reasons and possible solutions because they are legally responsible for reporting suspected child neglect.

Praxis Practice Test

1. According to the Assistive Technology Act, assistive devices are:

    a. Electronic devices that support learning such as computers, calculators, student responders, electronic self-teaching books and electronic reading devices.

    b. Any mechanical, electrical or electronic device that helps teachers streamline efficiency.

    c. Any device that could help a disabled student in school or life functions.

    d. Experimental, high-tech teaching tools that teachers can obtain by participating in one of 67 government funded research projects.

2. A seventh grader with mild intellectual disabilities is having considerable trouble with algebra. His stepfather is trying to help, but the more he drills the girl, the less she seems to understand. The teacher suggests:

    a. He continues drilling and enhances with pop quizzes. It may take the student longer to understand algebraic terms, expressions and equations, but with hard work she will eventually learn them.

    b. He calls a moratorium on at-home algebra work. The student is becoming less willing to work at school and the teacher is concerned she is losing confidence due to failure at home.

    c. He continues drilling but breaks the study sessions into no more than 3 five-minute periods per day.

    d. He substitutes fun activities for math drills. Incorporating algebra blocks, math games, and applications of algebra to real-life situations will make math more fun and more relevant.

3. Augmentative and Alternative Communication (AAC) devices, forearm crutches and a head pointer are assistive devices that might be used by a student with:

    a. Severe intellectual disabilities.

    b. Cerebral palsy.

    c. Tourette syndrome.

    d. Minor skeletal birth defects.

4. A four-year-old child has difficulty sorting plastic cubes, circles and triangles by color and shape, doesn't recognize patterns or groups and doesn't understand the relationship between little/big, tall/short, many/few. The child enjoys counting, but does not say the numbers in proper order nor recognize the meaning of different numbers. This child most likely:

    a. Is exhibiting signs of intellectual disabilities.

    b. Is developing within an acceptable range.

    c. Has dysgraphia.

    d. Has dyscalculia.

5. Response to Intervention (RTI) is:

    a. Parents, classroom teacher, special education teacher and other caring persons stage an intervention to express how a student's socially unacceptable behavior upsets them.

    b. An opportunity for a student to openly and freely respond to specific interventions without fear of reprimand.

    c. A strategy for diagnosing learning disabilities in which a student receives research-supported interventions to correct an academic delay. If the interventions do not result in considerable improvement, the failure to respond suggests causal learning disabilities.

    d. A formal complaint lodged by a parent or guardian in response to what they consider an intrusion by a teacher into private matters.

- 143 -

6. Sixth graders Alfie and Honesty ride the same bus. Honesty constantly teases Alfie. Alfie is embarrassed because he believes she is berating him. The bus driver told their teacher it was possible that Honesty is actually interested in Alfie, but doesn't express it well. The best form of conflict resolution would be for the teacher to:

a. Take Honesty aside and explain boys don't like overly aggressive girls.
b. Take Honesty aside and teach her less embarrassing methods of getting a boy's attention.
c. Explain to Alfie that Honesty probably teases him because she likes him and he should take it as a compliment.
d. Suggest to Alfie that if he is disturbed by Honesty's teasing, he have a calm, assertive conversation with her and tell her he doesn't like it and insist she stop.

7. When transitioning from one subject to another and when she becomes anxious, a student always taps her front tooth 5 times then opens and closes her eyes 11 times before leaving her desk. The child most likely has:

a. Repetitive Disorder
b. Obsessive Compulsive Disorder
c. Anxiety Disorder
d. Depression

8. By law, a child with a disability is defined as one with:

a. Intellectual disabilities, hearing, speech, language, visual, orthopedic or other health impairments, emotional disturbance, autism, brain injury caused by trauma or specific learning disabilities and needs special education and related services.
b. Intellectual disabilities, emotional disturbance, autism, brain injury caused by trauma or specific learning disabilities who needs special education and related services.
c. A child who is unable to reach the same academic goals as his peers, regardless of cause, and needs special education and related services.
d. The term "disability" is no longer used. The correct term is "other ability".

9. Which classroom environment is most likely to support a student with ADHD?

a. Students with ADHD become bored easily so a classroom with distinct areas for a multitude of activities will stimulate her. When she loses interest in one area, she can move to the next and continue learning.
b. Students with ADHD are highly aggressive and easily fall into depression. The teacher needs to provide a learning environment in which sharp objects such as scissors, tacks or sharpened pencils are eliminated. This ensures greater safety for both student and teacher.
c. Students with ADHD are highly creative. A room with brightly colored mobiles, a multitude of visual and physical textures (such as striped rugs and fuzzy pillows) and plenty of art-based games will stimulate and encourage learning.
d. Students with ADHD are extremely sensitive to distractions. A learning environment in which visual and audio distractions have been eliminated is best. Low lighting, few posters and a clean whiteboard help the student focus.

10. A resource teacher notices one of her students has made the same reading error numerous times the past few days. She decides the student wrongly believes that 'ou' is always pronounced as it is in the word *through.* She corrects this misunderstanding by showing the student word families containing words like *though, ought, ground.* This strategy is called:

    a. Corrective feedback
    b. Positive reinforcement
    c. Consistent repetition
    d. Corrective support

11. A kindergarten teacher has a new student who will not make eye contact with anyone so she doesn't appear to be listening. She often rocks back and forth and does not stop when asked or give any indication she has heard. She avoids physical contact. Sometimes the teacher must take her arm to guide her from one place to another. Occasionally the student erupts, howling in terror and fury. The most likely diagnosis is:

    a. Asperger's Syndrome
    b. Obsessive-Compulsive Disorder
    c. Autism
    d. Antisocial Psychosis

12. A special education teacher shows parents of a dyslexic child a study that examined brain scans of dyslexic and non-dyslexic readers. The study demonstrated that dyslexics use (the) _____ side(s) of their brains while non-dyslexics use (the) _____ side.

    a. Both, the left.
    b. Both, the right.
    c. Left, right.
    d. Right, left.

13. A student with _____ has a great deal of difficulty with the mechanical act of writing. She drops her pencil, cannot form legible letters and cannot decode what she has written.

    a. A nonverbal learning disorder
    b. Dyslexia
    c. Dyspraxia
    d. Dysgraphia

14. A resource room teacher has a middle school student recently diagnosed with depression. The student has been put on an antidepressant. The teacher knows the student may develop certain transitory reactions to the medication. One reaction might be:

    a. Extreme sleepiness.
    b. Increased, persistent thirst.
    c. Anxiety, coupled with an urge to verbalize a continuous inner dialogue.
    d. Inappropriate anger.

15. Reading comprehension should be evaluated:

a. Every two months using various informal assessments. Done more than twice a year, assessments place undue stress on both student and teacher and do not indicate enough change to be worth it.

b. With a combination of informal and formal assessments including: standardized testing, awareness of grades, systematically charted data over a period of time and teacher notes.

c. With bi-weekly self-assessment rubrics to keep the student aware of his progress.

d. By testing the student before reading a particular text to determine which vocabulary words he already knows and can correctly use.

16. A diabetic first grader is very pale, trembling and covered in a fine sweat. The teacher attempts to talk to the child, but the girl's response is confused and she seems highly irritable She is most likely experiencing:

a. Diabetic hypoglycemia.

b. Lack of sleep.

c. Hunger.

d. Diabetic hyperglycemia.

17. An intellectually disabled teen has been offered a job by an elderly neighbor. The neighbor wants the teen to work alongside her in the garden twice a week. They will plant seeds, transplant larger plants, weed, lay mulch, water and fertilize. Later in the season, they will cut flowers and arrange bouquets, pick produce and sell them at the neighbor's roadside stand. The neighbor, the teen's mother and special education teacher meet to discuss the proposal. The plan is:

a. Tentatively accepted. Because the teen is excited about having a job, her mother and teacher reluctantly agree. They both know the girl is likely to lose interest quickly and caution the neighbor that if she truly needs help she may want to look elsewhere. However, no one wants to disappoint the girl and all decide the experience will be good for her.

b. Rejected. Despite the teen's insistence she can manage these tasks, her mother and teacher believe she cannot. They fear trying will set her up for failure.

c. Rejected. The teacher and her mother are very uncomfortable with the neighbor's offer. They suspect the elderly woman is simply lonely or may be a predator who has selected an intellectually disabled victim because such children are particularly vulnerable.

d. Enthusiastically accepted. The adults discuss a background check and the possibility the teen might discover gardening is not for her and want to quit. However, this is most likely to happen early in her employment, giving the neighbor sufficient time to find another helper.

18. Dr. Gee reads the following sentence to a group of 5th graders: "The turquoise sky is reflected in the still lake. Fat white clouds floated on the lake's surface as though the water was really another sky. It was such a beautiful day. The students were to write the word "beautiful" in the blank. One student wrote 'pretty' instead. This suggests:

a. The student doesn't know the meaning of the word 'beautiful'.

b. The student is highly creative and believes he can substitute a word with a similar meaning.

c. The student did not know how to spell 'beautiful'.

d. The student did not hear what the teacher said. He heard 'pretty' instead of 'beautiful.'

19. Autism Spectrum Disorder is also known as:

   a. Pervasive Spectrum Disorder
   b. Asperger's Syndrome
   c. Variable Developmental Disorder
   d. Artistic Continuum Syndrome

20. A third grade boy is new to the school. His teacher has noticed he happily plays with other children, redirects his attention without upset when another child rejects his offer to play and doesn't mind playing on his own. However, the boy doesn't pay attention when academic instruction is given. He continues to speak with other children, draws, or distracts himself. The teacher reminds him repeatedly to listen and follow instruction. When he does not, she moves him to a quiet desk away from the others. When isolated, the boy puts his head on the desk and weeps uncontrollably, or stares at a fixed spot and repeats to himself, "I hate myself, I hate myself. I should be dead." During these episodes, the teacher cannot break through to the student; his disconnection seems complete. The teacher has requested a conference with his parents, but they do not speak English and have not responded to her offer of a translator. The teacher should:

   a. Establish a consistent set of expectations for the child. He needs to understand there are appropriate times for play and for learning.
   b. Isolate the boy first thing. His behavior suggests manipulation. By third grade children fully understand they are expected to pay attention when the teacher is speaking. The boy is punishing the teacher with tears and repetitive self-hate, consciously or unconsciously attempting to make the teacher feel guilty.
   c. Immediately refer him to the counselor. The boy is exhibiting serious emotional distress suggesting abuse or neglect at home or outside of school.
   d. Recognize the child's highly sensitive nature; offer comfort when he acts out self-loathing. Carefully explain why he must learn to pay attention so he will use reason instead of emotion when making future choices.

21. A student with Asperger's Syndrome is most likely to display which set of behaviors?

   a. He is confrontational, argumentative and inflexible.
   b. He is fearful, shy and highly anxious.
   c. He is socially distant, focused on certain subjects to the point of obsession and inflexible.
   d. He is flighty, tearful and exhibits repetitive, ritualized behavior.

22. A special education teacher working with a group of third graders is about to begin a unit on birds. She asks the children what they know about birds. They tell her birds fly, lay eggs and build nests. She asks the students to draw a picture of a bird family. Some children draw birds in flight; one draws a mother bird with a nest of babies; another draws an egg with the baby bird inside the egg. These pre-reading activities are useful because:

   a. They help assess prior knowledge.
   b. They establish a framework in which to integrate the new information.
   c. They create a sense of excitement and curiosity.
   d. All of the above.

23. Verbal dyspraxia is:

   a. Trouble with the physical act of writing.
   b. Refusal to speak.
   c. Misplacing letters within words.
   d. A motor skill development disorder which includes inconsistent speech errors.

24. A resource room teacher has a small group of second and third graders who are struggling with reading comprehension. A useful strategy would be to:

    a. Present a list of vocabulary words before students read a particular text.

    b. Ask students to create a play about the story.

    c. Read a story aloud. Ask students to raise their hands when they hear an unfamiliar word.

    d. Have each child keep a book of new vocabulary words. Whenever an unfamiliar word is seen or heard the student should enter the word in her personal dictionary.

25. Tourette syndrome is characterized by:

    a. Facial twitches, grunts, inappropriate words and body spasms.

    b. Inappropriate words, aggressive behavior and tearful episodes.

    c. Facial twitches, grunts, extreme shyness and refusal to make eye contact.

    d. Refusal to make eye contact, rocking, spinning of objects and ritualized behavior.

26. A second grader finds it impossible to remain in her seat. She wanders around the room, sprawls on the floor and rolls back and forth when asked to do math problems and jumps up and down when waiting in line. When the teacher tells her to sit down, she rolls her eyes in apparent disgust and looks to other students for support. When she finds a student looking back, she laughs and makes a face. The teacher has noticed when a reward is attached to good behavior; the girl is consistently able to control her actions for long periods of time. But when reprimanded without the promise of a reward, she becomes angry, tearful and pouts. This child is most likely manifesting:

    a. Tourette's Syndrome

    b. Attention Deficit Hyperactivity Disorder

    c. Lack of sufficiently developed behavior and social skills

    d. Psychosis

27. ADHD refers to:

    a. Attention Deficit Hyperactivity Disorder

    b. Anxiety/ Depression Hyperactivity Disorder

    c. Aggression-Depression Hyperactivity Disorder

    d. Atkinson, Draper and Hutchinson Disability

28. Rate, accuracy and prosody are elements of:

    a. Reading fluency

    b. Reading comprehension

    c. Math fluency

    d. Algebraic function

29. When a diabetic student goes into insulin shock, she should:

    a. Call her parents to come get her.

    b. Drink a soda or eat some hard candy.

    c. Drink a high-protein shake.

    d. Put her head on the desk and wait for the episode to pass.

30. Strategies to increase reading fluency for English Language Learners include:

    a. Tape-assisted reading.

    b. Reading aloud while students follow along in their books.

    c. Asking parents to read with the child each evening.

    d. A and B.

31. The Individuals with Disabilities Education Act (IDEA) requires that members of an IEP team include:

a. All teachers involved with the student, the parent(s) or guardian and the student (if appropriate).
b. The classroom teacher, a special education teacher, the parent(s) or guardian, a representative of the local education agency knowledgeable about specialized instruction, someone to interpret instructional implications, the student (if appropriate) and other people invited by the parents or the school.
c. The classroom teacher, a special education teacher, the principal or AP and the parent(s) or guardian.
d. All teachers involved with the student, the principal or AP, the parent(s) or guardian and the student (if appropriate).

32. At the beginning of each month, a student reads a page or two from a book he hasn't seen before. The resource teacher notes the total number of words in the section and the number of times the student leaves out or misreads a word. If the student reads with more than a 10% error rate, he is:

a. Reading with full comprehension.
b. Probably bored and his attention is wandering.
c. Reading at a frustration level.
d. Missing contextual clues.

33. A Cloze test evaluates a student's:

a. Reading fluency
b. Understanding of context and vocabulary
c. Phonemic skills
d. Ability to apply the Alphabetic Principle to previously unknown material.

34. A Kindergarten teacher is showing students the written alphabet. The teacher pronounces a phoneme and one student points to it on the alphabet chart. The teacher is presenting:

a. Letter-sound correspondence
b. Rote memorization
c. Predictive Analysis
d. Segmentation

35. A resource teacher wants to design a lesson that will help first and second graders learn sight words so all the students can read their lists. She should teach them how to:

a. Divide sight words into syllables. Considering one syllable at a time provides a sense of control and increases confidence.
b. Recognize word families. Organizing similar words allows patterns to emerge.
c. Sound out the words by vocalizing each letter. Using this approach, students will be able to sound out any sight word.
d. Memorize their lists by using techniques such as songs, mnemonic devices and other fun activities. By definition, sight words cannot be decoded but must be recognized on sight.

36. Phonological awareness activities are:

    a. Oral
    b. Visual
    c. Both A and B.
    d. Semantically based.

37. It is important to teach life skills to developmentally delayed students to prepare them for life after school. Which of the following skills sets should these students be taught?

    a. Count money, plan meals, grocery shop, recognize safety concerns.
    b. Count money, order delivery meals, dating skills, how to drive.
    c. How to drive, style and hygiene tips, social strategies, dating skills.
    d. Stock market investment, hairdressing, house painting, pet care.

38. A special education teacher has done intervention with an eighth grade student with a reading disability. The student can now successfully use tactics to understand the meanings of unfamiliar words, knows words such as *crucial, criticism* and *witness* have multiple meanings and considers what she already knows to figure out a word's meaning. These features of effective reading belong to which category?

    a. Word recognition
    b. Vocabulary
    c. Content
    d. Comprehension

39. Emergent writers understand letters represent sounds, words begin with a sound that can be written as a letter and writing is a way one person captures an idea another person will read. Emergent writers pass through the following stages:

    a. Scripting the end-sound to a word (KT=cat); leaving space between words; writing from the top left to the top right and from top to bottom of the page.
    b. Scripting the end-sound to a word (KT=cat); writing from the top left to the top right and from top to bottom of the page; separating the words from one another with a space in between.
    c. Leaving space between the initial letters that represent words; writing from the top left to the top right and from top to bottom of the page; scripting the final sound of each word and the initial sound (KT=cat).
    d. Drawing a picture beside each of the initial sounds to represent the entire word; scripting the end-sound to a word (KT=cat); scripting the interior sounds that compose the entire word (KAT=cat).

40. As defined by the Individuals with Disabilities Education Act (IDEA), Secondary Transition is a synchronized group of activities that are:

    a. Results-oriented and include post-school activities, vocational education, employment support and adult services and considers the individual's strengths, preferences and interests.
    b. Socially structured and consider the individual's strengths, preferences and interests and vocational requirements.
    c. Designed to support vocational training, results-oriented and have a strong social component.
    d. Selected by the parent(s) or guardian because the student cannot choose for himself.

41. A resource teacher can facilitate the greatest achievement in emergent writers who are scripting initial and final sounds by:

a. Suggesting they write a book to build confidence, teach sequencing, and encourage them to deeply explore ideas.
b. Suggesting they read their stories to other students.
c. Inviting a reporter to write about her emergent writers.
d. Inviting parents or guardians for a tea party at which the children will read their stories aloud.

42. At what point should the teacher in the above example offer the children picture books and ask them to read to her?

a. When the children are able to script initial sounds, end sounds and interior sounds. She should wait until this point to avoid frustration.
b. After the teacher has read the picture books several times, the children can 'practice reading' to her, while learning to handle books, turn pages, and pay attention to context clues.
c. After the children have learned the sight words.
d. From the first day of school. Picture walks help young readers understand books are arranged sequentially. Pictures provide narrative coherence and contextual clues. Holding a book and turning pages also gives young readers a familiarity with them.

43. How can a teacher teach spelling effectively?

a. Students who have an understanding of letter-sound association do not need to be taught to spell. If they can say a word, they can spell it.
b. Students who have an understanding of letter-sound association and can identify syllables and recognize when the base word has a Latin, Greek or Indo-European ancestry don't need to be taught to spell. They can deduce what is most likely the correct spelling using a combination of these strategies. A teacher who posts charts organizing words into their ancestor families, phonemic units and word-sound families is efficiently teaching spelling. The rest is up to the student.
c. Students who spell poorly will be at a disadvantage for the rest of their lives. It is essential students spend at least 15 minutes a day drilling spelling words until they know them forward and backward. The teacher should alternate between students individually writing a new word 25 times and the entire class chanting the words.
d. Students should be taught writing is a process. By applying spelling patterns found in word families, the spelling of many words can be deduced.

44. A special education teacher gives a struggling reader a story with key words missing:

The children were hungry. They went into the _____. They found bread, peanut _____ and jelly in the cupboard. They made _____. They __ _ the sandwiches. Then they were not _____ anymore.

The student is able to complete the sentences by paying attention to:

a. Syntax. Word order can provide enough hints that a reader can predict what happens next.
b. Pretext. By previewing the story, the student can determine the missing words.
c. Context. By considering other words in the story, the student can deduce the missing words.
d. Sequencing. By ordering the ideas, the student can determine the missing words.

45. Collaborative Strategic Reading (CSR) depends upon which two practices?

 a. Cooperative learning and reading comprehension.
 b. Reading and metacognition.
 c. Reading comprehension and metacognition.
 d. Cooperative learning and metacognition.

46. Before being assigned to a special education classroom, a student must:

 a. Agree to the reassignment.
 b. Have an Individualized Education Plan developed.
 c. Have an Independent Education Policy developed.
 d. Be seen by an educational psychologist to confirm her diagnosis.

47. When asked a question, the new student answers with as few words as possible. He prefers to draw airplanes over and over again rather than play with the other children. The classroom teacher isn't sure how to help the child. The special education teacher suggests the teacher:

 a. Leave the child alone. He is likely adjusting to the new situation and will come out of his shell soon enough.
 b. Remind other children in the class to include the new student.
 c. Observe the child over the course of a week or two. Draw him into conversation to determine if vocabulary is limited. Note how the child interacts with others in the class. Does he initiate conversation? If another child initiates, does he respond?
 d. Refer him to the school counselor immediately. It is likely the child is suffering from serious problems at home.

48. A special education teacher feels some of his strategies aren't effective. He asks a specialist to help him improve. The specialist suggests he:

 a. Begin a journal in which he considers strategies he has used. Which seemed to work? Which didn't, and why?
 b. Meet with the specialist to discuss the teacher's goals.
 c. Permit the specialist to drop into his classroom unannounced to observe. This will prevent the teacher from unconsciously over-preparing.
 d. Set up a video camera and record several student sessions to review. They can effectively collaborate at that time.

49. An eighth grade student is able to decode many words and has a borderline/acceptable vocabulary, but his reading comprehension is quite low. He can be helped with intervention offering:

 a. Strategies to increase comprehension and build vocabulary.
 b. Strategies to increase comprehension and learn to identify syntax.
 c. Strategies to improve understanding of both content and context.
 d. Strategies to develop vocabulary and improve understanding of both content and context.

50. Research indicates oral language competency in emergent readers is essential because:

 a. It enhances students' phonemic awareness and increases vocabulary.
 b. The more verbally expressive emergent readers are, the more confident they become. These students will embrace both academic and independent reading levels.
 c. Strong oral language skills invite students to consider a plethora of ideas. The more they ask, the richer their background knowledge.
 d. It demonstrates to students their ideas are important and worth sharing.

51. A teacher has shown a mentally challenged student a website that integrates music and video clips with a variety of educational games about a topic the student has shown interest in. The student is initially intimidated and fears interacting with the program might result in her breaking the computer. The teacher reassures her she cannot harm the machine and shows the girl how to manipulate the mouse and keyboard. The teacher reminds the student what she already knows about the subject. As the student becomes more comfortable with the mouse, she focuses on the images and sounds, at times responding to the program conversationally, telling it what she knows about dinosaurs. The teacher is using the computer along with which teaching strategy?

    a. Modular instruction.
    b. Scaffolding.
    c. Linking.
    d. Transmutation.

52. A student has been identified with a cluster of learning disabilities. She will be joining a special education classroom. She is understandably nervous about making the change to a different teacher and group of classmates. In order to help her make the transition, the child should:

    a. Have a party to which her new classmates are invited along with some friends from the fifth-grade class she is leaving.
    b. Prepare to begin classes with her new teacher the next day. Once the decision has been made, nothing will be gained by postponing the inevitable.
    c. Be brave and understand life will be full of transitions. This is an opportunity to learn new skills that will serve her well in the future.
    d. Visit the classroom, meet the teacher and her new classmates and be given the opportunity to ask questions about the change she is about to make.

53. A student is taking a reading test in which several words have been replaced with blanks. Below each blank is a series of three possible answers. The student chooses the right answer from each set. The student is taking:

    a. A Cloze test, which is a type of Maze test.
    b. A Maze test, which is a type of Cloze test.
    c. A multiple-choice quiz.
    d. A vocabulary test incorporating a type of multiple-choice quiz.

54. A teacher has a student with dyscalculia who has trouble organizing addition and subtraction problems on paper. She can best help him by:

    a. Encouraging memorization of number families. Committing them to memory is the only way.
    b. Demonstrating a problem in different ways. Write a problem on the board: 11 - 3. Gather 11 books and take 3 of them away. Draw 11 x's on the board and erase 3.
    c. Use graph paper to help him organize. Show him how to write the problems, keeping each number in a box aligned with other numbers.
    d. Make a game of addition and subtraction problems. Divide the class into groups and let them compete to see which group can solve the most problems.

55. A child has been losing strength in her muscles over a period of time. The loss is very gradual, but the teacher is concerned and would like the child to see a doctor. The possible diagnosis is:

    a. Cerebral Palsy
    b. Muscular Dystrophy
    c. Muscular Sclerosis
    d. Spastic Muscular and Nerve Disorder

56. A middle school student is preparing to transition from a self-contained special education classroom to a general education classroom. This transition should be made:

a. With proper preparation. A student this age needs to acclimate socially and can best do so with the same group of students in every class.

b. At the beginning of the next school year so the student doesn't have a stigma when joining the new group.

c. One class at a time with the special education teacher supervising academic and social progress.

d. By transitioning into classes he is most interested in because he is most likely to succeed with subjects he cares about. The confidence he gains from academic success will support him as he transitions into classes he's less interested in.

57. The four required activities described by the Assistive Technology Act (AT ACT) of 1998 are a public awareness program, coordinating activities among state agencies, technical assistance and training and

a. Specialized training for special education teachers and support.

b. Outreach to underrepresented religious groups, ethnicities and urban populations.

c. Outreach to underrepresented and rural populations.

d. New technologies training on a quarterly basis for special education teachers and support.

58. Behavior problems in special education students are most effectively handled with:

a. Zero tolerance.

b. Positive Behavioral Support (PBS)

c. Acceptance and tolerance

d. Positive Behavioral Control (PBC)

59. A teacher suspects one of her kindergarteners has a learning disability in math. Why would the teacher suggest intervention to the child's concerned parents rather than assessment as the first step?

a. She wouldn't; assessment should precede intervention.

b. She wouldn't; kindergarteners develop new skills at radically different rates. Suggesting either intervention or assessment at this point is premature. The teacher would more likely observe the child over a three month period to note her development before including the parents about her concern.

c. Assessing a young child for learning disabilities often leads to an incorrect conclusion because a student must be taught the subject before it's possible to assess her understanding of it. Intervention teaches the child specific skills to correct her misconceptions. If the intervention fails, assessment is the next step.

d. Assessment at this stage is unnecessary and wastes time and money. Since an assessment that resulted in a diagnosis of a learning disability would recommend

60. IDEA requires that students identified with learning disabilities or other special needs be educated in _____ learning environment appropriate for their needs.

a. The safest

b. The least restrictive

c. The most appropriate

d. The most desirable

61. Howard Gardner's theory of Multiple Intelligences organizes learners into what types of intelligences?

a. Verbal linguistic, mathematical, musically attuned, visual special, body embraced, interpersonal, naturalistic, existential.
b. Emphatic, recessive, aggressive, assertive, dogmatic, apologetic, determined, elusive.
c. Verbal linguistic, mathematical logical, musical, visual spatial, body kinesthetic, interpersonal, naturalistic, existential.
d. Dramatic, musical, verbal, mathematical, dance-oriented, sports-oriented, scientific, socially concerned.

62. Lead teaching, learning centers / learning stations, resource services, team teaching and consultation are all used in:

a. Innovative teaching
b. Strategic teaching
c. Collaborative teaching
d. Self-contained classrooms

63. A special education teacher has a child who doesn't understand the relationship between ones, tens and hundreds. He is a Bodily Kinesthetic learner. The teacher should:

a. Draw a colorful chart and put the numbers in the appropriate columns.
b. Teach him how an abacus works.
c. Create a song and dance about the numbers families.
d. Show him the relationship using Monopoly money.

64. Identifying specific skills deficient in special education math students is important so the teacher can decide how to remediate. Problems can include an inability to recall math facts, understand mathematical operations and formulas and how rules are used in solving problems or focusing on attention to details. Such students might be:

a. Able to solve math problems when they haven't been taught an operation required to do so.
b. Unable to locate errors in their own work.
c. Able to solve math problems in another language.
d. Unable to count higher than 100.

65. What steps are taken to identify specific skill deficits in math?

a. Standardized assessment tests, examining areas of weakness in student work to determine patterns, teacher observations, interviews with student.
b. Standardized assessment tests, examining areas of weakness in student work to determine patterns, teacher observations, interviews with parent(s).
c. Teacher observations coupled with examining areas of weakness in student work are sufficient.
d. None of the above.

66. A fifth-grade lead teacher and the special education teacher have scheduled a parent conference to discuss the behavior problems of the student. They anticipate the boy's mother will be anxious and defensive as she has been at previous conferences. The best approach for the teachers to take is to:

a. Draw the parent out about issues in her own life so that she will feel reassured and trusting. Point out possible connections between the mother's emotions about her own life and her son's behaviors and reactions.

b. Be very firm with the mother, explain the penalties and disciplines her son can expect if the behavior continues and stress neither the parent nor the child has input regarding punishment.

c. Stress the teachers will not do anything without the parent's approval since they do not want to face liability issues.

d. Begin by welcoming the mother and telling her about her son's academic improvements. Stress the teachers, the mother and the child share goals for the student's success. Explain the behavior problems and ask if the mother has any insights to share.

67. At the beginning of the week, a special education teacher asked a group of students to generate a list of verbs that make visual or sound pictures. She suggests students think of verbs that mean ways of walking, talking, eating, sitting and playing. The students spend the remainder of the week compiling the list. They notice interesting verbs as they read books, remark on less common verbs they hear in conversation or on television and locate interesting verbs in signs, magazines and other printed materials. One child begins to draw pictures to illustrate some of the verbs. Two children collaborate to create a play in which they demonstrate some of the verbs in a dance. A boy writes a song incorporating the list of verbs. The project is extremely successful. At the end of the week the students have created the following list:

TIPTOE, SCOOT, MUMBLE, MUNCH, LEAP, SPIN, DIVE, POUNCE, GLIDE, SLITHER, MOAN, WHISPER, GRUMBLE, NIBBLE, SHRILL, HOLLER, PERCH, LEAN, STOMP, MARCH, GIGGLE, HOP, STRUT, SLOUCH, GULP, HOWL, WHINE, SLURP, CROUCH, DRIBBLE, DROOL, HOOT, YELP, YOWL, GROWL, WHISTLE, SHRIEK, SNICKER, INSULT, COMPLIMENT, PLEAD, BARK, WIGGLE, TWIST, SLINK, TODDLE, TRUDGE, WANDER, STROLL.

The teacher's goal is to:

a. Enhance students' understanding of theme by encouraging them to make connections between categories of verbs.

b. Enhance students' vocabulary by encouraging them to find examples in the world around them.

c. Enhance students' understanding of context by encouraging them to explore verbs for contextual clues.

d. Enhance students' sense of curiosity by directing their attention to a number of different resources they may not have considered.

68. In the previous example, how could the teacher extend the lesson and apply it across the curriculum?

a. Create a Word Wall with the words the students collected.

b. Have students work on a class dictionary, putting the words in alphabetical order and explaining what they mean.

c. Ask students to create a chart noting which verbs have 1, 2 or 3 syllables, which verbs contain double letters, which verbs are also nouns and which verbs have common word-endings.

d. All of the above.

69. A classroom teacher has a student with learning disabilities that affect her ability to do math. The teacher consults with the special education teacher and decides she will modify the work the child is given by reducing the number of problems, let her have extra time to finish, and provide her with a multiplication chart. The teacher is:

a. Giving the student an unfair advantage. Letting her have extra time should be sufficient.
b. Giving the student an unfair advantage. Providing a multiplication chart should be sufficient. With that, she should get her work done on time.
c. Making appropriate modifications. Each child is different. In this case, she consulted with the special education teacher and concluded the child needs multiple supports.
d. Modifying the student's work because it makes it easier on the teacher. There is less to explain and less to grade.

70. Explain the philosophy of inclusion.

a. All children should be included in decisions affecting their education.
b. Children with special needs are as much a part of the educational community as any other child and necessary services that allow these students to participate in the learning community should be provided.
c. Parents are part of a child's learning community and should be included in academic decisions.
d. All teachers and support persons, including Para pros, translators and other assistants, should be allowed to participate in academic decisions.

71. The ADA is:

a. The Americans with Disabilities Act.
b. The Anti-Discrimination Act.
c. The American Diabetes Association.
d. The Alternatives to Discrimination Act.

72. A teacher working with students who have math disabilities has had success with a variety of multi-sensory techniques including:

a. Estimating, converting fractions, multiplication families, graphic organizers.
b. Graphic organizers, math textbooks, multi-step problems, converting fractions.
c. Memorizing tables, drawing graphs, converting fractions, charting information.
d. Power point presentations that include music, manipulatives, graphic organizers, clapping games.

73. The development of an IEP is a(n) _____ process.

a. Indirect.
b. Collaborative.
c. Mathematical.
d. Single.

74. From the age of 3 years to 5 years, a child's expressive vocabulary will usually:

a. Double
b. Increase by 25%
c. Increase by 50%
d. Triple

75. Which of the following is likely to be most disabling for a young child?
   a. Articulation errors
   b. Hearing loss
   c. Being of below average height
   d. Having slow dentition

Answers and Explanations

1. C: Any device that could help a disabled student in education or life functioning. The Assistive Technology Act of 1998 is the primary legislation regarding assistive technology for disabled students and adults. The act funds 56 state programs concerned with the assistive technology needs of individuals with disabilities. Assistive devices include wheelchairs, hearing aids, glare-reduction screens, Braille devices, voice-recognition software, screen magnifiers and a wealth of other tools.

2. D: He substitutes more enjoyable algebra activities for math drills. Incorporating manipulatives such as algebra blocks, math games and applications of algebra to real-life situations, will make math both more fun and more relevant. When both parent and child are enjoying the work, they will accomplish more in a shorter period of time and the child will feel happy and successful, which encourages her to embrace further learning opportunities.

3. B: Cerebral palsy. Cerebral palsy is an umbrella term that groups neurological childhood disorders that affect muscular control. It does not worsen over time and the cause is located in damaged areas of the brain that control muscle movement. Depending upon the severity of the disorder, a child with cerebral palsy might benefit from an AAC device to help in speaking, forearm crutches to assist in walking or a head pointer for a child whose best motor control is his head.

4. D: Dyscalculia. Dyscalculia defines a range of difficulties in math, such as the inability to understand numbers' meanings, measurements, patterns, mathematical terms and the application of mathematic principals. Early clues include a young child's inability to group items by size or color, recognize patterns or understand the meaning or order of numbers.

5. C: A strategy for diagnosing learning disabilities in which a student with an academic delay receives research-supported interventions to correct the delay. If the interventions do not result in considerable academic improvement, the failure to respond suggests causal learning disabilities.

6. D: Suggest to Alfie that if he is disturbed by Honesty's teasing, he might have a calm, assertive conversation with her in which he tells her he doesn't like it and insist she stop. By encouraging Alfie to act on his own, it shows him he has primary responsibility for taking care of himself. By offering social strategies, he learns a set of skills that will serve him throughout life. If Honesty continues to tease him, he can ask a teacher to step in, but doing so without his invitation is inappropriate.

7. B: Obsessive Compulsive Disorder (OCD). Children and adults with OCD typically engage in a series of highly ritualized behaviors that are rigidly performed when they feel stressed. Behaviors include tapping, snapping fingers, blinking, counting and so forth.

8. A: Intellectual disabilities, hearing, speech, language, visual, orthopedic or other health impairments, emotional disturbance, autism, brain injury caused by trauma, or specific learning disabilities who needs special education and related services. Children with one or more of these conditions are legally entitled to services and programs designed to help them achieve at the highest level of their ability.

9. D: Students with ADHD are extremely sensitive to distractions. A learning environment in which visual and audio distractions have been eliminated is best. Low lighting, few posters and a clean whiteboard will help minimize distractions.

10. A: Corrective feedback. Corrective feedback is offered to a student in order to explain why a particular error is, in fact, an error. Corrective feedback is specific; it locates where and how the student went astray so that similar errors can be avoided in the future.

11. C: Autism. Autistic children are typically very withdrawn, avoid eye contact and are not responsive to verbal or physical attempts to connect. Some autistic children fall into repetitive behaviors that are very difficult to arrest or prevent. These behaviors include rocking, spinning and handshaking.

12. A: Both, the left. Research using MRIs show dyslexics use both sides of their brains for activities such as reading, while non-dyslexics use only the left side.

13. D: Dysgraphia. Dysgraphic individuals cannot manage the physical act of writing. While many dysgraphics are highly intelligent and able to express themselves cogently, they have extreme difficulty holding a writing implement and shaping letters.

14. B: Increased, persistent thirst. Although there are a number of antidepressants available, most of them share the side effect of a dry, cottony mouth that lasts for a few weeks at the beginning. The student is likely to ask for water frequently because this type of thirst isn't easily quenched. The teacher and the student should understand this side effect will ease and disappear with time.

15. B: With a combination of informal and formal assessments including standardized testing, awareness of grades, systematically charted data over a period of time and teacher notes. Comprehension and vocabulary cannot be sufficiently assessed with occasional, brief studies. Continuous observation, high-stakes and standardized testing, attention to grades and closely tracking the outcomes of objective-linked assessments are interrelated tools that, when systematically organized, offer a solid understanding of students' strengths and weaknesses.

16. A: Diabetic hypoglycemia. Diabetic hypoglycemia, also known as insulin reaction, occurs when blood sugar falls to a very low level. It is important to treat it quickly or the diabetic could faint, in which case an injection of glucagon is administered.

17. D: Enthusiastically accepted. The adults discuss a background check and the possibility the teen might discover gardening is not for her and want to quit. However, this is most likely to occur early in her employment, giving the neighbor sufficient time to find another helper. The teacher is pleased because the girl will learn new skills through modeling and repetition. The mother is pleased because the experience will add to the girl's self-esteem as well as show her she is capable of learning. The elderly neighbor is pleased because she is both compassionate and truly needs help. The girl is delighted the neighbor recognizes her potential and sees her as valuable.

18. C: The student did not know how to spell 'beautiful'. It is doubtful the student heard "pretty" instead of beautiful since the two sound nothing alike. It is equally unlikely he doesn't know the meaning of the word 'beautiful' since his substitution, 'pretty', is a synonym for beautiful. It is likely this child is creative, but that alone wouldn't be sufficient reason to replace one word with another. The most logical answer is that he simply didn't know how to spell 'beautiful'. He does know that some words mean almost the same thing, and since he already knew how to spell 'pretty', he incorrectly believed a synonym would be acceptable.

19. A: Pervasive Spectrum Disorders (PSD) is another name for Autism Spectrum Disorders (ASD). PSD causes disabilities in language, thought, emotion and empathy. The most severe form of PSD is autistic disorder. A much less severe form is Asperger's Syndrome.

20. C: Immediately refer him to the counselor. The boy is exhibiting serious emotional distress suggesting either abuse or neglect at home or elsewhere. While his behavior may seem manipulative, the fact that the boy is unreachable once he's in the highly charged emotional state in which he repeats, "I hate myself" suggests emotional trauma. The fact the child is socialized with peers, playing with them when invited and not taking rejection personally, suggests his emotional distress may be caused by an adult who has convinced him he is unworthy. A trained counselor is the best choice.

21. C: He is socially distant, focused on certain subjects to the point of obsession and inflexible. Asperger Syndrome is a mild form of autism. Children with this disorder typically do interact with teachers, other adults and sometimes other children; however, the interaction is rather remote and without emotional expression. They are also very focused on subjects of great interest to the abandonment of all others. When asked to redirect focus, Asperger children often become emphatically obstinate, refusing to shift focus.

22. D: All of the above. This project gives the teacher the opportunity to evaluate what students already know, establishes a scaffold of accessible information to which the students can integrate new information and creates a sense of curiosity and excitement in the students, which encourages them to learn.

23. D: A motor skill development disorder which includes speech errors that don't clearly follow a pattern and so appear to be inconsistent. An example is a student who can pronounce /p/ when it is followed by a long i, as in pine, but not when followed by an ou diphthong, as in pout. Verbally dyspraxic individuals are unable to correctly place the tongue, lips and jaw for consistent sounds that can be organized into syllables. Dyspraxia appears to be a brain disorder in which the area that controls production of particular sounds is damaged.

24. B: Ask students to create a play about the story as the teacher reads aloud. This activity grounds the students in the story action as it is occurring. Acting it out insures understanding; otherwise, the students will most likely stop the teacher and ask for clarification. Furthermore, by acting it out, students are incorporating understanding physically. They will be more likely to retain the story and be able to comprehend the meanings incorporated in it.

25. A: Twitches, grunts, inappropriate words, body spasms. Children and adults with Tourette syndrome are rarely aggressive nor are they reluctant to make eye contact or otherwise engage others. Tourette syndrome is characterized by explosive sounds, sometimes in the form of inappropriate words, more often just as meaningless syllables; muscular twitches of the face or elsewhere in the body and the complete inability to control these spasms. Tourette sufferers often also suffer from Obsessive Compulsive Disorder.

26. C: Lack of sufficiently developed behavior and social skills. The child may or may not be hyperactive, but the fact that she can control her behavior for extended periods if a reward is involved suggests the child is overly indulged outside of class. In addition, she appears to act out in an effort to seek peer admiration; this excludes the possibility of Tourette syndrome and Attention Deficit Hyperactivity Disorder. In the first case, she would be unlikely to seek approval. In the second, she would be unlikely to be able to control herself under certain circumstances. There is nothing in her behavior to suggest psychosis.

27. A: Attention Deficit Hyperactivity Disorder. Children with ADHD exhibit a myriad of symptoms including: disorganization, easily distracted and frustrated, defensive, immature, impulsive, often interrupts conversations and hyperactive behaviors.

28. A: Reading fluency. Fluent readers are able to read smoothly and comfortably at a steady pace. The more quickly a child reads, the greater the chance of leaving out a word or substituting one word for another, i.e., wink instead of *sink*. Fluent readers are able to maintain accuracy without sacrificing rate. Fluent readers also stress important words in a text, group words into rhythmic phrases and read with intonation (prosody).

29. B: Drink a soda or eat some hard candy. Diabetes is a metabolic disorder that prevents proper processing of food, resulting in a lack of enough insulin for the blood to transport sugar. Insulin shock, also known as hypoglycemia, is typically brought on by a diabetic's failure to take insulin or to eat often enough. It is a serious condition that must be dealt with immediately.

30. D: A and B. Any opportunity for an ELL to hear spoken English while simultaneously seeing it in print will help facilitate reading fluency.

31. B: The classroom teacher, a special education teacher, parents or guardian, a representative of the local education agency knowledgeable about specialized instruction, someone to interpret instructional implications, the student if appropriate and other people invited by the parents or the school. IDEA defines the IEP team as a group of people responsible for developing, reviewing and revising the Individualized Education Program for a disabled student.

32. C: Reading at a Frustration reading level. At a Frustration reading level, a student is unable to unlock meaning from a text regardless of teacher support or strategies. The reader is at this level when he has less than 90% accuracy in word recognition and less than 50% in comprehension, retelling a story is illogical or incomplete and the student cannot accurately answer questions about the text.

33. B: Understanding of context and vocabulary. A Cloze test presents a reader with a text in which certain words are blocked out. The reader must determine probable missing words based on context clues. In order to supply these words, the reader must already know them.

34. A: Letter-sound correspondence. Letter-sound correspondence is the relationship between a spoken sound and the letters predictably used in English to transcribe them.

35. D: Memorize their lists by using techniques such as songs, mnemonic devices and other fun activities. By definition, sight words cannot be decoded but must be recognized on sight.

36. A: Oral. Phonological awareness is the understanding of the sounds within a spoken word. While phonological awareness contributes to fluent reading skills, activities designed to develop an awareness of word-sounds are, by definition, oral.

37. A: Count money, plan meals, grocery shop, recognize safety concerns. These are among the most basic life skills developmentally delayed students must master. Other life skills include specific occupational skills, home maintenance, clothes selection and care, food preparation and personal hygiene.

38. A: Word recognition. Elements of word recognition include strategies to decode unfamiliar words, considering alternate word meanings to decode a text and the ability to apply prior knowledge to determine a word's meaning.

39. A: Scripting the end-sound to a word KT=cat; leaving space between words; writing from the top left to the top right and from top to bottom of the page. Each of these steps is progressively more abstract. Scripting the end-sound to a word helps a young writer recognize words have

beginnings and endings. This naturally leads to the willingness to separate words with white space so they stand as individual entities. Once this step is reached, the child realizes English, writing progresses from left to right and from the top of the page to the bottom.

40. A: Are results-oriented, includes post-school activities, vocational education, employment support, adult services and considers the individual's strengths, preferences and interests. Additional activities that compose Secondary Transition are instruction, related services, community experiences, the development of employment and other post-school adult living objectives and, if appropriate, acquisition of daily living skills and functional vocational evaluation.

41. B: Suggesting they read their stories to other students. Emergent writers scripting initial and final sounds will gain the most immediate and relevant satisfaction by moving around the room, reading what they've written to other students.

42. D: From the first day of school. Picture walks give young readers the idea books are arranged sequentially. Pictures provide narrative coherence and context clues. Holding a book and turning pages gives young readers a familiarity with them.

43. D: Students should be taught that writing is a process. By applying spelling patterns found in word families, the spelling of many words can be deduced.

44. C: Context. By considering the other words in the story, the student can deduce the missing words. Referring to other words when a reader encounters an unfamiliar or missing word, can often unlock meaning.

45. A: Cooperative learning and reading comprehension. CSR is group of four reading strategies that students with learning disabilities can use to decipher and understand texts. Small groups of students at various reading levels support one another by going through the strategies as they read aloud or silently. Before reading, the group *previews*, applying prior knowledge and prediction. Next readers target words or syllables they didn't understand called *clunks* and apply a number of strategies to decode the *clunks*. Third, students *get the gist* by determining the most important character, setting, event or idea. Finally, the students *wrap it up* by creating questions to discuss their understanding of the text and summarize its meaning.

46. B: Have an Individualized Education Plan written for her. An IEP is a requirement of law. The plan, written by a team of individuals including her classroom teacher, the special education teacher, her parent s, the student if appropriate and other interested individuals, establishes objectives and goals and offers a time-line in which to reach them.

47. C: Observe the child over the course of a week or two. Draw him into conversation to determine if vocabulary is limited. Note how the child interacts with others in the class. Does he initiate conversation? If another child initiates, does he respond? Once the teacher has observed, she is in a better position to offer information to the special education teacher or counselor and to determine her best course of action.

48. B: Meet with the specialist to discuss the teacher's goals. It isn't possible to determine if strategies are effective or determine a future course unless the teacher has a firm grasp of his goals and expectations.

49. A: Strategies to increase comprehension and to build vocabulary. He should receive instruction focused on just the areas in which he is exhibiting difficulty. Improved vocabulary will give him

greater comprehension skills. Strategies focused on enhancing comprehension together with a stronger vocabulary will provide the greatest help.

50. A: It enhances students' phonemic awareness and increases vocabulary. Strength in oral language helps emergent readers because reading relies largely upon the ability to decode words with knowledge about what sounds the letters represent. A large vocabulary helps the reader recognize words whose sounds are properly decoded but whose meanings aren't familiar. Unfamiliar words slow reading fluency.

51. B: Scaffolding. Scaffolding is an umbrella teaching approach which offers a multitude of supports. Scaffolding includes prior knowledge, mnemonic devices, modeling, graphs, charts, graphic organizers and information needed prior to starting the lesson such as vocabulary or mathematical formulas.

52. D: Visit the classroom, meet the teacher and her new classmates and be given the opportunity to ask questions about the change she is about to make. When she is able to visualize what the classroom looks like, meet the people that will become her new educational 'family' and have her concerns and questions addressed, she will feel more confident about the transition.

53. B: A Maze test, which is a type of Cloze test. A Cloze test offers a text with key words blanked out and the student must determine the most likely words based upon context and his vocabulary. A Maze test offers a number of possible answers and the student must read very carefully in order to make the correct selection.

54. C: Use graph paper to help him organize. Show him how to write the problems, keeping each number in a box aligned with other numbers. This will help him determine which numbers are in the ones group, the tens group, the hundreds group and so on.

55. B: Muscular dystrophy. There are 20 types of muscular dystrophy, a genetically inherited disease that frequently first manifests in childhood. By contrast, muscular sclerosis almost never appears in childhood. Cerebral palsy is not a deteriorating disease, as is muscular dystrophy.

56. C: One class at a time, with the special education teacher supervising his academic and social progress. It is important to make this transition slowly, to permit the special education teacher to remain in the student's life as both academic and emotional support and the student to adjust to her larger classes and students she doesn't know as well.

57. C: Outreach to underrepresented and rural populations. The four required activities of the AT ACT of 1998 are: a public awareness program, coordinate activities among state agencies, technical assistance and training and outreach to underrepresented and rural populations.

58. B: Positive Behavior Support. The Individuals with Disabilities Education Act of 1997 is the recommended method of dealing with behavioral problems in children with disabilities.

59. C: Assessing a young child for learning disabilities often leads to an incorrect conclusion because a student must be taught the subject before it is possible to assess her understanding of it. Intervention teaches the child specific skills to correct her misconceptions. If the intervention fails, assessment is the next step. Many experts recommend such assessment should not be undertaken until a child is at least six years of age.

60. B: Least restrictive. IDEA requires the least restrictive environment (LRE) appropriate to a child's needs is the proper learning environment so children are not unnecessarily isolated from non-disabled children. The student's IEP team is responsible for determining the LRE.

61. C: Verbal linguistic, mathematical logical, musical, visual spatial, body kinesthetic, interpersonal, naturalistic, existential. Harvard Professor Howard Gardner cites his theory of multiple intelligences, also called learning styles, as an answer to how teachers can most effectively reach all their students. It is especially important to recognize the learning styles of students with learning disabilities and design lessons for those students accordingly.

62. C: Collaborative teaching. Classrooms with a lead teacher often include a specialized teacher to listen to the lesson then work with special needs children. Other methods are: learning centers or stations in which collaborating teachers are responsible for different areas, assigning special needs students into a resource room, team teaching and/or consultation by the special education teacher to the classroom teacher.

63. B: Teach him how an abacus works. An abacus gives both a visual/tactile demonstration of how numbers work and allows a child who processes information through hand/body movement to physically experience numerical relationships.

64. B: Unable to locate errors in their own work. This is the only logical answer. Answers a, c and d do not make sense in context.

65. A: Standardized assessment tests, examining areas of weakness in student work to determine patterns, teacher observations and interviews with the student. At this point the teacher is well-prepared to plan instruction.

66. D: Begin by welcoming the mother and discussing her son's academic improvements. Stress that the teachers, the mother and the child share goals for the student's success. Explain the behavior problems and ask if the mother has insights to share. It's important to keep communication open.

67. B: Enhance students' vocabulary by encouraging them to find examples in the world around them. Often children have richer vocabularies than they realize. This project simultaneously encourages students to remember words they already know and to learn other words with similar meanings.

68. D: All of the above. There is often a multitude of ways a teacher can apply skills and information learned in one lesson to other subjects. In this case, vocabulary building is enhanced with a word wall; logic and reasoning skills are developed by putting the words into alphabetical order then carefully considering how to define them; and both math skills and word recognition ability are improved by creating a chart demonstrating a variety of ways one can categorize a list of words.

69. C: Making appropriate modifications. Each child is different. In this case, she has consulted with the special education teacher and concluded the child needs multiple supports.

70. B: Children with special needs are as much a part of the educational community as any other child and necessary services that allow these students to participate in the learning community should be provided.

71. A: The Americans with Disabilities Act. The ADA is a federal act prohibiting discrimination based on disability in the areas of employment, state and local government, public accommodations, commercial facilities, transportation and telecommunications.

72. D: Power point presentations that include music, manipulatives, graphic organizers and clapping games. Multi-sensory techniques include visual, audio, tactile and kinesthetic approaches to teaching.

73. B: Collaborative. The creation of an Individualized Education Plan (IEP) involves classroom and special education teachers, family members, the student (if appropriate) and other interested parties who collaborate in the student's best interests.

74. C: From the age of 3 years to 5 years, a child's spoken vocabulary will typically increase by 50% (c). A typical 3-year-old will have a maximum expressive vocabulary of around 1,000 words*; by age 5, this will have increased to around 1,500 words. (*Children develop vocabularies of around 300 to 1,000 words in their first three years; the increase percentage here is based on the high end.) Vocabulary development is more rapid from age 1 to 3 since the child is starting from nothing and has more words to learn. If the child's earlier development has been optimal, the additional increase in spoken vocabulary by age 5 is 50%, making (a), (b), and (d) incorrect.

75. B: Having hearing loss (b) is likely to be most disabling for a young child as it will interfere with language and speech development. The drive to have universal newborn hearing screenings is based on statistics showing that children's academic progress is significantly impeded by hearing loss. Even when hearing loss is mild, children are much more likely to fail a school grade later without early intervention. Articulation errors (a) are quite common in young children and are generally resolved as children learn to speak. The norms for correct articulation of various speech sounds range from roughly ages 7 to 9, so 3- to 6-year-olds are likely to make articulation errors. Being of below average height (c) is not as disabling as hearing loss. Short stature has some social implications in older children, but has less impact in early childhood. There is enough natural variation in children's heights that it is normal to be shorter or taller than peers. Having slow dentition (d) means the child's teeth take longer than average to erupt; this is not significantly disabling like hearing loss.

How to Overcome Test Anxiety

Just the thought of taking a test is enough to make most people a little nervous. A test is an important event that can have a long-term impact on your future, so it's important to take it seriously and it's natural to feel anxious about performing well. But just because anxiety is normal, that doesn't mean that it's helpful in test taking, or that you should simply accept it as part of your life. Anxiety can have a variety of effects. These effects can be mild, like making you feel slightly nervous, or severe, like blocking your ability to focus or remember even a simple detail.

If you experience test anxiety—whether severe or mild—it's important to know how to beat it. To discover this, first you need to understand what causes test anxiety.

Causes of Test Anxiety

While we often think of anxiety as an uncontrollable emotional state, it can actually be caused by simple, practical things. One of the most common causes of test anxiety is that a person does not feel adequately prepared for their test. This feeling can be the result of many different issues such as poor study habits or lack of organization, but the most common culprit is time management. Starting to study too late, failing to organize your study time to cover all of the material, or being distracted while you study will mean that you're not well prepared for the test. This may lead to cramming the night before, which will cause you to be physically and mentally exhausted for the test. Poor time management also contributes to feelings of stress, fear, and hopelessness as you realize you are not well prepared but don't know what to do about it.

Other times, test anxiety is not related to your preparation for the test but comes from unresolved fear. This may be a past failure on a test, or poor performance on tests in general. It may come from comparing yourself to others who seem to be performing better or from the stress of living up to expectations. Anxiety may be driven by fears of the future—how failure on this test would affect your educational and career goals. These fears are often completely irrational, but they can still negatively impact your test performance.

> **Review Video:** 3 Reasons You Have Test Anxiety
> Visit mometrix.com/academy and enter code: 428468

Elements of Test Anxiety

As mentioned earlier, test anxiety is considered to be an emotional state, but it has physical and mental components as well. Sometimes you may not even realize that you are suffering from test anxiety until you notice the physical symptoms. These can include trembling hands, rapid heartbeat, sweating, nausea, and tense muscles. Extreme anxiety may lead to fainting or vomiting. Obviously, any of these symptoms can have a negative impact on testing. It is important to recognize them as soon as they begin to occur so that you can address the problem before it damages your performance.

Review Video: 3 Ways to Tell You Have Test Anxiety
Visit mometrix.com/academy and enter code: 927847

The mental components of test anxiety include trouble focusing and inability to remember learned information. During a test, your mind is on high alert, which can help you recall information and stay focused for an extended period of time. However, anxiety interferes with your mind's natural processes, causing you to blank out, even on the questions you know well. The strain of testing during anxiety makes it difficult to stay focused, especially on a test that may take several hours. Extreme anxiety can take a huge mental toll, making it difficult not only to recall test information but even to understand the test questions or pull your thoughts together.

Review Video: How Test Anxiety Affects Memory
Visit mometrix.com/academy and enter code: 609003

Effects of Test Anxiety

Test anxiety is like a disease—if left untreated, it will get progressively worse. Anxiety leads to poor performance, and this reinforces the feelings of fear and failure, which in turn lead to poor performances on subsequent tests. It can grow from a mild nervousness to a crippling condition. If allowed to progress, test anxiety can have a big impact on your schooling, and consequently on your future.

Test anxiety can spread to other parts of your life. Anxiety on tests can become anxiety in any stressful situation, and blanking on a test can turn into panicking in a job situation. But fortunately, you don't have to let anxiety rule your testing and determine your grades. There are a number of relatively simple steps you can take to move past anxiety and function normally on a test and in the rest of life.

Review Video: How Test Anxiety Impacts Your Grades
Visit mometrix.com/academy and enter code: 939819

Physical Steps for Beating Test Anxiety

While test anxiety is a serious problem, the good news is that it can be overcome. It doesn't have to control your ability to think and remember information. While it may take time, you can begin taking steps today to beat anxiety.

Just as your first hint that you may be struggling with anxiety comes from the physical symptoms, the first step to treating it is also physical. Rest is crucial for having a clear, strong mind. If you are tired, it is much easier to give in to anxiety. But if you establish good sleep habits, your body and mind will be ready to perform optimally, without the strain of exhaustion. Additionally, sleeping well helps you to retain information better, so you're more likely to recall the answers when you see the test questions.

Getting good sleep means more than going to bed on time. It's important to allow your brain time to relax. Take study breaks from time to time so it doesn't get overworked, and don't study right before bed. Take time to rest your mind before trying to rest your body, or you may find it difficult to fall asleep.

Review Video: The Importance of Sleep for Your Brain
Visit mometrix.com/academy and enter code: 319338

Along with sleep, other aspects of physical health are important in preparing for a test. Good nutrition is vital for good brain function. Sugary foods and drinks may give a burst of energy but this burst is followed by a crash, both physically and emotionally. Instead, fuel your body with protein and vitamin-rich foods.

Also, drink plenty of water. Dehydration can lead to headaches and exhaustion, especially if your brain is already under stress from the rigors of the test. Particularly if your test is a long one, drink water during the breaks. And if possible, take an energy-boosting snack to eat between sections.

Review Video: How Diet Can Affect your Mood
Visit mometrix.com/academy and enter code: 624317

Along with sleep and diet, a third important part of physical health is exercise. Maintaining a steady workout schedule is helpful, but even taking 5-minute study breaks to walk can help get your blood pumping faster and clear your head. Exercise also releases endorphins, which contribute to a positive feeling and can help combat test anxiety.

When you nurture your physical health, you are also contributing to your mental health. If your body is healthy, your mind is much more likely to be healthy as well. So take time to rest, nourish your body with healthy food and water, and get moving as much as possible. Taking these physical steps will make you stronger and more able to take the mental steps necessary to overcome test anxiety.

Review Video: How to Stay Healthy and Prevent Test Anxiety
Visit mometrix.com/academy and enter code: 877894

Mental Steps for Beating Test Anxiety

Working on the mental side of test anxiety can be more challenging, but as with the physical side, there are clear steps you can take to overcome it. As mentioned earlier, test anxiety often stems from lack of preparation, so the obvious solution is to prepare for the test. Effective studying may be the most important weapon you have for beating test anxiety, but you can and should employ several other mental tools to combat fear.

First, boost your confidence by reminding yourself of past success—tests or projects that you aced. If you're putting as much effort into preparing for this test as you did for those, there's no reason you should expect to fail here. Work hard to prepare; then trust your preparation.

Second, surround yourself with encouraging people. It can be helpful to find a study group, but be sure that the people you're around will encourage a positive attitude. If you spend time with others who are anxious or cynical, this will only contribute to your own anxiety. Look for others who are motivated to study hard from a desire to succeed, not from a fear of failure.

Third, reward yourself. A test is physically and mentally tiring, even without anxiety, and it can be helpful to have something to look forward to. Plan an activity following the test, regardless of the outcome, such as going to a movie or getting ice cream.

When you are taking the test, if you find yourself beginning to feel anxious, remind yourself that you know the material. Visualize successfully completing the test. Then take a few deep, relaxing breaths and return to it. Work through the questions carefully but with confidence, knowing that you are capable of succeeding.

Developing a healthy mental approach to test taking will also aid in other areas of life. Test anxiety affects more than just the actual test—it can be damaging to your mental health and even contribute to depression. It's important to beat test anxiety before it becomes a problem for more than testing.

Review Video: Test Anxiety and Depression
Visit mometrix.com/academy and enter code: 904704

Study Strategy

Being prepared for the test is necessary to combat anxiety, but what does being prepared look like? You may study for hours on end and still not feel prepared. What you need is a strategy for test prep. The next few pages outline our recommended steps to help you plan out and conquer the challenge of preparation.

Step 1: Scope Out the Test

Learn everything you can about the format (multiple choice, essay, etc.) and what will be on the test. Gather any study materials, course outlines, or sample exams that may be available. Not only will this help you to prepare, but knowing what to expect can help to alleviate test anxiety.

Step 2: Map Out the Material

Look through the textbook or study guide and make note of how many chapters or sections it has. Then divide these over the time you have. For example, if a book has 15 chapters and you have five days to study, you need to cover three chapters each day. Even better, if you have the time, leave an extra day at the end for overall review after you have gone through the material in depth.

If time is limited, you may need to prioritize the material. Look through it and make note of which sections you think you already have a good grasp on, and which need review. While you are studying, skim quickly through the familiar sections and take more time on the challenging parts. Write out your plan so you don't get lost as you go. Having a written plan also helps you feel more in control of the study, so anxiety is less likely to arise from feeling overwhelmed at the amount to cover. A sample plan may look like this:

- Day 1: Skim chapters 1–4, study chapter 5 (especially pages 31–33)
- Day 2: Study chapters 6–7, skim chapters 8–9
- Day 3: Skim chapter 10, study chapters 11–12 (especially pages 87–90)
- Day 4: Study chapters 13–15
- Day 5: Overall review (focus most on chapters 5, 6, and 12), take practice test

Step 3: Gather Your Tools

Decide what study method works best for you. Do you prefer to highlight in the book as you study and then go back over the highlighted portions? Or do you type out notes of the important information? Or is it helpful to make flashcards that you can carry with you? Assemble the pens, index cards, highlighters, post-it notes, and any other materials you may need so you won't be distracted by getting up to find things while you study.

If you're having a hard time retaining the information or organizing your notes, experiment with different methods. For example, try color-coding by subject with colored pens, highlighters, or post-it notes. If you learn better by hearing, try recording yourself reading your notes so you can listen while in the car, working out, or simply sitting at your desk. Ask a friend to quiz you from your flashcards, or try teaching someone the material to solidify it in your mind.

Step 4: Create Your Environment

It's important to avoid distractions while you study. This includes both the obvious distractions like visitors and the subtle distractions like an uncomfortable chair (or a too-comfortable couch that makes you want to fall asleep). Set up the best study environment possible: good lighting and a comfortable work area. If background music helps you focus, you may want to turn it on, but otherwise keep the room quiet. If you are using a computer to take notes, be sure you don't have any other windows open, especially applications like social media, games, or anything else that could distract you. Silence your phone and turn off notifications. Be sure to keep water close by so you stay hydrated while you study (but avoid unhealthy drinks and snacks).

Also, take into account the best time of day to study. Are you freshest first thing in the morning? Try to set aside some time then to work through the material. Is your mind clearer in the afternoon or evening? Schedule your study session then. Another method is to study at the same time of day that you will take the test, so that your brain gets used to working on the material at that time and will be ready to focus at test time.

Step 5: Study!

Once you have done all the study preparation, it's time to settle into the actual studying. Sit down, take a few moments to settle your mind so you can focus, and begin to follow your study plan. Don't give in to distractions or let yourself procrastinate. This is your time to prepare so you'll be ready to fearlessly approach the test. Make the most of the time and stay focused.

Of course, you don't want to burn out. If you study too long you may find that you're not retaining the information very well. Take regular study breaks. For example, taking five minutes out of every hour to walk briskly, breathing deeply and swinging your arms, can help your mind stay fresh.

As you get to the end of each chapter or section, it's a good idea to do a quick review. Remind yourself of what you learned and work on any difficult parts. When you feel that you've mastered the material, move on to the next part. At the end of your study session, briefly skim through your notes again.

But while review is helpful, cramming last minute is NOT. If at all possible, work ahead so that you won't need to fit all your study into the last day. Cramming overloads your brain with more information than it can process and retain, and your tired mind may struggle to recall even previously learned information when it is overwhelmed with last-minute study. Also, the urgent nature of cramming and the stress placed on your brain contribute to anxiety. You'll be more likely to go to the test feeling unprepared and having trouble thinking clearly.

So don't cram, and don't stay up late before the test, even just to review your notes at a leisurely pace. Your brain needs rest more than it needs to go over the information again. In fact, plan to finish your studies by noon or early afternoon the day before the test. Give your brain the rest of the day to relax or focus on other things, and get a good night's sleep. Then you will be fresh for the test and better able to recall what you've studied.

Step 6: Take a practice test

Many courses offer sample tests, either online or in the study materials. This is an excellent resource to check whether you have mastered the material, as well as to prepare for the test format and environment.

Check the test format ahead of time: the number of questions, the type (multiple choice, free response, etc.), and the time limit. Then create a plan for working through them. For example, if you have 30 minutes to take a 60-question test, your limit is 30 seconds per question. Spend less time on the questions you know well so that you can take more time on the difficult ones.

If you have time to take several practice tests, take the first one open book, with no time limit. Work through the questions at your own pace and make sure you fully understand them. Gradually work up to taking a test under test conditions: sit at a desk with all study materials put away and set a timer. Pace yourself to make sure you finish the test with time to spare and go back to check your answers if you have time.

After each test, check your answers. On the questions you missed, be sure you understand why you missed them. Did you misread the question (tests can use tricky wording)? Did you forget the information? Or was it something you hadn't learned? Go back and study any shaky areas that the practice tests reveal.

Taking these tests not only helps with your grade, but also aids in combating test anxiety. If you're already used to the test conditions, you're less likely to worry about it, and working through tests until you're scoring well gives you a confidence boost. Go through the practice tests until you feel comfortable, and then you can go into the test knowing that you're ready for it.

Test Tips

On test day, you should be confident, knowing that you've prepared well and are ready to answer the questions. But aside from preparation, there are several test day strategies you can employ to maximize your performance.

First, as stated before, get a good night's sleep the night before the test (and for several nights before that, if possible). Go into the test with a fresh, alert mind rather than staying up late to study.

Try not to change too much about your normal routine on the day of the test. It's important to eat a nutritious breakfast, but if you normally don't eat breakfast at all, consider eating just a protein bar. If you're a coffee drinker, go ahead and have your normal coffee. Just make sure you time it so that the caffeine doesn't wear off right in the middle of your test. Avoid sugary beverages, and drink enough water to stay hydrated but not so much that you need a restroom break 10 minutes into the test. If your test isn't first thing in the morning, consider going for a walk or doing a light workout before the test to get your blood flowing.

Allow yourself enough time to get ready, and leave for the test with plenty of time to spare so you won't have the anxiety of scrambling to arrive in time. Another reason to be early is to select a good seat. It's helpful to sit away from doors and windows, which can be distracting. Find a good seat, get out your supplies, and settle your mind before the test begins.

When the test begins, start by going over the instructions carefully, even if you already know what to expect. Make sure you avoid any careless mistakes by following the directions.

Then begin working through the questions, pacing yourself as you've practiced. If you're not sure on an answer, don't spend too much time on it, and don't let it shake your confidence. Either skip it and come back later, or eliminate as many wrong answers as possible and guess among the remaining ones. Don't dwell on these questions as you continue—put them out of your mind and focus on what lies ahead.

Be sure to read all of the answer choices, even if you're sure the first one is the right answer. Sometimes you'll find a better one if you keep reading. But don't second-guess yourself if you do immediately know the answer. Your gut instinct is usually right. Don't let test anxiety rob you of the information you know.

If you have time at the end of the test (and if the test format allows), go back and review your answers. Be cautious about changing any, since your first instinct tends to be correct, but make sure you didn't misread any of the questions or accidentally mark the wrong answer choice. Look over any you skipped and make an educated guess.

At the end, leave the test feeling confident. You've done your best, so don't waste time worrying about your performance or wishing you could change anything. Instead, celebrate the successful completion of this test. And finally, use this test to learn how to deal with anxiety even better next time.

> **Review Video: 5 Tips to Beat Test Anxiety**
> Visit mometrix.com/academy and enter code: 570656

Important Qualification

Not all anxiety is created equal. If your test anxiety is causing major issues in your life beyond the classroom or testing center, or if you are experiencing troubling physical symptoms related to your anxiety, it may be a sign of a serious physiological or psychological condition. If this sounds like your situation, we strongly encourage you to seek professional help.

Thank You

We at Mometrix would like to extend our heartfelt thanks to you, our friend and patron, for allowing us to play a part in your journey. It is a privilege to serve people from all walks of life who are unified in their commitment to building the best future they can for themselves.

The preparation you devote to these important testing milestones may be the most valuable educational opportunity you have for making a real difference in your life. We encourage you to put your heart into it—that feeling of succeeding, overcoming, and yes, conquering will be well worth the hours you've invested.

We want to hear your story, your struggles and your successes, and if you see any opportunities for us to improve our materials so we can help others even more effectively in the future, please share that with us as well. **The team at Mometrix would be absolutely thrilled to hear from you!** So please, send us an email (support@mometrix.com) and let's stay in touch.

If you'd like some additional help, check out these other resources we offer for your exam:

http://MometrixFlashcards.com/PraxisII

Additional Bonus Material

Due to our efforts to try to keep this book to a manageable length, we've created a link that will give you access to all of your additional bonus material.

Please visit http://www.mometrix.com/bonus948/priispedech to access the information.